Ronald R. Wlodyga

The Foolishness Of God

Is wiser than men (I Cor. 1:25)

Volume 2

Copyright Statement

Any articles may be reproduced in whole, but not the book in its entirety under the following provisions: proper credit of book title and author must be given at the end of each article. There can be no charge of articles to the recipient. It is my desire to encourage, and inspire the Christian into further study with the fundamental belief of giving freely.

ISBN 978-0-9996000-3-0

Published in 2020 by Ingram Printing

Acknowledgements

I am truly grateful for the many individuals who helped me in making the publication of this series possible, which has been in the making for the past forty-five years.

A special thanks to Professors Bill Koehn who edited the initial draft and Arlen Wilbers who helped in the proofreading and editing of the final manuscript. A heartfelt thanks to Ms. Terry Makowski for her labor of love in helping in the typing of the manuscript, and Eric Wilbers in formatting the final Jacket cover.

Last, but not least, I would like to express my warmest love to my devoted wife Ruth, who was extremely patient and understanding towards me as I have spent countless hours in the research and formatting of this series.

The Book Colors

Throughout this four volume series we will see that God has revealed his master plan for the salvation of the world through many different agencies. The many different types of *offerings* in the Old Testament are no exception to the *types* and a*ntitypes* of the Christian experience. Through the Sin-offering, Burnt-offering, Meat-offering and Peace-offering—we have God's blue-print plan for establishing WORLD PEACE!

There was only one *entrance* into the holy place from the court of the Gentiles to bring offerings. This was through a beautiful *four*-colored embroidery of blue, purple, scarlet and white.

Here again, we find deep *spiritual significance* to the seemingly irrelevant detail.

What did this **curtain** represent in *type?* Why *four* colors instead of five? Why blue, purple, scarlet and white instead of yellow, green, black and orange?

Firstly, the eye catching embroidery of brilliant Color was a *portrait* of our Savior being the ENTRANCE to God's throne. This understanding will be elaborated upon in volume 3.

What are we to envision by these *four* mysterious colors? Could they possibly depict the *four* gospels leading to salvation?

The color *blue* corresponds to the gospel of John as he described our Savior as the Son of God who came from *heaven* (Jn. 3:13,31; 6:32-33,58). The color of the sky and the vast reaches of the universe where GOD'S THRONE is located is thought to be blue.

The color *purple* correlates to the gospel of Matthew in that the GLORY of Jesus as *King of Kings* is strongly emphasized.

Purple is the color of *royalty* as observed by the robes of kings and magistrates.

The gospel of Mark presents our Lord and Savior as **"...the Son of man [who] came not to be ministered unto, but to minister and *to give His life* as a ransom for many" (Mk. 10:45).** Scarlet [red or crimson] is most often associated with *sin* or *blood*. This reminds us of the ATONEMENT for sin through the precious blood of Jesus Christ.

The fourth color was the *white* byssus fabric made of white cotton (Gen. 41:42). White being associated with RIGHTEOUSNESS (Rev. 19:8), corresponds to the gospel of Luke who designates Jesus as *sinless*, *holy,* or *spotless* in character. Notice the wording, **"That holy thing which shall be born" (Lk. 1:35), and "I find no fault in this man" (Lk. 23:4,14).**

Vol. 2

TABLE OF CONTENTS

Chapter One
God's Plan Revealed by His Trades   *Page*

1. God the Master Builder 1
2. God the Great Metallurgist 8
3. God the Master Potter 13
4. God the Master Jeweler 18
5. God the Master Tailor 21

Chapter Two
God's Plan Revealed by His Businesses

1. God the Loving Animal Husbandryman 25
   a. Clean and Unclean Meats 28
   b. The Carnivorous Lion 32
   c. Becoming Bold as Lions 36
2. God the Great Shepherd 38
3. God the Master Chef 43
   a. Milk and Strong Meat 45
   b. The Unpardonable Sin 45
   c. God's Plan Revealed by Offerings 46

Chapter Three
God's Plan Revealed by His Recreations

1. God the Master Gardener 55
    a. Types of Spiritual Fruit 58
    b. Christian Trees 61
2. God the Great Musician 65
3. God the Wonderful Astronomer 68
4. God the Amazing Artist 74
    a. The Breastplate of Judgement 75
    b. The Precious Stones 78
    c. The Urim and Thummim 82

Chapter Four
God's Plan Revealed by His Professions

1. God the All-Wise Financial Advisor 85
    a. Cause of Poverty 87
    b. Giving Offerings..............................90
    c. Is it wrong to have Riches......................91
    d. Insurance.. 97
2. God the Benevolent Physician 98
    a. Is it God's Will to Heal? 100
    b. Why God doesn't Heal 106
3. God the Magnificent Army Officer.................... 109
4. God the King of Kings................................. 114

Chapter Five
God's Plan Revealed by the Galilean Parables

1. The Sower... 120
2. The Wheat and Tares................................. 123
3. The Lamp Under a Bushel 125
4. The Grain of Mustard Seed.......................... 126
5. The Kingdom Like Unto Leaven.................... 128
6. The Seed Growing of Itself......................... 132
7. The Treasure Hid in a Field......................... 134
8. The Pearl of Great Price............................. 135

9. The Net Cast into the Sea............. 136
10. The Householder's Treasure......... 137

Chapter Six
Parables of Israel's History

1. The Wicked Husbandmen............................. 140
2. The Parable of Two Sons............................... 143
3. The Barren Fig Tree Accursed........................ 144
3. The Barren Fig Tree....................................... 148
4. The Wineskins and Rent Garment.................... 149
5. The Changing of Administration...................... 152

Chapter Seven
Evangelistic Parables

1. The Ten Virgins... 159
2. The Royal Marriage Feast for the Kings Son......... 161
3. Biblical Weddings..165
4. The Lost Sheep... 172
5. The Lost Coin... 173
6. The Prodigal Son... 174

Chapter Eight
Prophetic Parables

1. The Parable of the Fig Tree........................... 177
2. The Watchful Porter......................................178
3. The Marriage Supper of the Lamb.................... 179
4. The Bride becomes Christ's Army.................... 180
5. The Harvest of Souls.................................... 181
      a. One Shall be Taken............................... 184
      b. The New Covenant made with Israel............. 189
      c. The dead to rise first............................. 190
      d. Resurrections to occur in stages?.................... 191

Chapter Nine
Parables of Christian Admonition

1. The Good Samaritan.. 195
2. The Pharisee and the Publican......................... 197
3. The Two Debtors... 200
4. The Unforgiving Servant.............................. 201
5. The Lowest Seat at the Feast......................... 202
6. The Great Supper... 203
7. The Unprofitable Servant............................. 204
8. The Parable of the Pounds........................... 205
9. The Parable of the Talents........................... 208
10. The Parable of the Vineyard........................ 213
11. The Friend at Midnight............................... 217
12. The Unjust Judge.. 218

Chapter Ten
The Futility of Riches

1. The Moths and Thieves................................. 221
2. Lazarus and the Rich Man........................... 223
3. Sole Sleep... 228
4. The "Worm that dieth not"........................... 229
5. The Rich Fool.. 230
6. The Unjust Steward...................................... 232

Chapter Eleven
Numbers and their Spiritual Significance........ 239

Chapter Twelve
Prophetic Numbers

1. The Hebrew Calendar.................................. 261
2. Cycles of 70.. 272
3. Fifty, the Jubilee.. 273
   a. Jubilee and Atonement........................... 277
   b. Jubilee and Pentecost............................. 283
4. 2520 and the Prophetic Sentence.....................285
   a. The Gentiles Seven Times Punishment......... 286

   b. Israel's Seven Times Punishment............... 291
   c. Ezekiel's Living Legend…....................….. 292

Chapter Thirteen
Daniel's Seventy Weeks Prophecy

1. The first 69 Weeks…..................…………297
   a. Persian Decrees…..................………….301
   b. Ezra's Commission…............................. 203
   c. Israel's 70 Years of National Captivity……… 310
   d. The Historical-Messianic Interpretation……...315

Chapter Fourteen
Daniel's Seventieth Week Prophecy

1. Daniel's 70th Week
   a. The Seventieth Week and Christ............... 325
   b. The Anti-Christ Version….....................…326
   c. The Seventy Weeks and Israel…..............…330
   d. Joseph in Egypt and 7 Years of Famine…….333
   e. The "Times of Jerusalem"…................. 334

Chapter One

GOD'S PLAN REVEALED BY HIS TRADES

God the Master Builder

This is a most exciting chapter. Here is where we find out how the ALL Omnipotent God has revealed His GRAND DESIGN through physical occupations.

The Great Creator God uses every-day occupations such as a carpenter, potter, tailor, jeweler; etc. to illustrate His beautiful plan.

Each of these mundane jobs contains vital physical tasks that can be applicable to spiritual principles.

God the Father and Jesus Christ are Master Builders, or contractors. It is probably no coincidence that Jesus and His physical father, Joseph, were also contractors.

We shall see how God the Father has sub-contracted His work to Noah, Moses, Solomon, etc, in building physical things which have *revealed* God's spiritual plan!

The physical universe and all that it contains, including the earth, was created by God through Jesus Christ as we have shown in Volume one.

Noah's Ark

It was God's Spokesman Jesus Christ, God the Son who gave Noah a detailed plan to build the Ark as recorded in (Genesis 6:14). Noah was given the blueprints including the type of wood to use and the dimensions from the second member of the God-head.

We shall see in the chapter on "The Days of Noah" in Vol. 4 that the dimensions, type of wood, pitch, door and where the Ark settled—contain deep spiritual truths!

The Tabernacle

God, the Great Builder, instructed Moses in how to build the Tabernacle as recorded in (Exodus 25).

Here again, we will conclusively prove in the chapter on "The Sanctuaries of God" [vol. 3], that each component of the Tabernacle was highly significant. The holy place, Ark, Mercy Seat, Altar of Incense, Veil, Shewbread Candlestick, and Offerings, all point to spiritual entities!

The Great Pyramid

God reveals in (Jeremiah 32:18-29) that He **"hast set signs and wonders in the land of Egypt, even unto this day."** But what *signs and wonders* are in Egypt?

There are over 80 pyramids in Egypt, the most famous are the pyramids of Giza; the largest is the Great Pyramid. The Great Pyramid is the only remaining one of the seven wonders of the ancient world

Isaiah 19:19-20 states, **"In that day shall there be an altar to the Lord in the midst of the land of Egypt, and a pillar [Hebrew *'matstsebah'* correctly translated means monument] at the border thereof to the Lord. And it shall be for a sign, and for a witness unto the Lord of Hosts in the land of Egypt."**

The only spot in Egypt that completely fulfills this description, both geometrically and geographically, is the precise place where the Great Pyramid actually stands.

The Great Pyramid was placed in the exact center of all the land area of the world. Lines drawn through the north-south and east-west axis (31° 9' meridian east of Greenwich is the longest land meridian, and the east-west axis 29° 58' 51' north), the longest land parallel.

That the Architect knew where to find the poles of the earth is evidenced by the high degree of accuracy in orienting the building true north. Modern man's best effort, the Paris Observatory, is six minutes of a degree off true north. The Great Pyramid today is only off three minutes and that after 4,200 years, due mainly to subsidence.

Such near perfect orientation is exceedingly hard to secure, even with modern astronomical equipment, and seemingly impossible without it. If knowledge of the magnetic needle was known, it would have been of little value. It points to the magnetic north, not to the true north. The celestial pole is a point, usually a star, through which the polar axis of the earth would pass were it projected to the star sphere.

The Great Pyramid is the largest building in the world and covers slightly over 13 acres. It contains nearly 90,000 cubic feet of masonry, enough to build 30 Empire State buildings!

Who built the Great Pyramid?

The *Cambridge Ancient History*, vol. 1, page 281, declares of the Great Pyramid: "...its perfect building compels our admiration; its alignment [with the points of the compass] is mathematically correct; often one cannot insert a pen-knife between the joints of the stone."

"The Great Pyramid is so incredibly precise that compass errors can be checked against it," writes Leonard Cottrell in his book, *The Mountains of Pharaoh.*

But who built the Great Pyramid at Giza, Egypt and why has this been a mystery to most pyramidologists?

At the true entrance to the Great Pyramid is the hieroglyphic carving containing the name of the builder. His name in Egyptian is spelled Khufu by modern writers. The Greeks spelled his name CHEOPS.

The Egyptians like to boast about their pyramids. Yet the

greatest pyramid of all they admit, was not built by an Egyptian. The Egyptian historian Manetho, who lived in the third century before Christ, wrote that Khyfu, "was of a *different race*" from Egyptians (*Wathens' Arts and Antiquities of Egypt*, p. 54).

Manetho explains in *Cory's Ancient Fragments*, p. 68, that..."...there came up from the East, in a strange manner, men of an ignoble race, who had the confidence to invade our country, and easily subdued it by their power without a battle. Ruling over all this nation was style Hycsos, the Shepherd Kings."

Archbishop Ussher, in his chronology, refers to the migration of the Shepherd Kings from Arabia into Egypt.

Herodotus, the famous Greek historian of the 5th century B.C. states that the builders of the Great Pyramid were SHEPHERDS *(Euterpe* 5128).

The Bible says that the Egyptians were not shepherds (Gen. 46:31-34). Who then was this Cheops, who was not an Egyptian and came from Arabia with Shepherds to build the Great Pyramid?

At least one historian states that Cheops was a young contemporary of King Zoser of Egypt. Zoser (1737-1718 B.C.) built the "step pyramid" shortly before Cheops built the Great Pyramid (Budge, *A History of Egypt*, vol. 11, p.9.).

History informs us that King Zoser recorded the seven years draught in Joseph's time. Notice: "My heart is in great anxiety, for in my time the Nile has not overflowed for a period of SEVEN YEARS" (*Cambridge, Ancient History,* p. 309-310, vol. 1).

Now the surprise of history is that king Zoser ruled part of lower Egypt at the same time Joseph was Prime Minister under Pharaoh Amenemhet III, king of upper Egypt. Ancient Egypt was a confederation of small city states. Amenenhet III was king of upper Egypt and Pharaoh of all Egypt. But under him were lesser kings, among whom was Zoser.

The name given Joseph by King Amenemhet III was "Zaph-nath-paaneah" (Gen. 41:45). The Egyptians called Joseph "yousuf".

A noted man who helped Cheops in building the Pyramid

was named Souf. He was "Chief of the works of Khufu" (*Rawlinson's Egypt*, chp. 14).

In Maspero's *Dawn of Civilization*, p. 363-364, he is called "Sufhotep" Meaning "Saf the servant". He was apparently one of 12 brothers who built the Labyrinth—the "Pentagon" of ancient Egypt for Amenemhet III (*Wathen's Antiquities*, p. 142).

Although all of the evidence from ancient history appears to indicate that Joseph, youngest son of Jacob's 12 children, who dwelt in Egypt, second under Pharaoh during the famine helped Cheops build the Great Pyramid—recent archaeological evidence suggests otherwise. The Great Pyramid appears to a much older structure than when the Israelites dwelt there.

Why The Great Pyramid was built?

In 1798 the French discovered the corner sockets, peculiar to no other pyramid, and also the relationship of the Pyramids structure and dimensions to astronomical science. Colonel Howard Vipe was next to make significant discoveries in 1830. Later, John Tailor, a London publisher who was a gifted mathematician and amateur astronomer, indicated the relationship of certain measurements to Biblical prophecies including Christ's birth, death and resurrection.

Mr. Robert Menzies, of Leith Scotland, is given credit for being the first to attract general attention to the assertion that the Great Pyramid was a treasury of Divinely given wisdom, embodying chronological, meteorological, astronomical, mathematical, historical and Biblical truth.

There seems to be a relationship between the dimensions of the Great Pyramid and the earth, the suns' distance from the earth, the density of the earth, mean temperature etc.

Many dimensions correlate to certain Biblical prophecies. Although the Pyramid numbers are geometric, there is one arithmetical number that is prominent in the Pyramid, and that number is 5. The number 5, and multiples, powers and geometrical proportions of it runs through the Great Pyramid.

Periods of 5 years, are the integral units with which the

whole structure of prophetic chronology is built up in the Bible.

5,10,15,40,65,70,100,120,360,390,(1260,or 42 months), 1335,2300, and the "Seven Times" (7 years or 2520) are all multiples of 5.

Multiples of 5 were also dimensions of Noah's Ark, the Wilderness Tabernacle and Solomon's Temple as we will view under "Numbers and their Spiritual Significance."

A Common Source of Inspiration

There is a correspondency between the King's Chamber and the Holy of Holies and between the Ante-Chamber and the place called Holy in the Bible Tabernacle. These significant correspondences seem to suggest that the designers of each must have had a common source of inspiration.

In its original position, the Coffer sat midway between the north and south walls of the King's Chamber—with its sides parallel to the respective sides of the Chamber and its axis coinciding with the Pyramid's own north-south axis. That is to say that the Coffer's axis, which was due north and south, would be geometrically 286.1 inches west of the axis of the passage system.

Symbolic of God's ensuing government, the top piece, or capstone, was never set, having been rejected by the builders. It should be pointed out that the capstone [Head Stone] is also the chief cornerstone, since all the four corners of the building converge in that one stone at the top. Thus, it alone, of all stones in the structure, is the only one that is over all the four corners.

The Bible tells us in (Matthew 21:42) that **"The stone which the builders rejected, the same is become the head of the corner: this is the Lord's doing, and it is marvelous in our eyes."**

In (Ephesians 2:20-22) we read where **"Jesus Christ Himself being the chief corner stone; in whom all the building fitly framed together unto an holy temple in the Lord: in whom ye also are builded together for an habitation of God through the Spirit."**

And in the Psalms we read that, **"The stone which the builders rejected, the same is become the head of the corner. This is the Lord's doing, it is marvelous in our eyes"** (Ps. 118:22,23).

When Christ returns to establish God's Kingdom, **"He shall bring forward the Top-Stone amid shouts of Grace unto it"** (Zech. 4:7).

Jesus Christ is the STONE which the builders [Israel] rejected who is the HEAD of the pyramid structure representing His Kingdom here upon earth.

Conclusion

The Great Pyramid was constructed in accordance with astronomical observations of great accuracy. To achieve such exactness without modern scientific instrumentation is seemingly unbelievable.

The perfect accuracy of all the various geodetic and astronomical statistics, which man was unable to ascertain until modern times after the development of trigonometrical knowledge, is evidence of DIVINE REVELATION. God gave this divine knowledge to those who supervised its construction. Not that God directly inspired it, but certainly the mathematical genius to build it was given to man by the greatest Architect of all—Almighty God, the Creator of the Universe!

Could ancient men have been smarter than we think or smarter than us?

For further indepth details of the significance of the Great Pyramid, the reader is encouraged to read the works of Adam Rutherford on *Pyramidology*, Books 1,2,3,4 which can be obtained by writing to:

The Institute of Pyramidology,
31 Station Road, Horpenden,
Hertfordshire, A15 4xb
Great Britain

God—The Great Metallurgist

Metallurgy is the science of extracting a metal from its ore and refining it to be used for a specific purpose.

God, the Greatest Metallurgist, uses the precious metals of the earth with their various physical properties to describe *spiritual* principles.

The following metals of the Bible portray deep *spiritual* significance as used in relation to their unique physical features.

Gold: Of all the metals of the earth, gold is surely the most treasured. Its physical attributes range from beauty, warmth, non-corrosiveness, endurance, to extreme malleability. It therefore represents the *divine* in scripture.

There are countless references to gold in the Bible. The Ark of the Covenant, Mercy Seat, Candlesticks, Altar and various vessels in the Holy of Holies were all overlaid with gold.

All of these were *emblematic* of the holy, just and PERFECT character of Jesus Christ! What better metal to be used to describe the *glory* of our majestic Savior?

Because of its precious nature—gold is used to describe the streets and framework of the Holy City when the New Earth is created (Rev. 21:15; 18; 21). This will be spiritual gold, being transparent as glass.

Gold was also used to describe the Babylonian empire in King Nebuchadnezzar's dream. Recall how the prophet Daniel interpreted the head of gold to mean the Babylonian dynasty in prophecy. The Babylonian Empire was superior to all other empires to follow in splendor—yet inferior in physical strength.

Christians are told to build with it, the Laodiceans are to buy it! Here is the connection—God *pictures* the Christian character we are to build as spiritual gold.

A Christian of high character and FAITH is more valuable to God than best gold purified by the refiner (1 Pet. 1:7). Faith is our foundation for building character (1 Cor. 3:11).

To Christians who were self-satisfied and complacent with their own spiritual works, God instructed: **"I counsel you to buy from Me gold refined in the fire, that you may be rich" (Rev. 3:18).**

Gold's soft, yellow luster and glow make gold objects attractive. Gold bracelets, necklaces, rings and earrings capture our visual attention with an appeal far above that of other metals. Likewise, a Christian with the character of "spiritual gold" stands out from others. A deeply converted, growing Christian has a special quality of spirit nothing else can match—the inner glow of God's Spirit radiating God's character.

Gold makes surfaces highly reflective; this is another of its valuable assets. Our goal is to become like Jesus Christ, who at all times *mirrored* to the world God's very nature—and we should *reflect* Jesus' example as SHINNING LIGHTS to this darkened world.

Pure gold is extremely soft, malleable and ductile. A pound of pure gold can be drawn into wire so thin it would stretch 900 miles. However, it is not brittle like pottery or glass, or hard and unmanageable like iron. Gold can be fashioned as the craftsman desires.

God is our Master Craftsman, and we are to become spiritual gold, yielded, humble, receptive to His correction and instruction without resisting or breaking.

We are to be molded into God's character for His purpose to be fulfilled in our lives.

When heated, gold compound breaks down, yielding the bright yellow metal we are all familiar with. Not only does heat remove impurities from the metal by forming slag that can be skimmed off the top, but it also changes the chemical composition of gold compounds and returns gold to its pure, metallic state.

God also intends the heat of our trials and test to bring out the best in our Christian character. Gold tried in the fire is pure and refined. When we experience personal trials, we should remember that God is REFINING us to bring out the best, the gold of His character in us.

God builds His character in Christians just as He created

the gold to be mined from the earth. It requires effort to acquire both. It is not enough to want godly character—we must be willing to work for it with all our being. Remember, the gold is there—all we have to do is dig for it!

Silver: Beside gold, silver is second in beauty. Many of the Proverbs compare gold and silver *figuratively* [the most precious of metals] to that of God's truth: **"The words of the Lord are pure words; as silver tried in a furnace of earth, purified seven times" (Ps. 12:6).**

Today, the adage "silver haired" or "silver tongued" depicts a unique and special trait about a person.

Jesus was betrayed for 30 pieces of silver (Matt. 26:15), and the temples honoring Diana [Semiramis] were made of silver (Acts 19:24).

Because silver is less precious than gold, yet harder and stronger—the Persian Empire of Nebuchadnezzar's dream was described as silver.

God, the Great Metallurgist appears to have spiritual significance behind everything He does—therefore, silver surely has a spiritual meaning. The question must be raised then, "why use silver to represent the payment of the atoning sacrifice of Jesus Christ?" Due to the fact that all of the metals, colors and stones point to some aspect of the *glory* of Jesus' redeeming work—silver must have some spiritual connotation!

If gold represented His holy and *perfect* nature, silver must *symbolize* His REDEEMING character for the atonement of sin! It is also highly significant that in God's Holy City "New Jerusalem" there is gold, but no silver. We will learn the reason for this in a latter chapter.

Brass: Brass is a yellow metal alloy consisting of copper and zinc in varying percentages. Oftentimes brass is used interchangeably in the Bible for bronze. Bronze is a man-made alloy of copper and tin.

Bronze was used to overlay many parts of the altar for burnt offerings. Many of the vessels including pots, shovel, grate and laver were made of bronze. All of these pointed to

JUDGMENT!

The serpent that Moses lifted up in the wilderness *pointing* to Christ was made out of bronze (Num. 21:9). The feet of the resurrected and *glorified* Christ appear as brass in the fire (Rev. 1:15). Surely brass is *symbolic* of the tried, tested and proven Christ—who *suffered* for us and withstood the fiery trials in our stead!

The Grecian Empire of Nebuchadnezzar's dream was described as bronze because of its inferior beauty to gold and silver—yet harder in substance!

Brass, or copper generally represents *judgment* in scripture.

Iron: Daniel had just described the first three world ruling empires of the earth as the precious metals of gold, silver and brass. Now he describes the fourth as iron, being inferior to the others, yet stronger in military might. This represented the fierce military machinery of the Roman Empire that would be extant to the days when Christ would intervene in human affairs!

The first Biblical reference to iron is found in (Genesis 4:22) where Tubal-Cain was a worker of brass and iron.

The Israelites feared the Canaanites because they had chariots of iron (Josh. 17:16,18). Goliath's spearhead weighed nearly 20 pounds of iron (1 Sam. 17:7).

Although iron has been used for many constructional purposes, its use for WAR in the Bible is most notable. The prophet Isaiah foretold of the day when iron will be used for only good, as, **"...he shall judge among the nations, and shall rebuke many people: and they shall beat their [iron] swords into plowshares, and their [iron] spears into pruninghooks: nation shall not lift up sword against nation, neither shall they learn war any more" (Isa. 2:4; Micah 4:3).**

Rebuilding the Kingdom of God will require preparation of proper food-stuffs, and the right education. It will begin by planting seed with farm instruments made out of weapons.

Steel remelted from spears of warfare will have to be metallurgically hardened. Steel is heated to "red hot" temperatures and then *quenched* in water. This makes the steel *hard* but is very brittle!

Steel is then *tempered* by heating it up slowly at much lower temperatures for a certain length of *time*. If steel is not tempered it will CRACK because of *stress*. During this process, a little bit of hardness is lost—but a great deal of TOUGHNESS is gained!

There are many spiritual lessons a Christian can learn from this metallurgical process.

We need to be made HARD and TOUGH to be rulers in the Kingdom of God, and that's the reason God puts us through trial and testing. Christians need to be *tempered* to lose the hard and stony hearts of human nature.

After we as Christians endure the fiery trials of this life, we will no longer be weapons of destruction—but rather productive tools in our loving Father's hands!

God—The Master Potter

God, the *Master Potter,* has revealed the maturing process of Christian character development, through the beautiful *analogy* of a physical potter.

Many times, Christians go through PAINFUL and agonizing experiences in this life without understanding why. Sometimes we even get to the point of almost cursing God for placing such heavy burdens upon us. We see known offenders prospering—and ask inside ourselves, is God fair?

Why do we get sick when we are trying to maintain our bodies by watching what we eat? Why do some get healed and some don't? Why are we in financial straights when we are tithing and giving generous offerings? Why do we have problems with our children when we try to raise them God's way? Why are we persecuted when we are trying to live godly? Have you ever said, *"why me Lord?"*.

Obviously, there is an explanation, and the apostle to the Gentiles declares God's motives:

Thou wilt say then unto me, Why doth he yet find fault? For who hath resisted his will? Nay

> **but, O man, who art thou that repliest against God? Shall the thing formed say to him that formed it, 'Why hast thou made me thus'? Hath not the potter power over the clay, of the same lump to make one vessel unto honor, and another dishonor? (Rom. 9:19-21).**

Clearly, God is compared to a MASTER POTTER molding His creation of clay. Trials and tests are for the *perfection* of God's plan in each of us. But we must learn *why* God puts us through these adversities.

Isaiah understood this intricate relationship between humankind and its creative designer. He compared the grand design of God through the fashioning of a potter forming his clay: **"O Lord, thou art our father; we are the clay, and thou our *potter*; and we all are the work of thy hand" (Isa. 64:8).**

Job's friend Elihu also comprehended God's plan to that of a potter. He said: **"I also am formed out of the clay" (Job 33:6).**

There is a deep spiritual meaning that can be understood about God's plan of salvation from the mechanical working of physical clay. From this relationship, Christians can better understand why we are compared to clay—being formed by the Master Potter into His *image* and *likeness*!

Basically, there are *seven* stages in which a sculptured piece of pottery must go through, that can be compared to Christian "clay models."

- **Selecting the clay:** There are various types of clay a potter can select for his particular masterpiece. Each type contains different physical properties such as color, malleability and moisture content that enhance its use.

Perhaps you can already surmise the spiritual *analogy* of "Christian clay" being formed by our Heavenly Potter!

Just as there are different types of clay with varying physical properties—there are many types of human beings with various physical attributes. Some are more intelligent, better speakers, more humorous, avid musicians, superb athletes, etc.

Each of us have been endowed with special gifts by our Creator as the *Parable of the Talents* illustrates metaphorically. That is why our God chooses certain types of individuals to perform His work over others! God has chosen some to be apostles, prophets, evangelists, pastors, teachers, etc. (Eph. 4:11).

It is God who *chooses* us to carry out His plan as Jesus reiterated to His disciples: **"Ye have not chosen me, but I have chosen you, and ordained you"** (Jn. 15:16). Jesus further stated of human clay: **"No man can come to me, except the Father which hath sent me draw Him"** (Jn. 6:44-45).

We are merely "clay models" that God is using to fulfill His master plan of salvation! As the Master Potter chooses the material He desires to work with—God is calling the foolish, base, and weak things of this world to confound the wise (1 Cor. 1:27-28). As Master Potter, this is God's choice! We have no right to complain as Paul wrote in (Romans 9).

God has chosen each of us for a specific purpose in His wonderful kingdom plan. Christians have been preparing to fill roles in God's soon coming government to RULE the earth with Jesus, the Christ! This has not been done at random, like spiritual roulette—rather by *selective design*, by the Master Potter!

- **Aging the Clay:** After the potter has chosen the type of clay he chooses to work with—it must be *aged*. This is similar to fermenting or souring, because the clay will virtually reek with a pungent odor.

As clay is placed in a container for several months with plenty of moisture—it begins to decompose into organic compounds that "smell." This is due to bacterial action that promotes plasticity (*The Complete Book of Pottery Making*, John B. Kenny).

As clay becomes plastic through aging, it is much easier to work with. This is also true of Christians on a spiritual plane. Before God can begin fashioning us into His character—we must have WILLING HEARTS and yielding attitudes!

We must perceive ourselves useless without God in our lives and the need for repentance! Jesus said without reservation; **"I am not come to call the righteous, but sinners to repentance" (Matt. 9:13).**

Before God can begin to *mold* character in us—He must have material that is like putty in His hands! He can only use people who are of a HUMBLE spirit!

- **Kneading the Clay:** Next, the potter must knead or *beat* the clay before it can be ready for use. By continuously wedging the clay, pockets of air and hard lumps are removed. This process gives the clay added plasticity and consequently it is easier to work with.

What is the Christian parallel to kneading? Christians are constantly being CHASTENED by our loving Father in order to toughen us up. Through trials, we begin to root out the wrong living habits we have acquired through the world's vain philosophies. Christians must recognize that trials are for our good and to "rejoice" in them as Peter proclaimed (I Pet. 1:6-7).

Without trials, we would not see ourselves as we really are—helpless, dependent, foolish, vain, ignorant, self-righteous! Trials begin to remove the spiritual lumps of sin in our lives.

Now we are ready for the fourth step in character building!

- **Shaping the Clay:** Now that the lumps and air pockets have been removed by the potter through kneading—he can begin *forming* the clay into whatever shape he desires.

Because the clay is still not workable enough—moisture in the form of water or oil is added.

As already shown, water and oil are *analogous* to God's

Holy Spirit. By maintaining a constant supply of God's HOLY SPIRIT, Christians can remain MALLEABLE in God's hands!

Christians must thirst for the "living waters" of God's Holy Spirit. Jesus declared of this:

> **...If any man thirst, let him come unto me, and drink. He that believeth on me, as the scripture hath said, out of his belly shall flow rivers of living water. [But this spake he of the Spirit, which they that believe on him should receive: for the Holy Spirit was not yet given; because that Jesus was not yet glorified] (Jn. 7:37-39).**

In order to be fashioned into His "image" and "likeness"—we must receive enough *spiritual water* to allow our Heavenly Potter to conform us into His model!

- **Firing the Clay:** After the clay has been molded by the potter, it is ready to go into the kiln. The kiln is a *furnace* that will heat the clay till it dries completely to a permanent fixture. Initially the baking is at low heat so the piece will not crack. Then the temperature is gradually increased so adequate *hardness* is attained.

Firing the clay is a delicate operation. Too little heat will render an uncured piece that will be soft and pliable—while too high a temperature can cause cracking and warping.

Likewise, our loving Father, "chastens every son He loves" in order to develop mature clay models (Heb. 12:6-11). Spiritually speaking, this chastening must be at just the right temperature. If the trials we are subjected to are not fiery enough—we will not become hardened! If they are too severe—we will explode! God knows the medium temperature range for each of us!

One thing we can rest assured—our Master Potter will *never* subject His spiritual clay to temperatures [trials] beyond their capabilities (1 Cor. 10:13). So, count it all joy when you fall into different trials—realizing it is all for character maturing (Jas. 1:2-3).

- **Glazing the Clay:** When the moisture in the clay is driven off in the kiln—it becomes permanently hard! Now we are ready for the final FINISH TOUCHES. Here is where added highlights, perhaps in silver or gold are brushed on to make the piece even more stunning. Once the piece has cooled to room temperature, it is given final decorations, glazed and baked again. This second firing bakes the decorations into the piece permanently!

Now for the spiritual *parallel* to Christians. Oftentimes God puts finishing touches on our character and personality through additional trials. This is to polish us up spiritually and remove any ROUGH EDGES from our character.

These added trials may be in the form of the same trial or different ones. But always keep in mind God's modus operandi. He is trying to create a beautiful masterpiece!

Our Heavenly Potter may glaze us over several times before the added spiritual dimensions shine through. Just when we think our trials are over—new ones appear on the horizon. Why? Because our Master Potter realizes that more beautiful god-like features are still needed to make us into His "image" and "likeness."

- **Evaluating the Finished Piece:** At last our piece is ready to be criticized. Has it ENDURED the firing without cracking? Have the decorations taken after glazing a second or third time? The potter is now ready to *evaluate* the piece to see if it is fit for his eventual purpose.

God, the Master Designer of the human race, will ultimately JUDGE each of us to see if we are fit for His creation. If we have not warped or cracked spiritually—God will use us as a king or priest in His soon coming kingdom (Rev. 5:10; 20:6).

What a marvelous reward for those who endure to the

end! (Matt. 24:13). When its all over and done—the Master Potter will have created a *unique* son or daughter of God that will be able to share and inherit all His goods! (Rev. 21)

God—The Master Jeweler

God, the Master Jeweler, relates many spiritual lessons about His purpose for the world from the precious gems He has created. Notice Proverbs 20:15: **"There is gold, and a multitude of rubies: but the lips of knowledge are a precious jewel."**

God demonstrates through the parable in (Ezekiel 16:11) of how He dressed ancient Israel [fine bracelets, chains around her neck, jewels on her forehead, and earrings in her ears, and a beautiful crown upon her head, decked with gold and silver] until she played the harlot.

Pearls were considered by the ancients among the most precious of gems and were highly esteemed as ornaments. This is probably the reason the word is used *metaphorically* for anything of great value, and especially for wise sayings.

God's Word speaks of the Kingdom of heaven like a merchant man, seeking goodly pearls, who, when he had found one pearl of great price, went out and sold all that he had, and bought it (Matt. 13:45). This parable is *analogous* to the Christian who is willing to give up everything for God's truth (a precious pearl). The Eternal admonished Christians not to cast their pearls [truth] before swine (Matt. 7:6).

"New Jerusalem" [the spiritual city composed of "resurrected"Christians is described in earthly terms of precious stones such as jasper, saphire, chalcedony, emerald, sardonyx, sardius, chrysolyte, beryl, topaz, chrysoprasus, jacinth, amethyst, with pearls on the gates (Rev. 21:19-21).

God's Spokesman commanded Moses to make the names of the children of Israel in precious stones to be worn by Aaron and his sons in a breastplate (Ex. 28:4-21). One of the stones mentioned is a diamond which has many spiritual *parallels* to a Christian.

How Christian Diamonds Are Made

Christians are much like a piece of charcoal that has gone through a *process* to become a beautiful diamond. They may look like a rough piece of charcoal now, but someday they will astound the world with their BRILLIANCE! God is producing *spiritual* diamonds who are far more enduring and priceless.

Beautiful gems are made through the crucible of time under extreme heat and pressure! Jesus is in the process of making precious jewels for His spiritual diadem out of Christians (Mal. 3:16-17).

When He is finished—they will possess the following characteristics similar to that of a physical diamond. In fact, only diamonds can polish other diamonds because of their extreme hardness. The Bible tells us that "iron sharpens iron" (Prov. 27:17), and therefore Christians must sharpen each other.

Hardness: The diamond is the *hardest* substance in nature known to man. It is derived from carbon that has been subjected to the extreme heat and pressure of the earth over thousands of years.

Under this intense heat and pressure, the carbon atom actually *moves* or rearranges itself to form an entirely *different* substance! Graphite, coal and charcoal are all forms of carbon, yet these are not gems! Only when the carbon atom is *reconstructed* through heat and pressure is a beautiful diamond produced! God first finds the raw material [Christians] by mining a rock [Stone] into a beautiful jewel (Isa. 51:1).

Now how does this process apply spiritually to Christians? Followers of Christ are *reconstructed* through the heat and pressure of trials. Christians should **"...endure *hardness*, as a good soldier of Jesus Christ" (11 Tim. 2:3).** Emulators of Christ should *rejoice* in fiery trials as they are for our good (1 Pet. 4:12).

Christians must be *unmovable* in the faith in order to be of value in God's Kingdom (1 Cor. 15:58). Only through a toughening-up process is a steadfast character matured!

Cleaned: Once diamonds are formed, they are divided from the ones that have flaws. Similarly, God removes the flaws from His Church by cleaning off our bad character traits through trials.

Brilliance: Diamonds come in various colors, the blue-white being the most sought after. Words can hardly express the feeling one gets from looking at the "sparkle" of a beautiful diamond. It is simply magnificent!

As sparkling lights that shine in a perverse world, Christians are to let their lights be blameless (Phil. 2:15). Jesus exhorted His followers to "let their lights shine" among men (Matt. 5:16).

Refraction: Diamonds have the ability to take in light and *multiply* that light, then push it back to our eyes. This is called refraction. Christians also have refractory power, **"...because the love of God is shed abroad in our hearts by the Holy Spirit which is given unto us" (Rom. 5:5).**

The love of God comes from God to us and we shed it to others by examples. God's Word goes forth and does not return to Him void. It prospers or bears fruit due to the efforts of sincere Christians (Isa. 55:11).

Christians are like the small mirror-like surfaces of a diamond, and must have new direction or reflection of God's character.

Rarity: It takes tons of earth to get one blue diamond. This makes diamonds a *rare* commodity! Christians are also a rare species. Jesus called His church a "little flock" (Lk. 12:32).

Setting: Once diamonds are formed through the crucible of heat and pressure, and providing they don't crack—they are *chosen* because of their brilliance to be put into a beautiful setting.

Likewise, Christian diamonds are now being selected to be put into God's Crown Jewels (Mal. 3:16-17). God will then put His jewels in a particular position of service in His eternal ruling family. Then we will be priceless spiritual gems!

Summary

Diamonds are valuable because of the 3 C's (cut, color and clarity). God is calling Christians to comprise His Son's royal spiritual diadem.

They are being *reconstructed* through trials and testing to fit in that beautiful spiritual crown. Then their character will be as HARD as a diamond, and as BRILLIANT as the shining sun—flawless! They will express the relationship of beauty and rare excellence because of their CHARACTER.

The day is also fast approaching when the present earth will melt away with fervent heat and create a *new* heaven and a *new* earth (Rev. 21:1; 11 Pet. 3:10).

Someday, this earth will be a gem of spiritual gold and crystal (Rev. 21:11). Only then will God the Father dwell with His glorious creation forevermore! (vs. 3).

God—The Master Tailor

Our wonderful Father in heaven has revealed much about Himself, and His plan for humankind through *types* of clothing.

It was God's Spokesman who clothed Adam and Eve with coats of skins after they had sinned (Gen. 3:21). This was *symbolic* of the *sins* they tried to *cover*. The Hebrew word for "naked" implies bareness in a bad or negative way.

The personage who later became Jesus Christ also told the Levites how to dress themselves for serving at the Temple (Ex. 28:2-43). Through His servant Moses, God explained how to make the curtains for the Tabernacle (Ex. 26:1).

God tells us through Paul's writings to put on the whole armor of God to be protected spiritually (Eph. 6:11-18).

Our benevolent God promises to provide for us even as He clothes the lilies of the field (Matt. 6:28-30).

However, just before our Lord returns those who have a lukewarm attitude will have to go through the Great

Tribulation in order to receive *white raiment*, which is *symbolic* of purity (Rev. 3:18).

In (Matthew 22:12), God shows through a parable of a physical marriage, that a certain garment is required in order to be at the marriage supper. This is in reference to the spiritual marriage that is to eventually take place between Jesus Christ and His spotless Bride [clean and white] (Rev. 19:8).

Joshua, the high priest needed a change of raiment because of his many sins! After he repented, God gave him a change of garment, representing forgiveness of sin:

> **Now Joshua was clothed with filthy garments [he had many sins] and stood before the angel. And he answered and spake unto those that stood before Him, saying, take away the filthy garments from him. And unto him he said, Behold, I have caused thine iniquity to pass from thee, and I will clothe thee with change of raiment (Zech. 3:4).**

This verse clearly shows that only when we have forsaken our man-made garments—which are as "filthy rags" to God, will we receive the garments of righteousness! This is not to say that it is our "works" that determine forgiveness, but God's Grace!

Linen—the Clothing of Righteousness

Several different Hebrew and Greek words are used in the Bible for linen, all denoting "fine" or "white". The Biblical references of linen show that it was used for a myriad of uses including nets and burial shrouds.

Linen was chosen over cotton for clothing in warm climates because of its cool feeling.

The Israelites were forbidden to wear a garment made of two sorts of thread such as linen and wool (Lev. 19:19; Deut. 22:11). They were also commanded *not* to mix kinds of seed, fruit or animal. This was all done by their Sustainer to teach them the importance for PURITY of kinds! Ultimately, God wanted to impress upon them the significance of preserving their race by not intermarrying with Gentile nations!

Likewise, Christians are exhorted to separate themselves from the unrighteous (11 Cor. 6:14).

The garments used in the Aaronic priesthood such as tunics, breeches and girdles were made solely of linen (Ex. 28:39; 39:27-29). This was commanded for the purpose of "sanctifying" them from everyone else.

Angels are always described as clothed in linen (Ezek. 9:2; 10:2; Dan. 10:5; 12:6). Linen is used *figuratively* in describing the RIGHTEOUSNESS of those saints who have been *redeemed* from the earth (Rev. 19:8,14).

Clearly, linen's spiritual significance stands for *purity* or *righteousness* in God's eyes!

The veil of the Temple was constructed out of "fine linen" modeled after the "Righteous One" Jesus Christ! He alone was righteous and "was made sin for us, that we might be made the righteous of God in Him."

Following in our elder brother's example, Christians will put on the royal robe of righteousness, symbolic of His spotless character woven in heavens loom!

Chapter Two

GOD'S PLAN REVEALED BY HIS BUSINESSES

God—The Loving Annimal Husbandryman

There are innumerable animals mentioned in the Bible and certain ones *bear* [pun intended] specific relationships to deep *spiritual* meanings as we will now make more apparent.

The book of *Leviticus* contains God's instructions for Moses concerning the kinds of animals the Israelites were to bring for Offerings. God mentioned four kinds: 1) Bull (vs. 5); 2) Sheep (vs. 10; 3) Goat (vs 10); and 4) Turtledove or pigeon (vs. 14). Jesus of course is *envisioned* in all of these offerings *symbolically*. This concept will be covered in greater detail under "The Offerings" in (volume 3).

Although highly speculative, Swiss Reformer Heinrich Bullinger, one of the most influential theologians of the Protestant Reformation in the 16th century, has assigned a sign of the Zodiac to each of the children of Israel.

Bull: A bull represents UNTIRING labor and patience. Jesus is depicted as such because He had endless *patience* and *endurance*—as He taught, preached and healed people (Mk. 1:35; 6:30). Taurus [the bull] of the Zodiac is assigned to Joseph [Ephraim & Manasseh] as part of the character of Christ. The understanding of God's plan as revealed through the signs of the zodiac will be covered shortly under, "God the Astronomer."

Sheep: A sheep is a very MEEK animal and is *symbolic* of the character of Jesus who was led as a lamb to be *slaughtered (Isa. 53)*. The only account that mentions Jesus as being "the lamb of God" is found in (John 1:29). Aries [the ram or lamb] of the Zodiac is assigned to the tribe of Gad.

Goat: Jesus was represented by a scapegoat on the Day of Atonement. A *scapegoat* is someone who is willing to take the BLAME for others. Jesus laid down His life for our sins and was accused unjustly by Caiaphas the Jewish high priest (Jn. 18:13). Yet, Christ said **"... I lay down my life..." (Jn. 10:17)**. Capricorn [the fish-goat] of the Zodiac is assigned to the tribe of Naphtali.

Turtledoves: Turtledoves are noted for their AFFECTION for each other. Two turtledoves were offered to God when Jesus was born (Lk. 2:24). Jesus had compassion toward the needs of others as witnessed on many occasions. Can you see why they were used *symbolically* to represent Christ?

Eagle: Israel was carried away from Egypt by God on eagles wings (Ex. 19:4; Deut. 32:11). The New Testament Church of God escapes the Great Tribulation and the Devil by using the gift of "two wings of a great eagle" (Rev. 12:14). Both events are *symbolic* of supernatural DELIVERANCE.

The eagle is a large hawk-like bird having a powerful beak, wings and feet.

Dove: The dove is *symbolic* of PEACE. The Holy Spirit came upon Jesus "like a dove" (Matt. 3:16). One of the fruits of the Holy Spirit is *peace* (Gal. 5:22).

Dogs: In Bible times, dogs were generally despised OUTCASTS known for their ravenous and filthy habits (Prov. 26:11). Jesus said not to give that which is holy [the truth] to dogs (Matt.

15;27). Paul warned Christians to "beware of dogs [evil workers]..." (Phil. 3:2). The prophet Isaiah made reference to Israel's religious leaders who were not performing their duty, much like many of todays preachers because of greed (Isa. 56:10-11).

Individuals that fail to repent once enlightened by God's Holy Spirit are described as dogs going back to eat their own vomit (1 Pet. 2:22). Such individuals, like dogs, and sorcerers, and whoremongers, and murderers, and idolaters, will not inherit the Kingdom of God (Rev. 22:15).

The second and third constellations under the sign of Gemini are Canis Major and Canis Minor (the dog and the second dog). This sign is attributed to the tribe of Benjamin.

Leopard: A Leopard [panther] is more savage and malevolent than a lion. It possesses great fighting ability and is wary, treacherous, highly intelligent and subtle. Daniel and John used it in a *figurative* sense to describe the Grecian Empire as it was CUNNING and fleet-footed.

Bear: Daniel and John described the Medo-Persian Empire as a bear because it was slow moving, yet DELIBERATE as a war Machine. Issachar is identified with the Zodiac sign Cancer whose first and second constellation is Ursa Minor [the lesser bear] and Ursa Major [the great bear].

Fish: The numerous references to fish and to fishing in the Gospels give clear indication of their commercial importance in Palestine. Many of the apostles were fisherman and Jesus used fish as *analogous* to catching PEOPLE (Lk. 5).

The Zodiac sign Pisces [the fishes] is attributed to the tribe of Simeon.

Serpent: The Bible has many references to serpents which imply POISONOUS qualities. The serpent is commonly used as a *symbol* of evil and Satan was called a serpent (Num. 21:4-9; Jn. 3:14; Rev. 12:9; 20:2). The tribe of Dan is rightfully depicted by the Zodiac sign of a serpent [Scorpio] as he was prophesied to be "a serpent by the way" (Gen. 49:17).

Swine: Although the names "hog" and "pig" are not named in the Bible, "swine" are referred to numerous times. Swine were forbidden to eat by the nation of Israel and labeled "unclean" animals although they part the hoof. In every single instance where the Bible refers to swine, it depicts metaphorically a DEGENERATE state, or the lowest state to which any person can stoop.

The prodigal son in (Luke 15:15), was reduced to a complete state of depravity, that of feeding swine! We are told in (Matthew 7:6) not to cast pearls [God's Truth] before swine. God compares a woman who does not practice discretion, to the snout of a swine (Prov. 1:22)..

Clean and Unclean Animals

In (Leviticus 11, and Deuteronomy 14), God classifies animal meats as either clean or unclean for the nation of Israel to eat. Most religious organizations refute the fact that these laws are still in effect today, and believe they were only given to the nation of Israel to teach spiritual lessons. It is not our intention to answer this question here, only to explain why Christians have disagreement. We shall provide several New Testament scriptures which are the basis for discussion.

One of the first arguments is that the Old Testament was for the Jews, and this was done away with when Jesus started the New Testament. But if these laws were only for the Jews or the ancient Israelites—why were they known to Noah even before the nation of Israel was even established, and there were no Jews present? (Gen. 7:2).

Acts 10: 9-14

This scripture is where God supposedly ordained "unclean meats" in the New Testament. The apostle Peter was given a *vision* of a great sheet let down from heaven with all sorts of creatures. Peter, in a trance, was asked to kill and eat what he saw. He immediately responded: **"No, Lord; for I have never eaten anything that is 'common' or 'unclean'."** What is the meaning of the word "common" in this verse and why not simply "unclean"?

Peter used two distinct Greek words to express two distinct matters, *koinos* and *akathartos,* The Greek word *"koinos"* means "common" and the Greek word *"akathartos"* means "unclean."

In (Romans 14:14) translated in the KJV **"...nothing is unclean of itself..."** the Greek word is *akathartos,* meaning "common" and not "unclean" and is improperly translated. There is a big difference in the two meanings. Paul's statement should have been translated, **"that nothing is common of itself."**

Clean farm animals, torn of beasts, were commonly eaten by the Gentiles. But God inspired Moses to instruct Israel to avoid eating any torn clean animal because of blood in the animal (Exodus 22:31).

Sometimes a clean animal died of itself. What did the law say: **"You shall not eat anything that dies of itself...for you are a people holy to the Lord your God" (Deut. 14:21).** Here again, clean farm animals that died of themselves were forbidden to Israel.

Such practice among the Gentiles would give rise to the expression that meats could be "common"—*[koinos]* in Greek—that is forbidden—though eaten by Gentiles commonly and in their spiritual ignorance.

Sheep, goats, calves, doves and pigeons—creatures sacrificed at the temple of God—are clean animals by nature. When killed by wild beast or upon natural death, they become *common.* That is why Paul wrote that **"there is nothing common of itself."** It is a circumstance that happens to the flesh that renders it *common* to God's people.

Another act that rendered a clean animal *common* was offering it to an idol (Acts 15:29). Later, as the Greek converts understood that an idol was nothing, it was permitted (see 1 Cor. 8).

Greek vegetarians converted to Christ thought all meat was improper to eat, that is, *common.* That is why Paul wrote **"...nothing is common in itself; but it is common for anyone who thinks it common. If your brother [a vegetarian] is being injured by what you eat, you are no longer walking in love..." (Rom. 14:14-15, RSV corrected).**

Acts 10:9-14 can easily be explained by understanding its context. Note that it was a VISION (vs. 17) and Peter did not actually eat any unclean animals. The answer to this *vision* is found in (vs. 28), where this vision was referring to a man, and not an animal.

See also (Chapter 11:17-18,34,36) where God is trying to get the point across to the apostle Peter who was Jewish, as were all of the early church—that now the Gentiles who were "unclean" by nature [spiritually speaking because they were not Jews by birth]—could now become "clean" or have a chance for salvation!

This descriptive language is what was needed for Peter to understand a deep spiritual principle through the *analogy* of "unclean" meats by God!

Mark 7:19

Most religious organizations understand that "unclean meats" were done away with based on Jesus' own words in (Mark 7:19). Let's read this account starting at verse 18: **"...whatsoever thing from without entereth into the man, it cannot defile him; Because it entereth not into his heart, but into the belly, and goeth out into the draught, purging all meats"** (or **margin, making all meats clean KJV).**

The next point of interest is to notice the real issue. The real issue here is not whether we can eat unclean meats—but whether or not washing or not washing one's hands before each meal made one "defiled," as was thought by the hypocritical Pharisees (vs. 1-6).

Jesus was simply trying to explain to the Pharisees and His disciples, that the Pharisees were wrong once again in their whole approach to understanding. They were once again trying to put their own interpretation on God's laws. Jesus was trying to show them how wrong they were. That there was no such commandment ever given as to washing one's hands before eating in the Old Testament.

Jesus was trying to show them through the analogy of food passing through the system—that it did not come in contact with the heart (vs. 19). That food coming into one's body does not defile one's mind because it passes right on out.

Jesus was telling the Pharisees that it was their spiritual attitude [heart or mind] that was perverted. By putting so much emphasis on little matters [such as washing one's hands before eating]—the Pharisees made "a mountain out of a molehill" or into a commanded ceremony similar to a physician scrubbing up before an operation. The Pharisees neglected the most important spiritual matters once again. They would eventually add hundreds of legalistic laws to show their righteousness.

Meats Offered unto Idols

The apostle Paul said, **"Let no man judge you in meat or a holyday" (Col. 2:16).** That it was ok to eat meats offered up unto idols (1 Cor. 8:4, 8:13); and that nothing was unclean of itself (Rom. 14:14). He told Titus, **"Unto the pure, all things are pure" (Tit. 1:15).**

Paul told Timothy: **"For every creature of God is good and nothing to be refused, if it be received with thanksgiving. For it is SANCTIFIED by the Word of God and prayer."** (1 Tim. 4:4-5).

What did Paul mean by these seemingly contradictory statements? The key word here is *sanctified* which means "set apart." Unclean meats were "set apart" by the Word of God in (Leviticus 11 and Deuteronomy 14) as shown previously. But for whom and for what purpose?

These confusing scriptures can be clarified once one realizes that Paul was writing to people who were familiar with "clean and unclean meats", and understood the meaning of what "common" meant.

Paul related, although meat may have been offered to a false god in a heathen temple—this did not make the meat unfit to eat physically, if one had a pure mind or understanding of God's laws.

The apostle Paul showed further, that he could actually go into one of these heathen temples to eat meat that was offered by heathens—and it didn't bother him in the least, for he knew a temple or a heathen's offering could not hurt him (1 Cor. 8:4, 8:13).

Paul did caution however that although all things are lawful to do within God's laws, all things are not always helpful, nor do they build up (1 Cor. 6:12; 10:23). A Christian should not do things whereby his brother would be offended and stumble (Rom. 14:20-21).

The argument is made, that if Christ made it so abundantly clear that "unclean" meats could now be eaten though Peter's vision—why didn't Peter practice this supposed "new teaching" 20 years later in the book of Galatians where we find Paul rebuking Peter for his hypocrisy of avoiding eating with

Gentiles?

The acceptance of Gentile Christians was reaffirmed during the Jerusalem Council in which specific laws of circumcision, abstaining from meats offered to idols, fornication; etc. were to be either followed or not (Acts 15:1-29). Specifically, the keeping of the law (dietary laws included) was not to be binding upon the Gentiles (verse 24). However, when some Jews arrived in Antioch from Jerusalem, Peter gradually began to withdraw from eating with the Gentile Christians, and instead ate with the Jewish Christians. Galatians 2:12 says he did this because he feared these Jews. These were Jews that James said were teaching a false gospel (Acts 15:1).

The apostle Paul called Peter out in front of everyone. As the text says, his primary sin (as well as the other Jews who followed his lead) was that he "walked not uprightly according to the truth of the gospel" (Gal 2:14). In other words, he was teaching a false gospel. He believed in salvation by grace, but by withdrawing from the Gentile Christians, he was showing with his actions that he believed Jewish traditions were superior. He was "nullifying the grace of God" (Gal 2:21).

Because of this action, Paul called Peter a hypocrite. He believed one thing, but did something else. As a leader in the church, he was to set a good example for others, but instead, his hypocritical actions led others astray (other Jews followed his lead including "even Barnabas" (Gal 2:13).

Paul rightly confronted and condemned Peter's sinful actions.

The Carnivorous Lion

Lion: Lions by their size and majestic bearing have won the title "King of the Beasts." Usually they are friendly, travel in small groups, share prey peaceably, and kill only what they intend to consume. The tribe of Judah is represented by the Zodiac sign Leo (lion).

Animal noises fit their build and it is only fitting that the MIGHTIEST of the beasts makes a loud roar! The Bible *pictures* Satan, God's archenemy, as a *roaring* lion out to devour whom he may (1 Pet. 5:8). Jesus is also *symbolically* represented by a lion; being the lion of the tribe of Judah (Rev. 5:5). Daniel and John described the Babylonian Empire as a winged lion because of its *swiftness* in battle.

Because Satan would have us for breakfast (Lk.22:24), there are invaluable lessons we can understand about this ENEMY by observing the strengths and weaknesses of lions.

Strengths: A lion is capable of running the 100 yard dash in 4 seconds flat! There's no way in the world a human being can outrun a lion (even with steroids)! Lions are as STRONG as a bear and have been known to run with a small deer in their mouth! They can rip and tear their prey apart with their razor sharp teeth in a matter of minutes. Because of their tan and white coloring, lions are easily *camouflaged* from their victims.

Lions are excellent swimmers and have a keen sense of smell. This cunning beast is patient in waiting for, and moving towards its prey. They have the uncanny ability to perceive distance in attacking different prey. Lions only roar at night, not when they are hunting!

Weaknesses: Although lions have many strengths—they also have several limitations! It is imperative that all Christians understand these weaknesses, in order to stand off the lion-like attacks of Satan.

Because of their prodigious size, weighing between 300-500 lbs.—lions become TIRED very easily and have little *endurance*. If there is any *resistance* from their prey—lions will back off!

They also will turn away and give up if they cannot get close enough to their prey. That is why they usually go after the weak and sickly in a herd—because these feeble ones put up little resistance! There are six groups that can become a lions prey:

- **Lamb:** Oftentimes lions will seek out a *crippled* lamb in the flock. Understanding this, Christians should prevent becoming spiritually crippled by allowing themselves to slip back into old doctrinal beliefs. The parable of the *Old Wine Skins* is *analogous* to this (Matt. 9:16).

- **Weak:** Lions will seek out the *weak* in the flock because they put up little resistance. Spiritually speaking, Christians must eat a balanced diet of [prayer, Bible study, meditation, fasting, fellowship] in order to remain spiritually strong! Followers of Christ become spiritually sick by allowing our RESISTANCE to be lowered from unforgiving attitudes such as hatred, pride, selfishness, covetousness, discontentment, rebellion, promiscuousness, criticism, disobedience doubting, accusative; etc. May God help us to be strong minded, **"Lest Satan should get advantage of us: for we are not ignorant of his devices"** (11 Cor. 2:11).

- **Young:** Many times, lions will look for the young *babies* in a herd because they cannot run fast. Satan's tactics are similar in that he tries to UPROOT newly enlightened Christians. This is made clear through the parable of *The Sower* (Matt. 13:4).

- **Old:** Another easy victim for lions are the *old* in a herd. They too cannot run fast enough to escape this killer. The analogy to older Christians is just this. Often times, older members tend to get "burned out" spiritually and have little drive left in them. They become WEARY of well-doing and begin to slip back into their old ways! This is exactly what Satan the roaring lion desires— Christians are admonished to not fall into his trap!

- **Sleeping:** The carnivorous lion will oftentimes stalk those who are *slumbering* in a flock. Before they wake up, this beast is at their throats! Satan, the Christian predator also seeks to devour those who have "dozed off" spiritually! The Bible gives stern warnings to those who are *sleeping* spiritually. The parable of the *Ten Virgins* in (Matthew 25) is most sobering! Paul cautions LUKEWARM Christians to **"...awake out of sleep, now is salvation near"** (Rom. 13:11). Christians should not allow themselves to become too comfortable in this world—our enemy is watching us intensely!

- **Fringers:** Those who would *stray* from the main flock are easy victims for the fleet-footed lion! The *analogy* to Christians is quite simple. Those who think they can go it *alone* will be devoured by the insidious Satan in no time at all. Avoiding Christian fellowship and the spiritual weapons of prayer and Bible study is most dangerous!

Summary

Satan hates RESISTANCE just like a lion on the prowl! The Bible speaks of our spiritual predator: **"...Resist the devil, and he will flee from you, Draw nigh to God, and he will draw nigh to you. Cleanse your hands ye sinners; and purify your hearts, ye double minded. Be afflicted [fast], ...humble yourselves...speak not evil one of another..." (Jas. 4:7-11).**

Christians can understand some vital points from these verses. Satan will flee from us—not visa versa if we RESIST! Resist does not mean to give in! How do we resist? By using the spiritual weapons of prayer, fasting, and repentance! This is how we remain spiritually strong!

If we do these things—Satan will FLEE from us like a wounded lion licking his wounds! Be careful to *never* allow yourself to fall into any of these six categories because of NEGLIGENCE! In the meantime, enjoy life while your enemy cannot attack you—because you are close to God!

Christians are especially appetizing to Satan because they are a part of God's plan and therefore are big game! But a member who has some besetting spiritual weakness is like a wounded animal who doesn't have a chance against the spirited lion!

The prey animals, over a long distance, can usually outrun a lion. During daylight, the prey spot the lion and run away before the lion gets close enough to begin its charge. That's why most daylight hunting attempt by lions fail! *Darkness* gives the lion the edge and that is why lions, in general, prefer to hunt at night.

Do you see the spiritual analogy? Satan is sometimes called the "prince of darkness" because he likes to keep people in the dark spiritually! Jesus tells us how to come out of darkness by following Him, **"I am the light" (Jn. 8:12).** When we are close to that light source, Satan will not be able to overtake us! When we wander away from that light source—danger lurks behind the spiritual bushes and trees!

The Lion, Lamb and Child

There is a scripture in Isaiah that describes the restoration of God's government to the earth. Notice it in Isaiah 11:6: **"The wolf also shall dwell with the lamb, and the leopard shall lie down with the kid; and the calf and the young lion and the fatling together; and a little child shall lead them."**

Here we find described a lion, a lamb and a little child leading them—*picturing* the RESTORATION of GOD'S GOVERNMENT to the earth! Each of these entities picture a phase of Christian development that we must all go through *before* we enter God's Kingdom.

Becoming bold as Lions

The Bible *pictures* a lion as being STRONGEST among beasts...like a king whom there is no rising up (Prov. 30:29-30). Young lions *roar* after their prey and seek their meat from God (Ps. 104:21).

The fear of a king is as a roaring lion (Prov. 20:2). Here we find a relationship between royalty and lions. King Solomon had 12 lions made to stand close to his throne (1 Kings 10:16-20).

The nation of Israel is described as a lion in (Ezekiel 19:19). Its history is filled with zeal, setting Christians an example of a "roaring lion." She is a lion among nations (Num. 24:5,9), and will soon understand her rightful role of leadership among nations in God's Kingdom.

The remnant of Jacob shall be among the Gentile nations in the midst of many as a lion (Micah 5:8). The standard of the tribe of Dan was represented by a lion (Duet. 33:22).

The Eternal's voice will be heard as a roaring lion, who is *unafraid* of anyone (Isa. 3:4).

Jesus Christ is also described as the lion of the tribe of Judah (Rev. 5:5).

The RIGHTEOUS are to become bold as a lion (Prov. 28:1). Keeping of God's law is how to become righteous (Ps. 119:172).

The righteous are BOLD as a lion, because they are *self-confident*! They are self-confident because they have built *character*! They have built character because they have been faithful to God!

Christians must come *boldly* before God's throne of Grace and Truth, that we may obtain mercy (Heb. 4:16). We must study God's Word daily and *boldly,* never allowing anything to distract us.

Can we *boldly* say, **"…the Lord is my helper, and I will not *fear* what man shall do unto me?"** Christians must not cave into man's threats of breaking His laws—we must become bold as Lions!

Christian Lambs

Our Savior Jesus Christ is *pictured* as an innocent lamb being brought before the slaughter (Isa. 53:7; Jn. 1:29; Rev. 5:6).

The marriage supper between Christ, the Lamb, and His Church will take place upon His return (Rev. 19:7-9).

Christians are *portrayed* as a little flock of lambs (Lk. 12:32). Jesus told Peter to "feed my lambs" (Jn. 21:15). Today, Christians are being fed by God's ministry!

Upon His return, Jesus will feed His flock (Isa. 40:10-11). He was the good Shepherd who laid down His life for His sheep (Jn.10:14-15). His sheep hear His voice, and no man can pluck them out of His Father's hand (Jn. 10:27-30).

Christ's ministry is *pictured* as *sheep* among wolves (Lk. 10:3). Christ's Church is protected as a lamb (Isa. 16:1).

Becoming as "Little Children"

The final entity of Isaiah's prophecy pictures a little child leading a lion and a lamb. This "little child" is *reminiscent* of the "childlike" characteristics that all Christians must put on in order to qualify for God's Kingdom.

The nation of Israel is *envisioned* as a child of God in (Hosea 11:1 and Deuteronomy 1:30-31).

Jesus, our *example* and spiritual leader was the Father's Child as the Father said, **"This is my beloved Son in whom I am well pleased" (Matt. 3:16-17; Jn. 5:20).**

Christians are pictured as "little children" or "Sons" of God (Jn. 13:33; 1 Jn. 3:1; 4:4).

The Lion, Lamb and little Child leading them in Isaiah's prophecy represent in *type*—the *restoration* of *God's government* on the earth!

The little Child is a *type* of Jesus, who is leading Christians today! Christians are qualifying for leadership responsibilities in the future Kingdom of God. Jesus said further of Christians "we must become as little children" [in our relationships with God], if we want to enter the Kingdom of God!

Christians are to develop the humble, corrective, unassuming, receptive, innocent attitudes of little children?

God—The Great Shepherd

There are many scriptures in the Bible which describe God as a Shepherd and true Christians as His sheep. Thus, God reveals His FAMILY Plan through the analogy of a shepherd and his sheep.

If we study the physical relationship of a shepherd to his sheep, we can learn a great deal about God's plan for us. Let's notice: God in the form of Jesus Christ is depicted as the Chief Shepherd. See (Ps. 23:1; Jn. 10:14; Heb. 13:20; 1 Pet. 5:4). Ultimately, Christians will follow in their elder Brother's footsteps in the Kingdom of God. Therefore, Christians have not been called to become ballistic experts to "zap" people into obedience to God's laws—but to become gentle Shepherds (Jn. 23:4).

Concerning the Kingdom of God ruled by Jesus Christ, the Word of God says, **"...he shall rule them with a rod of iron; as the vessels of a potter shall they be broken to shivers..." (Rev. 2:27).** Truly, Jesus is to smite the nations with a sharp sword upon His return, and Rule the nations with a rod of iron (Rev. 12:5; 19:15).

However, many have interpreted these scriptures to mean that Jesus is to "rule" as a modern-day dictator. The Greek word used for "rule" is *poimaino*, and means to act as a shepherd (gentle, kind, feeding, supervise, guide). This verb describes the governing power exercised by our Loving Shepherd. It will be of firm and gentle character! Jesus will hold a sceptre of royalty!

Likewise, Christians are to now be "ruling" our families as a loving shepherd king with love and compassion?

Spiritual Relationships

During His absence, Jesus told Peter to feed His sheep [Christians] (Jn. 21:16; 1 Pet. 5:2). Jesus [the very first Christian] was described as "a sheep being led to the slaughter" (Acts 8:32). The Passover lamb is *emblematic* of Jesus Christ's sacrifice.

The Passover Lamb should have special significance to all Christians, and the Old Testament Passover ceremony brings out many of these relationships:

- **Preselected:** The lambs were selected on the 10th day of the first month (Ex. 12:3). Jesus was selected before the creation of the world as "the Lamb slain from the foundation of the world" (Rev. 13:8).

- **Without blemish:** The lambs had to be without blemish, healthy and flawless in appearance. Jesus was without the blemish of sin: he lived a perfect, sinless life (1 Pet. 1:19; Heb. 4:15).

- **Died without a struggle:** The lambs didn't struggle against their executioners. They went to death in silence (Isa. 53:7). Jesus also died without a struggle. He did not defend himself (Matt. 26:51-63).

- **Deliverance by blood:** The lambs blood was placed on the door jambs and headers. This saved the Israelite firstborn from the death plague (Ex. 12:7, 13). It prepared the way for Israel to journey to the promised land (Ex. 12:31-33). When Jesus' blood is applied to our sins, we are no longer under the death penalty (Eph. 1:7). This reconciles us to God and prepares us for salvation through the life of Jesus (Rom. 5:9-10).

- **Flesh provides sustenance:** The flesh of the lambs was roasted in fire. Once eaten, it became a source of strength to start Israel's journey to the promised land (Ex. 12:8-11, 41-42). The flesh of Jesus was beaten and broken before His death (Matt. 20:17-19). Along with the shedding of His blood, His body is part of His supreme sacrifice for sin (Heb. 10:10, 12). It is a source of strength necessary for eternal life as Jesus stated, **"Whoever eats My flesh and drinks My blood has eternal life, and I will raise him at the last day" (Jn. 6:54).**

There are many spiritual relationships that we can glean from a sheep's *wool* that can also apply to Christians. From the pen of God's prophet, we read in (1 Kings 3:4) that wool was used as tribute because of its *value*. White wool in particular was a sign of wealth (Ezek. 27:18). Here are some additional physical properties of wool that can also be equated with a Christian's character:

- **Durability:** Wool is especially long lasting, or enduring. Christians must also *endure* many trials of testing to the end.

- **Wrinkle resistant:** Christians, like wool must be *resilient* and bounce back after spiritual setbacks.

- **Elasticity:** Wool can stretch or compress easily and return to its original form. This *parallels* the Christian who must also be *flexible* and open-minded in their Biblical studies.

- **Warmth:** If we looked at a wool fiber under the microscope, we would see that the very center of the fiber has an air cylinder which gives it very good insulating properties of warmth. Likewise, Christians must show much *warmth* in the attitude of love toward each other and humankind.

Huddle Together

Jesus gives the analogy of a sheep being lost and then found in (Luke 15:4-7). This was in retrospect to that of a Christian who leaves the flock and returns upon repenting. The basic nature of sheep is to *stay together* in a flock in order to be PROTECTED from wild animals that would devour them.

A wolf or lion will always go after the strays from the flock. The Bible describes Satan as a roaring lion trying to devour whomever he may! That is why it is vital that Christians stay together in the flock or in the Church for protection!

At the height of a storm, sheep will huddle together in the middle of the field. Those in the middle of the flock are the *safest*, and those on the outside try to squeeze into the middle. The sheep know by instinct, that when they are alone during a storm they are vulnerable to the elements, and that there is safety in numbers!

The lesson—don't stray from the flock!

Sheep are *valuable* for food and clothing. Sheep *herd together*, unlike cows or horses that wander. Because sheep are unable to protect themselves—*they need a protector*! They cannot run very fast and a wolf or lion could easily devour them. Likewise, Christians should stay away from the wolves and lions of Satan's world!

There is a beautiful analogy of Christ leading His sheep [Israel] to its final grazing pasture to feed forever in (Ezekiel 34). During the Millennium, the land will be the most beautiful grazing land for His lost and sick sheep (verses 11-16). This reminds us of the parable in which Christ said, **"Other sheep are of my fold" (Jn. 10:16).**

Notice the wording in Jeremiah which many commentators believe is a millennial setting regarding the time when Christian Shepherds will feed the nation of Israel after Jesus gathers His sheep out of captivity:

> **Woe be unto the pastors that destroy and scatter the sheep of my pasture! saith the LORD. Therefore, thus saith the LORD God of Israel against the pastors that feed my people; Ye have scattered my flock, and driven them away, and have not visited them: behold, I will visit upon you the evil of your doings, saith the LORD.**
>
> **And I will gather the remnant of my flock out of all countries whither I have driven them [after the Great Tribulation, emphasis mine], and will bring them again to their folds; and they shall be fruitful and increase. And I will set up shepherds [resurrected Christians] over them**

> which shall feed them: and they shall fear no more, nor be dismayed, neither shall they be lacking, saith the LORD (Jer. 23:1-4).

Sheep need a Shepherd

God's people are pictured as *sheep* and therefore have need of a shepherd (Matt. 25:32). True believers have always been equated with sheep and therefore need a shepherd to guide them, notice in (Num. 27:16).

Jesus also equated Christians with sheep in (Matt. 9:35-36). The Bible describes Christians as "sheep" among "wolves" (Matt. 10:16), and that Satan's ministers appear as wolves in sheep's clothing (Matt. 7:15) These are false shepherds (Jer. 23) that cannot understand God's truths, or guide His flock into salvation (Isa. 56:9-12).

The Eternal doesn't mince words when He describes these "false shepherds" who feed themselves instead of His flock (Ezek. 34).

As a young boy, King David learned a great deal about his future responsibility as Israel's King, from herding sheep (11 Sam. 12:1-5).

Jesus admonished His disciples to "feed" His lambs in (Jn. 21:15). These were young lambs destined to become older sheep with the help of His ministers (shepherds). The Greek word here for "feed" is *bolki* and means to feed, lead, guide, defend, govern, and protect the flock!

One of the prime responsibilities of God's Shepherds is to protect His flock from ravening wolves [false teachers], who would enter the flock and devour it through heresies (Acts 20:28-29).

God's ministerial Shepherds are to therefore feed the flock spiritual food so they won't be tossed to and fro by false doctrine, and also set the right example (1 Pet. 5:2-4).

The 23rd Psalm, **"The Lord is My Shepherd"** was written from the perspective of how a Christian sheep views the Chief Shepherd. Notice the words, **"The Lord is my shepherd: I shall not want" (vs. 1).**

Characteristics of a Good Shepherd

- A good shepherd is **concerned** about his individual sheep (Acts 15:36). They visit them frequently to see how they are doing. The sheep hear only the good Shepherd's voice and he calls them by name (Jn. 10:3). God's sheep follow Him only and He goes after the one in 99 who is lost (Matt. 18:12). A good shepherd gives encouragement. Our Eternal Shepherd knows His sheep (Jn. 10:14).

- A good shepherd gives his sheep **rest.** God provides us with His weekly (spiritual) rest to get spiritually rejuvenated for future hardships.

- A good shepherd **provides** his sheep with daily sustenance. God the Father, our spiritual Shepherd, provides His flock with food, clothing, shelter and protection.

- A good shepherd **leads** his flock, and guides it with proper leadership (Isa. 40:10-11). He should feed the flock and lead it with gentleness (Jn. 10:3-4). God's ministers lead them in paths of righteousness (Deut. 32:2), and teach them to fear no evil! (Ps. 23) quotes "I will fear no evil, your rod and staff protect me."

God—The Master Chef

God, the Master Chef, has revealed His glorious plan for humankind around food—(see chapters on Offerings and Holy Days in Vol. 3).

Our High Tribunal of the universe can also be described as a manager of a restaurant, and His ministry as a Cook. The restaurant is *analogous* to the Church, and the Bible is His recipe book. Each minister can make a different menu from it, or as in any restaurant—each individual Cook [minister] can make a different menu [sermon] from the same food stuffs (Bible).

There are many scriptures in God's Word that make this analogy very clear. Our High Priest said we should pray for our daily bread (Matt. 6:11). Jesus further stated the most important part of the meal is he that sits at meat [the Church] (Lk. 22:27).

The chef [ministry] can serve *milk* or strong *meat* (1 Cor. 3:2; Heb. 5:12). A Christian's meat is to do the will of Him that sent Him (Jn. 4:34).

As in any good restaurant, the chef can burn the meat or make it too well-done! However, this does not mean the restaurant [Church] is not a five-star restaurant, or the food [Bible] is no good! We can enjoy the restaurant and the food regardless of how lousy the waiter or the Cook!

The ministry [Cook] must serve whosoever enters the restaurant (whoever God the Manager allows in—or whom He calls).

Milk and Strong Meat

The apostle Paul makes reference in (1 Corinthians 3:1) that carnal babies in Christ need *milk* and not strong meat. He further says in (Hebrews 5:13) that: **"For every one that useth milk is unskillful in the word of righteousness: for he is a babe (baby). But strong meat belongeth to them that are of full age [maturity], even those who by reason of use have their senses exercised to discern both good and evil."**

What exactly did Paul mean by these glaring words—and what is meant by spiritual milk and strong meat?

The Milk of the Word

On a physical level, you wouldn't give a little baby pizza or something hard to digest. Besides it's digestive system, there are also physical differences in speech, writing, etc. Because it can't speak yet, a little baby *cries* when it is discomforted with gas.

On a spiritual level, new-born babies in Christ must grow on spiritual pabulum—or the basic spiritual tenants of Christianity.

Notice Paul's wording to this effect: **"Brethren, be not children in understanding: howbeit in malice [hate] be ye children, but in understanding be men" (1 Cor. 14:20).**

Little children don't have any malice!

Our Savior said we must become like little children [in humility] (Matt. 18:1-3). King David was like a little child in the attitude of repentance (Ps. 131:1).

The apostle Peter also admonished babes in Christ: **"Wherefore laying aside all malice, and all guile, and hypocracies, and envies, and all evil speakings, As newborn babes, desire the sincere milk of the word, that ye may grow thereby" (1 Pet. 2:1-2).**

Paul elaborates in the book of Hebrews as to what exactly constitutes a "babe in Christ." He says, anyone who is UNSKILLFUL in the Word of God, and needs a teacher himself—is considered a spiritual baby!

Strong Meat

Now that we understand what the Bible considers as the "milk" of the Word—what is "strong meat"?

Once again the apostle Paul provides us with a clear definition: **"But strong meat [solid food] belongeth to them that are of full age [mature]...to discern both good and evil" (Heb. 5:14).**

A person who is able to digest "spiritual meat" is one who can exercise his senses in both good and evil because he or she is *skillful* in using the Bible or Word of God!

Paul further writes,

> **...let us go on unto perfection, not laying again the foundation of repentance from dead works, and of faith toward God, of the doctrine of baptisms, and of the laying on of hands and of resurrection of the dead, and of eternal judgment [basic church doctrines] (Heb. 6:1-2).**

Spiritual growth is stagnated if we haven't proven the basic doctrines of the Church. On the other hand, Paul, speaking to Jewish believers goes on to say that those who commit sin are *knowledgeable*—but don't produce growth [fruit] in their lives (Heb. 6:4-7). But this admonition must be applied to Gentiles as well!

Notice the admonition in Hebrews 10:26: **"For if we sin wilfully after we have received the knowledge of the truth, there remaineth no more sacrifice for sins."** These people (Jewish and Gentile Believers) commit what many have termed "the unpardonable sin" after they have received the knowledge of the truth!

The Unpardonable Sin

Needless to say, this passage has been very controversial among Christian opinions and commentators. One belief is that the passage is not intended to describe those who are true Christians, but only those who have been awakened and enlightened, and who then fall back. The other concept maintains that it refers to those who are true Christians, and who then apostatize. We will now quote several commentators so the reader can come to his own conclusion. Barnes' Notes on the Bible says:

> **The contending parties have been Calvinists and Arminians; each party, in general, interpreting it according to the views which are held on the question about falling from grace. I shall endeavor, as well as I may be able, to state the true meaning of the passage by an examination of the words and phrases in detail, observing here, in general, that it seems to me that it refers to true Christians; that the object is to keep them from apostasy, and that it teaches that if they should apostatize, it would be impossible to renew them again or to save them. That it refers to true Christians will be apparent from these considerations.**
>
> **(1) Such is the sense which would strike the great mass of readers. Unless there were some theory to defend, the great body of readers of the New Testament would consider the expression used here as describing true Christians.**
>
> **(2) The connection demands such an interpretation. The apostle was addressing Christians. He was endeavoring to keep them from apostasy. The object was not to keep those**

who were awakened and enlightened from apostasy, but it was to preserve those who were already in the Church of Christ, from going back to perdition. The kind of exhortation appropriate to those who were awakened and convicted, but who were not truly converted, would be 'to become converted;' not to warn them of the danger of 'falling away.'

(3) This interpretation accords, as I suppose, with the exact meaning of the phrases which the apostle uses. An examination of those phrases will show that he refers to those who are sincere believers. The phrase 'it is impossible' obviously and properly denotes absolute impossibility. It has been contended, by Storr and others, that it denotes only great difficulty. But the meaning which would at first strike all readers would be that 'the thing could not be done;' that it was not merely very difficult, but absolutely impracticable.

The word - ἀδύνατον adunaton - occurs only in the New Testament in the following places, in all which it denotes that the thing could not be done; Matthew 19:26; Mark 10:27, 'With men this is impossible;' that is, men could not save one who was rich, implying that the thing was wholly beyond human power. Luke 18:27, 'the things which are impossible with men are possible with God'… These passages show that it is not merely a great difficulty to which the apostle refers, but that he meant to say that the thing was wholly impracticable; that it could not be done. And if this be the meaning, then it proves that if those referred to should fall away, they could never be renewed.

Jamieson-Fausset-Brown Commentary states:

Illumination, however, was not supposed to be

the inseparable accompaniment of baptism: thus Chrysostom says, 'Heretics have baptism, not illumination: they are baptized in body, but not enlightened in soul: as Simon Magus was baptized, but not illuminated.' That 'enlightened' here means knowledge of the word of truth, appears from comparing the same Greek word 'illuminated,' Heb 10:32, with Heb 10:26, where 'knowledge of the truth' answers to it.

Now, a final quote from Matthew Henry's Concise Commentary on Hebrews:

6:1-8 The apostle is not speaking of the falling away of mere professors, never convinced or influenced by the gospel. Such have nothing to fall away from, but an empty name, or hypocritical profession. Neither is he speaking of partial declinings or backslidings. Nor are such sins meant, as Christians fall into through the strength of temptations, or the power of some worldly or fleshly lust. But the falling away here mentioned, is an open and avowed renouncing of Christ, from enmity of heart against him, his cause, and people, by men approving in their minds the deeds of his murderers, and all this after they have received the knowledge of the truth, and tasted some of its comforts. Of these it is said, that it is impossible to renew them again unto repentance. Not because the blood of Christ is not sufficient to obtain pardon for this sin; but this sin, in its very nature, is opposite to repentance and every thing that leads to it. If those who through mistaken views of this passage, as well as of their own case, fear that there is no mercy for them, would attend to the account given of the nature of this sin, that it is a total and a willing renouncing of Christ, and his cause, and joining with his enemies, it would

> **relieve them from wrong fears. We should ourselves beware, and caution others, of every approach near to a gulf so awful as apostacy; yet in doing this we should keep close to the word of God, and be careful not to wound and terrify the weak, or discourage the fallen and penitent. Believers not only taste of the word of God, but they drink it in. And this fruitful field or garden receives the blessing. But the merely nominal Christian, continuing unfruitful under the means of grace, or producing nothing but deceit and selfishness, was near the awful state above described; and everlasting misery was the end reserved.**

As stated previously, there are many opinions on this subject. Is the writer of Hebrews speaking solely to zealous Jews going back to a form of "ceremonial works of the Law" instead of accepting the grace of God, or are they Christians who have fallen from grace? Or is it a question of "once saved always saved"? We will cover this subject further in Volume 3.

How do we learn the Word of God?

By studying the Word of God and testimonies of God (Ps. 119:9-16).

Then we must exercise them by putting His word into practice!

God's Word [the Holy scriptures] are designed to make us wise from childhood (11 Tim. 3:14).

The Eternal has given us many vital spiritual tools to bring us to spiritual adulthood. His Holy Spirit helps us to discern both good and evil and then to put the good into practice (Gal. 5:22).

God has also provided us with His ministry to help perfect His Saints, so they can grow up and measure up to the spiritual perfection of our elder Brother Jesus Christ (Eph. 4:11-15).

God's Plan revealed by
what we put in Our Mouth

Under the New Testament, bread [leavened and unleavened], and wine have spiritual significance! See (Feast days Vol. 3).

In fact, the Old Covenant annual Feast days of God required certain foodstuffs to be eaten or restricted for spiritual understanding of God's master plan.

On the day of Pentecost [Firstfruits], you could eat whatever you wanted, but on Trumpets, fresh corn, and new grain was stressed. When the day of Atonement came, *nothing* was to be eaten at all! During the Feast of Tabernacles, one could eat *whatsoever his heart desired*, but meat and strong drink were emphasized. This was a time of *feasting* on the best meats and drink money could buy!

Manna was a part of Israel's diet in the wilderness experience. When Christians go through a "burnt-offering" spiritually [a trial], we don't get anything back (no reward). Through trials, God wants to see if we are willing to continue in His way of life UNCONDITIONALLY! Remember how God instructed our first parents not to eat of the tree of knowledge of good and evil?

God is trying and *testing* each of us continually to PROVE our FAITHFULNESS and loyalty to Him under any circumstance. Then He will give us Eternal Peace! Lucifer was a faithful son until he refused to give any more "burnt-offerings" and wanted only "peace-offerings."

Contrariwise, even though Abraham showed weakness in lying that his wife was his sister, he obeyed God without even knowing where he was going (Heb. 11:8).

Job was also faithful in offering Burnt-offerings (Job. 1:5). God saw Job in his affliction (Job 42:5), and told Job to make a "Burnt-offering" (vs.8). God accepted Job after he gave his offering because he did what God said—regardless of what he thought or *personal satisfaction*. Job passed his trial and God gave him back twice as much as he had before (Job.42:10).

The Eternal is trying to teach us a spiritual lesson from the offering of physical things. Whether they be food, money, or service in the form of GIVING ourselves as a "living sacrifice" (Rom. 12:1)—the principle is the same. We have to learn to give to others out of the goodness of our heart! It may be very difficult at times and even inconvenient, but this is our duty to do (Lk. 17:10).

If we want to quit before we finish God's purpose for us, we will certainly feel better. One may feel better quitting a game when the score is tied, or quitting school in their senior year. You may feel better because you don't have to go through a trial, and the pressure is released—but when you've won the game or graduated, it's all worth it!

Likewise, the trials and tests we go through now, cannot be compared to the glory God has in store for us!

God's Plan Revealed by Offerings

The Old Testament contains some twenty-four Hebrew words which are more or less *synonymous* with "Offer" or "Offering." These Hebrew words have variable meanings and therefore it is imperative to understand the exact Hebrew word translated in each instance.

These various Hebrew words are referred to in the marginal reference column of some Bibles and are usually translated as "burnt-offering," "peace-offering," "heave-offering," etc.

The following Hebrew words and their meanings in regard to "offerings" are given from the *Companion Bible,* Ap. 43.

1. The **VERB** "to offer".

I. KARAB means to draw near, but in the Hiphil conjugation, to make to approach, or draw near: hence, to bring near. See Korban, No. 1 below.

II. NAGASH to come near, after having been so brought i,e., to enjoy the presence which the Korban [see below 11. i.]) has secured. Cp. Jer. 30: 21 where we have both words. Hence used of coming near with offerings. Cp. Greek engizo Heb. 7:19, and prosphero Matt. 2:11; 5:23; 8:4. Mark 1:44. Luke 5:14. John 16:2. In the Epistle to the Hebrews it is used twenty times in a sacrificial sense, except Heb 12: 7, "God brings you near as sons". See also Heb. 9:14,28. Used also of the sinner's approach to God by offering, Heb. 4:16; 7:25; 10. 1, 22; 11:6.

III. ASAH to make ready or prepare a victim for sacrifice; to make a victim a specific offering. Hence to offer. First occurrence in Ex. 10:25 (sacrifice). Then Ex. 29:36,38,39 (offer) .&c.

IV. ZABACH to slay [and offer up]; hence to offer what has been slain; to sacrifice. Hence No. XII. below.

V. SHABAT to kill or slay [as a butcher]; used of men as well as of animals. Judg. 12:6, 1 Kings 18, 40. First occurrence Gen. 22:10; 37:31, Then Ex. 12:6.

VI. ALAH to offer up, especially a burnt offering, from its name in 11.11. below.

VII. KATAR to burn or turn into vapour. Used of the incense which —Kethoreth, but also of the "Olah" '(ll.ll) and parts of the Minchah (11. 111). and the Zebach (II. XlI.) because these ascended to Jehovah.

VIII. SARAPH is used of burning up [or rather, down] the sin-offering, because nothing ascended up to God in that offering.

IX. RUM, to offer up as a heave-offering.

11. The **NOUN** "offering"

I. KORBAN a gift. or an admittance-offering; from I, i. above. It is the present brought, to this day in the East, in order to secure an audience, or to see the face of the superior, and find access to his presence. Hence called to-day, "the face- offering". When the admittance has been secured and entrance has been obtained, then the real offering or present has to be given. Hence KORBAN is essentially an admittance-offering; securing the entree. Cp. the verb, Judg. 3:18. Cp. its use in New Testament, Matt. 5:23; 8:4; 23:18. Mark 7:11. Heb. 5:1.

II. OLAH the burnt offering: so-called from the Hiphil of the verb alah, to cause to ascend (as the flame and smoke ascend by burning). In Greek holocausta which conveys its meaning as being wholly burnt.

III. MINCHAH the Meal offering, a present as such. Hence a gift-offering, not necessarily to secure admittance, but to secure favour. It might be sacrifice by blood, or more generally and later, without blood. It is used of the offerings of Cain and Abel (Gen 4:3,4,5), of Jacob's present to Esau (Gen. 32:13-21), & c. In Exodus and Leviticus it acquires a special limitation, and is the only word rendered "meat", or better (with R.V..). "meat offering" though it has a wider signification than literal "meat").

IV. SHELEM the Peace offering, from the root Shalam, which conveys the idea of peace on the ground of perfection of compensation or recompense. Hence connected with the thought of rendering payment of vows or praises because of peace enjoyed. Sometimes combined with Zebach (No. XII, below). It is eucharistic rather than propiatory.

V. CHATTATH the Sin offering, from chata, to sin by coming short of, by missing the mark in sins of commission. In the Piel it means to purge from sin (Ps. 51:7). In the Olah (ll.ii) the blood went upward, in the chattath it went downward and outward "without the camp." The former was burnt up on the altar, the latter went down on the ground.

VI. ASHAM the Trespass offering. Relates to sins of omission, while chattath relates to sins of commission, sin in general; Asham sin in relation to Mosaic Law; sins of error arising from ignorance or negligence.

VII. NEDABAH Free will or Voluntary offerings. See Lev. 22:18, & e. It refers not to the nature or mode of the offering, but to the motive. Not the same as Lev. 1:4. "voluntary will", which "for his acceptance".

VIII. TERUMAH the Heave offering. So-called because it was lifted up on high in presentation to Jehovah for Himself alone. See 1. ix, above and Ex. 29:27.

IX. TENUPHAH the Wave offering, because it was waved to and fro (not up and down like No. viii), and presented for the four quarters of the earth.

X. NESEK the Drink offering. From nasak, to pour out. Cp. Ps. 2:6 (set). Phil. 2:17, 2 Tim. 4:6.

XI. ISHSHEH any offering made by fire (ep. Ex. 29:18. Lev. 24:7,9).

XII. ZEBACH any offering slain (from No. 11. iv. above). The proper word for a victim, slain and offered. The Hebrew name for altar (mizbeah) is derived from the same root, and denotes the place of slaughter. Cp. Gen. 22.

God's Plan Revealed through Food

- **Clean and unclean meats** (has a spiritual meaning to "clean" and "unclean" people).
- **Milk and strong meat** (God's Word).
- **Manna** (represents God's spiritual food through His Word).
- **Harvests** (Reveal God's plan through the Feast Days).
- **Bread and Wine** (The Passover *symbols)* reveal the spiritual meaning of our Lord's body and blood.
- **Unleavened Bread** (one of the annual Feast Days that *symbollicaly* relates to the removal of sin from a Christian's life).
- **Lamb** (*symbolic* of our Lord Jesus Christ—Our Passover Lamb slain for our sins).

Chapter Three

GOD'S PLAN REVEALED BY HIS RECREATIONS

God—The Master Gardener

God's great plan for humankind can be demonstrated as *picturing* God as a MASTER GARDENER. Interestingly, the first thing God did after the creation—was to plant a garden in Eden!

There are countless *analogies* to gardening in the Bible that picture the Christian growth experience and salvation!

Ancient Israel is portrayed as a vineyard bringing forth fruit in the fifth chapter of Isaiah.

Jesus prayed in a garden before He was betrayed and later crucified.

During the Millennium, a tree will be planted in a garden for the healing of nations (Rev. 22:2). Everyone will have his own fig tree during this time!

Analogous to Christians

A Christian's life can be compared to the development of a literal garden in many ways. Let's note these striking parallel points:

- **Plow the ground**: God prepares the ground in Christians by calling us. The ground is then ready to plant the seed.

- **Plant the seed**: God plants the seed (His Word) in us through His ministry (parable of the Sower—Matt. 13:1-9). As in a physical garden, fertilizer is needed to enhance GROWTH. God says of His spiritual garden, He will dung [fertilize] Christians through *trials* to make them mature (Lk. 13:8). Our loving Father brings forth this character in us through *chastening* so we can bring forth fruit (Heb. 12:11).

Christians should be *growing* toward Jesus Christ, the firstfruit (Eph. 4:11-13). He is the *Vine* of His Father's vineyard. God purgeth the good fruit so it will bring forth more fruit! The word "purge" means to "prune" or thrash to produce more fruit. The Church is as a Branch (Jn. 15:2). It is being grafted into the Olive tree consisting of Jew and Gentile (Rom. 11).

- **Sunlight:** Photosynthesis [the formation of carbohydrates from carbon dioxide and a source of hydrogen such as water, in the presence of chlorophyll] only occurs in the presence of sunlight.

Jesus is the LIGHT of the world that produces Christian growth. He said: "...I am the light of the world: he that followeth me shall not walk in darkness, but shall have the light of life" (Jn. 8:12). A tree cannot grow in the dark, and neither can a Christian without the white light of Christ!

Sunlight is to a tree as God's Holy Spirit is to a Christian. Light illuminates your path. "Then shall the righteous shine forth as the *sun* in the kingdom of their Father..." (Matt. 13:43).

- **Cultivation:** After planting the seed, cultivation, or *removal of the weeds* must take place. God will remove the weeds from His Church as indicated from the parable of the tares (Matt. 13:24). The ground is in our hands, not God's. The quality of the ground depends upon us. Plants are weaker than weeds, and therefore need more fertilizer.

- **Pray for rain:** Once the seed has been planted, cultivated and amidst plenty of sunlight—it cannot grow unless there is *water*. Water is what makes the seed grow toward maturity. God uses His ministry to plant the seed in His spiritual garden [the Church], then watering it brings forth Christian character, but it is God alone who grants the increase (1 Cor. 3:6). We cannot bring forth fruit apart from the Vine.

Christians cannot branch out on their own and expect to get water [God's Holy Spirit] to grow (Jn. 15:11). Water is the catalyst that makes trees grow even as God's HOLY SPIRIT makes Christians mature spiritually (1 Cor. 2).

Our loving God says we must bring forth fruit! (Jn. 15:16). The fruit is our way of life producing the *fruits* of the Spirit (Gal 5:22). Jesus said, "By their fruits you shall know them" (Matt. 7:16-20). To God, a mature Christian is "like a tree planted by the rivers of water, that bringeth forth fruit in his season; his leaf also shall not wither; and whatsoever he doeth shall prosper" (Ps. 1:3).

- **Harvest it:** Our patient Husbandman [Gardener] waits for the precious fruit of the earth [Christians] until He receives the early [Church] and the latter [world] rain (Jas. 5:7).

Christ is the "first-fruit" of them who are in their graves (1 Cor. 15:20-23). Afterwards, every man will be RESURRECTED in his own order (1 Cor.15:42). Our great God begat us [planted a seed] and we are "a kind of first-fruits" (Jas. 1:18). God's Word tells us Christians are God's husbandry or [margin *tillage*] (1 Cor. 3:9).

We have been *planted* together in the likeness of His death, and we shall also be in the likeness of His resurrection (Rom. 6:5). The first-fruits (Rev. 14:4) will be *gathered* at the end of this age (Matt. 13:39-40; Rev. 17:15-20). The Bible declares that the *harvest* is great (Matt. 9:35-38). Christians are now helping to *sow* the *seed* and will also help to *reap* it—we are sowing the seed in all the world as a witness (Matt. 24:14).

The first harvest will be the Church or first-fruits—then the seed will grow as a *mustard seed* in all the world, fulfilling the dispensations of Pentecost, Tabernacles and the Last Great Day.

- **Burning of bad fruit**: There are flagrant warnings in the Word of God that declares every plant that is not planted by the Gardener [God] shall be rooted up (Matt. 15:13).

The apostle that Jesus loved tells us every branch that beareth not fruit shall be BURNED (Jn. 15:2). This "burning" corresponds to the "lake of fire" or the "second" and final death that will consume all unrepentant sinners (Mal. 4:1). Paul cautions us without partiality, "You will reap what you sow!" (Gal. 6:7).

Yes, God is a great Master Gardener, and He will *try* and *test* us so we can bring forth much fruit. But He never promised us a rose garden!

Types of Spiritual Fruit

Jesus declared to His followers: "I am the true vine, and my father is the *husbandman*. Every branch in me that beareth not fruit he taketh away: and every branch that beareth fruit he *purgeth* it, that it bring forth more fruit" (Jn. 15:1-2).

He continued: "Herein is my father glorified, that ye bear *much* fruit; so shall ye be my disciples" (verse 8).

Once fruit has been harvested God must prune or "PURGE" His vineyard to bring forth more fruit.

Branches that are not producing fruit must be "CUT OFF" or pruned in order for the rest of the tree to produce "more fruit".

Otherwise, such branches become "suckers" or sap the juices from the other branches, thereby preventing their *full maturity*.

Pruning does three things to enhance the tree to bear more fruit: 1) it equalizes development, 2) it secures a certain form, and 3) it produces more fruit.

Do you see the spiritual analogy to Christians? There are many different kinds of fruits in nature that are analogous to Christians. Certain scriptures relate these spiritual characteristics to that of physical fruit. Our heavenly Husbandman desires that we bear MUCH fruit! The following are various kinds of

Christian fruit.

- **Blemished Fruit:** Blemishes on fruit are not very appealing to the buyer—and neither are they to our heavenly purchaser! Christians who are *spiritually blemished* with SIN are a sore spot in God's eye! All of us sin occasionally, for:

If we say that we have no sin, we deceive ourselves, and the truth is not in us. If we confess our sins, he is faithful and just to forgive us our sins, and to cleanse us from all unrighteousness (1 Jn. 1:8-9).

Jesus is represented in the Bible by a lamb without spot or *blemish* (1 Pet. 1:19). The Church of the living God is now being prepared to follow in Christ's footsteps and be His SPOTLESS Bride: "That he might present it to himself a glorious church, not having spot, or wrinkle, or any such thing; but that it should be holy and without *blemish"* (Eph. 5:27). God is desperately trying to help us clean up our act—but we must also do our part!

- **Diseased Fruit:** Diseased fruit is not fit to eat—and spiritually sick Christians can only become well through proper spiritual nourishment! Jesus warned us in Matthew 7:15:

Beware of false prophets, which come to you in sheeps clothing, but inwardly they are ravening wolves. Ye shall know them by their fruits. Do men gather grapes of thorns, or figs of thistles? Even so every good tree bringeth forth good fruit: but a corrupt tree bringeth forth evil fruit...Every tree that bringeth not good fruit is hewn down, and cast into the fire. Wherefore by their fruits ye shall know them.

Christians become MALNOURISHED spiritually by reading false literature and listening to false prophets! Jesus said to *beware* of them! You can tell if a tree is healthy if it has good fruit—not by its branches or roots! Many Christians become diseased spiritually when they are enticed by a "little twig" of truth some organization has—instead of looking at the main trunk!

Christians must be aware of becoming a diseased fruit?

- **Rotten Fruit**: Blemished, diseased, shriveled and rotten fruit stand in danger of being *discarded* by their user! Spiritually speaking, the same logic can be applied to Christians. Ancient Israel was described as a beautiful fig tree to God (Hosea 9:9; Nahum 3:12). But then she became *rotten* spiritually because of continual REBELLION! Stern warnings are given to Christians as well!

Ripe fruit and rotten fruit will fall from a tree when shaken as they exist on the same tree. But the day is fast approaching when the *gathering* in of *good* fruit will be separated from the *bad*. Then the bad or rotten will be discarded forever! Let us heed this warning!

- **Seedless Fruit:** Fruit that contains *no seed* cannot germinate to produce more fruit. This kind of fruit stops growing at the seedling stage. The *parable of the Sower* depicts this type of Christian fruit as one whose seed is uprooted by the Devil (Lk. 8:12).

- **Underdeveloped Fruit:** Fruit that is underdeveloped does not get enough water for it to grow. Christians who do not receive enough water in the form of God's HOLY SPIRIT will likewise cease to mature. This type of Christian is represented *symbolically* in the *Parable of the Sower*—by the seed that fell upon a rock and withered away because it lacked *moisture* (Lk. 8:6).

- **Overripe Fruit:** Overripe fruit is oftentimes so sweet you can't stand it! Overripe Christians can also be very hard to tolerate when they become "SELF RIGHTEOUS." The Word of God cautions: "Be not righteous over much: neither make thyself over wise: why shouldest thou destroy thyself?" (Eccl. 7:16).

- **Green Fruit:** Green fruit is still in the bitter stage and not yet fit for human consumption. Neophyte Christians who are GROWING in grace and in knowledge are green spiritually (11 Pet. 3:18). God, the Great Gardener, will do everything in His power (fertilize it, etc.) to make this fruit become *sweet* and delicious (Lk. 13:8).

From this description of the kinds of fruit—Each Christian is admonished to examine themself as to which one applies to us? Are we a diseased, shriveled, rotten, seedless, underdeveloped, overripe, green—or are we a sweet, succulent and ripe fruit, spiritually in God's eyes? God knows His children and is not fooled by those who appear to be Believers to us!

Christian Trees

God's Word compares a righteous person to a tree. Trees certainly are a glorious example of God's handiwork, and God has quite a lot to say about them in His Word, the Bible.

For instance, Psalm 91:12 says, "The righteous shall flourish like a palm tree, he shall grow like a cedar in Lebanon."

God here and in many other places in the Bible compares a righteous person to a tree.

Tiny seed, insignificant as it seems, holds within itself LIFE. It possesses the potential to become a mature tree. All it needs is moisture, warmth, air and light for germination to take place and growth to begin.

In the same way, our spiritual growth as Christians begins when God plants in our minds the seed of His Holy Spirit, which has life inherent in it—SPIRITUAL LIFE.

John 6:63 shows us that it is "the Spirit that gives life." God has to call us first (verse 44), then, when we repent, He gives us His Holy Spirit (Acts 2:38). The Holy Spirit is like a seed, with life—eternal life—inherent in it. As we overcome, God gives us more and more of His Holy Spirit, and we grow like spiritual trees.

For a seed to grow into a healthy tree, certain conditions need to be fulfilled. And for us to grow as God's people (11 Peter 3:18), certain spiritual elements are essential.

Psalm 1 is a good example of the comparison between a

righteous person and a tree. In verse 3, David wrote, "He shall be like a tree planted by the rivers of water."

What does water *symbolize* spiritually? Jesus made the answer clear in (John 7:37-39), where He portrayed God's Holy Spirit as rivers of living water. Notice Isaiah 44:3-4:

> **For I will pour water on him who is thirsty, and floods on the dry ground; I will pour MY Spirit on your descendants, and My blessings on your offspring, they will spring up among the grass like willows by the watercourses.**

The Holy Spirit helps us grow *spiritually* just as water helps a tree grow *physically.*

Another factor vital to the growth of a tree is *light.* Through photosynthesis, leaves use sun-light to produce carbohydrates for growth.

What does light *symbolize* in our Christian lives? Proverbs 6:23 shows that God's law is a light to our lives. We need it for our growth. We obtain more of this light through personal Bible study and by listening to messages from God's ministers.

Warmth is another factor necessary for growth in a tree. Trees slow down their rate of growth in the winter, but spurt ahead in warmer weather.

Spiritually, we need the warmth of fellowship with other Christians. We can know all about the Bible and God's true doctrines in an academic way, but our growth will be stunted if we don't spend time interacting with others in God's Church, learning from them, helping and sharing our lives with them, enjoying the beautiful, growth-motivating warmth of Christian fellowship.

Another force that influences the growth of a tree is weather. Sometimes howling storms lash the limbs and strip off the leaves, and even break a branch here and there, but the tree has to stand there, solid and firm.

And so we, as stouthearted spiritual trees, have to stand firm against the trials that assail us, and patiently endure, even though tempestuous storms sometimes shake our spiritual branches and knock off lots of leaves.

In (Colossians 2:6-7), Paul tells us to walk in Christ's way of life, **"rooted and built up in him."**

These roots anchor the tree to the ground and also search out and absorb available nutrients in the soil. We need to be deeply rooted and well-founded spiritually (Matt. 7:24-27).

Sometimes someone has to step in and aid the process by pruning a tree to improve its performance. Jesus talked about this in John 15:1-2:

> **I am the true vine, and My Father is the Vinedresser. Every branch in Me that does not bear fruit He takes away; and every branch that bears fruit He prunes, that it may bear more fruit.**

God prunes us spiritually by correcting us, by testing us in trials that seem tough and severe at the time, but that result in better growth later.

That's the idea of pruning. It's a bit of a paradox, really, to cut back the tree to make it produce more, but good gardeners know it works, bringing forth bigger and better fruit!

Trials are a paradox like that, too, but they cause God's people to be able to bring forth more fruit in the future.

In (John 15:8), Jesus went on to discuss the most important aspect of our lives as spiritual trees—the overriding reason for our existence: "By this My Father is glorified, that you bear much fruit: so you will be My disciples." In verse 16, He added, "I chose you and appointed you that you should go and bear fruit, and that your fruit should remain."

The fruits we are to produce—the fruits of the Spirit—are listed in (Galatians 5:22-23). As Christians, we are to look at this list often, meditate on it, consider these qualities carefully and ask our-selves, "Am I developing each of these attributes, and expressing them toward the people with whom I come in contact?"

Notice Jeremiah 17:7-8:

> **Blessed is the man who trusts in the Lord, and whose hope is the Lord. For he shall be like a tree planted by the waters, which spreads out its roots by the river, and will not fear when heat comes; but her leaf will be green, and will not be anxious in the year of drought, nor will cease**

from yielding fruit.

If we aren't bringing forth these fruits, we are not God's people! So, God looks on us as spiritual trees. As He looks down from heaven upon us, what does He see?

Olive Trees

As a husbandman, God seems to have a special interest for the olive tree. It is used for many physical analogies in the Bible as we shall see and for good reason. There are many physical properties of the olive tree that are helpful in relating to spiritual lessons.

I want to draw your attention to (1 Kings 6:23,31) where the inner sanctuary representing God's heavenly throne, had two cherubim as well as doors, made out of "olive trees."

Why did God specifically use olive trees for this purpose and not gopher wood, as He told Noah to use in building the Ark? This will become apparent as we learn more about the unusual qualities of the olive tree.

The olive tree has a twisted arthritic look to it, but once worked with, it is very *hard* and BEAUTIFUL and *useful*. This analogy holds true to Israel as well as Christians.

God began working with the nation of Israel who was like an unfinished piece of ugly olive wood. When God is finished working with Israel, she will be extremely beautiful. Notice a scripture to this affect in Hosea 14:6, "His branches [Israel] shall spread, and his *beauty* shall be as the *olive tree*..."

Olives are very *useful* as food, oil, cosmetics and medicinal purposes. Israel and Christians will also be very *useful* to God, serving in His kingdom!

James admonishes Christians to go before the elders of the Church to be anointed with oil when they are sick (Jas. 5:14). The oil used for anointing purposes was very likely olive. Turn now to the account in (Matthew 25) where it appears the church age just prior to our Lord's return during the last Church age [Laodician] will not have enough oil in their lamps. Here, oil is used *symbolically* for God's Holy Spirit. The oil used in a lot of lamps to give off *light* in Biblical times was olive.

As we have already read in Volume 1, the "Two Witnesses" are *symbolically* described as two olive trees in (Rev. 11:4 and

Zech. 4:3). They will be representative of the properties contained in the olive tree. They will be able to have God's STRENGTH and perform *miracles*!

Another attribute characteristic of the olive tree is ENDURANCE. Olive trees live to be very old. This characteristic is *symbolic* of eternal life as King David wrote in Psalm 52:8, "But I am like a green olive tree in the house of God: I trust in the mercy of God *for ever and ever*." The olive tree is *symbolic* of long life or *eternal life*, just as its oil represents God's Holy Spirit which imparts eternal life!

When Christ returns to the Mount of Olives in Jerusalem, there will be many olive trees there. This *symbolizes* His coming government with all the characteristics of the olive tree—strength, beauty, usefulness, and endurance!

God—The Great Musician

Believe it or not, there are examples of proper and beneficial music in the Bible.

The Psalms were written to be sung by the priests as praises to God (Ps. 100:1 2). String instruments such as the harp were stressed along with the timbrel and trumpet (Ps. 150:1-6). This was also accompanied with dancing.

The Psalms were sung to make a melody in ones heart to the Lord (Eph. 5:19). They make one merry (Jas. 5:13; Col. 3:16).

Our Lord sang with the apostles just prior to His arrest on the Passover night—displaying His approval of good music (Matt. 26:30). Christians will sing the song of Moses with the Lamb upon Christ's return (Rev. 15:2). The apostle Paul and Silas sang while they were in prison (Acts 16:25).

Clearly, the Bible is not against music or dancing as some puritan organizations contend. Recall how the prodigal son's father danced for joy upon his return (Lk. 15). This is a *type* of God the Father rejoicing over a repentant sinner.

Satan "The Prince of The Air"

Like anything else God has created for man's good and benefit, music has been perverted by Satan the devil!

Music can be good or bad—we wake up to it, make love to

it, and eat to it.

Satan is LITERALLY the "prince of the air" (Eph. 2:2). That is, he controls the air and what is going on in the air. He broadcasts through wave-lengths just as the ones coming over the air to TV or radio. Satan's wave-lengths go into our mind and react with our human spirit and cause us to have moods of rebellion, resentment—HE APPEALS TO HUMAN EMOTIONS! Satan appeals to human nature (vanity, lust, greed, jealousy, envy, hatred).

Satan is in contact with us 24 hours a day whether we realize it or not. When we turn on the radio, or TV—he's there! When we read a book or newspaper—he's there!

By filling our minds with good music, we will not fall prey to Satan' devices. We must be aware that Satan uses these methods to penetrate our minds and therefore have to be cognizant of his crafty devices. Satan is a thief—and he is trying to steal our minds!

Today's Music

Scientifically, it is known that loud music affects our eardrums, and sounds above 80 decibels can damage them. Rock concerts are in the 175 decibel range. According to Dr. Diamond, the beat of rock music is the opposite of the heart beat, which more closely resembles a waltz beat.

One has to wonder if it is a contributing factor of why we have so many hyper-active children these days. In an interview on September 4th, 1986 with Rexella Van Impe, ex-occultist Johanna Michaelsen and Mike Warnke expressed their fears for those involved with Rock music.

During this nationwide television interview, they said that drugs, sex and Rock music were inextricably tied together. Heavy metal and acid Rock were the main themes.

Miss Michaelsen had been involved with a psychic surgeon in New York City for 14 months. During this time, she observed brain surgeries—and the removal of cancers by a woman who could diagnose accurately with her eyes closed, verified by surgeons.

Mr. Warnke, who appeared on 20/20 as a high priest of Satan in San Bernadeno California, said that his group played Rock music prior to their sacrifices. He said, "you can only feed yourself with these things so long—for you are what you eat!" Mike further said to his children, "you can't put manure on your roses and come in and not *smell* like manure. You do drugs and pretty soon drugs do you."

(3) Basic concerns of hard Music

- **Rebellion Against Society.** The Bible tells us the "carnal mind is against God's law" (Rom. 8:7). Some vocal groups blatantly admit that "rebellion" is part of what makes their group successful. In fact, the more bazare, the more successful the group even if much of it is staged. Can you see why the Bible associates "rebellion" with the "sin of witchcraft"? (1 Sam. 15:23). The acronym KISS was rumored to stand for Knights in Satan's Service, but, as KISS bassist Gene Simmons explained in his autobiography, the rumors were just rumors, even if the band didn't exactly go out of its way to discourage them. Regardless, groups like this have had an influence on our culture and not necessarily in a positive way.

- **Occult Worship.** Charles Manson admitted the "Beatles" music inspired him to kill. On the cover of their album "Seargent Peppers Lonely Heart Club Band," they have a picture of Alester Crowley, the individual most involved in the occult over the last 100 years. Their song "My Sweet Lord" was dedicated to Hari Krishna. Prosecutor Vincent Bugliosi has arrived at his conclusions after interviews with several Manson family members and describes the Beatles songs *Revolution and Helter Skelter* having an influence on him on pages 238-245 of his book *Helter Skelter*.

Alice Cooper it was rumored, got his name from the ouija board although admits this was only legend. The hit album Hotel California song by the Eagles, had affiliation with Anton La Vey, founder of the church of Satan and author of the Satanic Bible. La Vey is called "the black pope" or "high priest of Satan."

- **Blatant Sex.** Can wild music with drugs have an affect on

THE FOOLISHNESS OF GOD

ones mind? Elvis epitomized sex through his music and sexy style. He read books on the occult, and his favorite movies were "The Omen" and "The Exorcist." His life ended because of drugs!

The Bible shows how wild music can make one go temporarily insane. Read (Exodus 32:17), where the nation of Israel stripped naked in a wild orgy during wild music!

God—The Wonderful Astronomer

For more than two thousand five hundred years the world was without written revelation from God. The question is, did God leave Himself without a *witness* of His plan before it was written?

In (Romans 1:19), it is declared:

...that which may be known of God is manifest in them; for God hath showed it unto them. For the invisible things of Him from the creation of the world are clearly seen, being understood by the things that are made, even His eternal power and Godhead; so that they are without excuse.

The apostle Paul was saying here that God made Himself known to the people of the Old Covenant by the things that were made. But what things? How were these "invisible things" of God—His plans, His purposes, and His counsels known since the creation of the world?

There is only one answer and that is THE HEAVENS! Psalm 19 says: "The heavens declare the glory of God...In them hath He set a tabernacle for the sun (vs. 4). By them is thy servant warned" (vs. 11).

Through (Isaiah 40:26 and Psalm 147:4) God, says He created the stars and gave them all a name. In the Book of Job there are references to the stellar revelation, Sign of the Zodiac and the names of several stars and constellations are mentioned. Notice Job 9:9: "Which maketh Arcturus [the Bear], Orion and Pleiades, and the chambers of the south." The margin has these words in Hebrew as Ash, Cesil and Cimah.

GOD'S RECREATIONS

Job 38:31,32 says,

> **Canst thou bind the sweet influences [cluster] of the Pleiades [margin, the seven stars, Cimah], or loose the bands of Orion [margin, Cesil]. Canst thou bring forth Mazzaroth [margin, the twelve signs R.V.: "the twelve signs"]: and [margin, the signs of the Zodiac] in his season? or canst thou guide Arcturus with his sons [R.V.; the Bear with her twin], and (margin, Hebrew, sons).**

Isaiah 13:10 says, "...the stars of heaven and constellations, ... thereof."

In Amos 5:8 we read, "Seek him that maketh the seven stars [R.V.; the Pleiades] and Orion."

Then we have the term "Mazzaroth," which refers to the twelve signs of the Zodiac in Job, while (11 Kings 23:5) refers to the "Planets" (margin—twelve signs or constellations). God declares in Genesis 1:14, **"They [the sun, moon and stars] shall be for signs [things to come] and for cycles" (appointed times).**

Here then, we have a distinct declaration from God, that the heavens contain not only a revelation concerning things to come in the "Signs" but also concerning appointed times in the wondrous movements of the sun, moon, and stars.

Thus, we see that the scriptures are not silent as to the great antiquity of the *signs* and constellations. If we turn to history and tradition, we are at once met with the fact that the twelve signs are the same—both as to the meaning of their names and as to their order in all the ancient nations of the world.

The Chinese, Chaldean, and the Egyptian records go back to more than 2,000 years B.C. Indeed, the Zodiacs in the Temples of Denlerah and Esneh, in Egypt, are doubtless copies of zodiacs still more ancient—which from internal evidence, must be placed nearly 4,000 B.C. when the summer solstice was in Leo.

Josephus, the Jewish historian of the first century, hands down to us what he gives as the tradition of his own nation—corroborated by his reference to eight ancient Gentile authorities, whose works are lost. He says that they all assert that, **"God gave the Ante diluvians such long life that they might perfect those things which they had invented in astronomy."**

Astronomy has been mixed in with *astrology (a form of nature worship)* mainly by the Babylonians and has confused God's plan revealed by true astronomy. The word Zodiac itself is a Greek word from the Hebrew root word "Sodi" which means "a way." It denotes "a way" or step, and is used for the way or path in which the sun appears to move amongst the stars in the course of the year.

To an observer on the earth, the whole firmament, together with the sun, appears to revolve in a circle once in twenty-four hours. But the time occupied by the stars in going around, differs from the time occupied by the sun.

The difference amounts to about one-twelfth part of the whole circle in each month, so that when the circle of the heavens is divided up into parts, the sun appears to move each month through one of them. The path which the sun thus makes amongst the stars is called the Ecliptic.

Each of these twelve parts [consisting each of about 30 degrees] is distinguished, not by numbers or by letters, but by pictures and names, and this, as we have seen, from the very earliest times.

They are preserved to the present day in our almanacs, and we are taught their order in the familiar rhymes: "The Ram, the Bull, the heavenly twins, and next the Crab, the Lion shines, the Virgin, and the Scales; the Scorpion, Archer, and SeaGoat, the Man that carries the Water-pot and Fish with glittering scales."

These signs have always and everywhere been preserved in this order, and have begun with Aries. They have been known amongst all nations, and in all ages, thus proving their common origin from one source.

The figures themselves are perfectly arbitrary. There is nothing in the groups of stars to even suggest the figures. Take for instance the sign of VIRGO, and look at the stars. There is nothing whatever to suggest a human form; still less is there anything to show whether that form is a man or a woman, and so with all the others.

The picture, therefore, is the original, and must have been drawn around or connected with certain stars, simply in order that it might be identified and associated with them; and that it might thus be remembered and handed down to posterity.

The Zodiac and the Twelve Sons of Jacob

"There is a striking parallel between the 12 signs of the Zodiac and the blessing of Jacob's 12 children (Gen. 49; Deut. 33). In (Genesis. 37:9) Joseph sees the sun and moon and eleven stars bowing down to him, he himself being the twelfth.

"It is more than probable that each of the Twelve Tribes bore one of them on its standard. We read in Numbers 2:2, 'Every man of the children of Israel shall pitch by his own STANDARD, with the Ensign of their father's house' (R.V. 'with the ensign of their fathers' houses').

"This 'Standard' was the Degel on which the 'Sign' was depicted. Hence it was called the 'En-sign.' Ancient Jewish authorities declare that each tribe had one of the signs as its own, and it is highly probable, even from Scripture, that four of the tribes carried its 'Sign'; and that these four were placed at the four sides of the camp.

"If the Lion were appropriated to Judah, then the other three would be thus fixed, and would be the same four that equally divide the Zodiac at its four cardinal points.

"The second chapter of Numbers describes how the 12 tribes of Israel were arranged in the camp.

"If we compare the blessing of the twelve tribes given in (Genesis 49 and Deuteronomy 33) we will see a definite fulfillment. Levi, for example, had no standard, and he needed none, for he kept 'the balance of the Sanctuary,' and had the charge of that brazen altar on which the atoning blood out weighed the nation's sins.

"The four great signs which thus marked the four sides of the camp, and the four quarters of the Zodiac, are the same four which form the Cherubim (the Eagle, the Scorpion's enemy, being substituted for the Scorpion). The Cherubim thus form a compendious expression of the hope of Creation, which, from the first, has been bound up with the Coming One, who alone should cause its groanings to cease.

"But this brings us to the Signs themselves and their interpretation. These *pictures* were designed to preserve, expound, and perpetuate the one first great promise and prophecy that all hope for Man, all hope for Creation, was bound up in a coming Redeemer.

"One who should be born of a woman; who should first

suffer, and afterwards gloriously triumph. One who should first be wounded by that great enemy who was the cause of all sin and sorrow and death, but who should finally crush the head of 'that Old Serpent the devil' (Gen. 3:15).

"These ancient *star-pictures* reveal this Coming One. They set forth 'the sufferings of Christ and the glory that should follow.' Altogether there are forty-eight of them, made up of twelve SIGNS, each sign containing three CONSTELLATIONS."

For a diagram that shows a brief outline of the 12 SIGNS and their CONSTELLATION, with a brief explanation of their connection to God's plan for salvation for humankind, the reader is encouraged to read, *The Witness Of The Stars*, by E. W. Bullinger.

The Genesis of Astrology

The origin of astrology dates back to the Babylonians. We read on page 26 of *Langer's Encyclopedia of World History*:

The most characteristic and influential features of Babylonian religion aside from it's mythology, were the elaborate systems of magical practices and the interpretation of omens [divination], particularly the movements and position of the heavenly bodies [astrology], the actions of animals, and the characteristics of the liver of sacrificial victims.

It was a Babylonian belief that the future could be forecast by the arrangement of the heavenly constellations. They named five of their most sacred planets after five of their most reverend gods.

By the time of the Roman Empire, astrology, had been developed into a very precise mathematical science. The Roman astrologers changed the names of the Babylonian gods to their most important gods. The Babylonian Marduk was changed to Jupiter, Nabu was altered to Mercury, Ishtar [the Babylonian name for Semiramis, became Venus, the "Queen of Heaven."

However, it was the Greeks who took the Babylonian concepts of astrology and derived the Zodiac and it's division into 12 signs. Each sign was associated with a group of fixed stars within each division called a constellation.

The Zodiac is an imaginary belt in the sky in which the sun, moon and planets appear to travel. The sun's path, called the ecliptic is it's middle line.

Although astrology was perpetrated because of man's superstitions, it has spawned the modern science of astronomy in which eclipses can be predicted.

Astrology had been developed to enhance paganistic beliefs, but the stars hold a GREAT REVELATION of the PLAN OF GOD.

God had revealed tremendous truths to His servants through the stars—long before the Babylonians even conceived there was any understanding in the arrangement of the stars.

As the Jews were taken off to exile in Babylon in the sixth century BC, Daniel was a slave among the Babylonians, but he was also chosen by God to teach them about the one true God of all creation. King Nebuchadnezzar was plagued by a troubling dream and only Daniel was able to solve the mystery. No Magician (magi) or astrologer (reader of the stars) or sorcerer could explain to the king the mystery of the dream (Dan.2).

As a result, King Nebuchadnezzar fell prostrate before Daniel, saying, "Surely your God is the God of gods and the Lord of kings and a revealer of mysteries" (2:47). King Nebuchadnezzar elevated God's servant Daniel to be ruler over his kingdom, making him the chief or lord over all the other wise men (magi) of Babylon (vs. 48). But could magi tell signs in the heavens?

There are many who have connected the story in Matthew 2 concerning the "star in the East" that the magi saw to be an event that the heavens declared. Many believe these magi were not pagan astrologers whose observations of the heavenly bodies led them to the infant Jesus, but rather, God-fearing descendants of the exiled house of Israel who were led to Bethlehem miraculously, observing a prophesied star to come out of Jacob (Num. 24:17). This "star" was most likely an angel, just as they were "divinely warned" to flee back to their homeland (Matt. 2:12).

God—The Amazing Artist

You may never have given it much thought before—but much understanding of GOD'S PLAN OF SALVATION can be understood through certain colors. The following colors demonstrate this amazing truth:

Red: The color red has long been *associated* with violence, war, blood, hatred, the devil, evil, etc.
 The Bible associates sin with the color red (Isa. 1:18) as well as war (Rev. 6:4) and the devil (Rev. 12:3).
 Wine [red] was used to *symbolize* the blood of Christ as the New Testament *symbol* during Passover.

White: White has always been *synonymous* with purity, cleanness, wisdom and righteousness. The Bible identifies white with righteousness (Isa. 1:18; Dan. 12:10; Rev. 2:17, 4:4, 7:9,13, 15:6, 19:8,14).

Black: The color Black is usually *related* with death or coldness. The Bible uses a black horse to describe death during the Great Tribulation (Rev. 6:5).
 Although Ham's [Heb.*burnt*] son Nimrod was presumably Tan/Black, this may be only coincidental in regards to sin—for we know Black is beautiful when describing the color of ones skin.

Blue: Blue is usually *connected* with royalty, calmness, peace, love, and tranquility. The blue sky and water are representative of this peacefulness.
 The priestly garments of the Levites were blue (Ex. 28:31, 39:22), as well as the curtains of the Tabernacle (Ex. 26:1).

Yellow: The color yellow was used by God to *describe* when certain diseases were still uncured (Lev. 13:30-36).

Green: Green has had the *connotation* with life [grass, trees, herbs]—see (Gen. 1:30).

Purple: Purple is a color derived from mixing blue with red. In many ways it has the same *association* as blue (royalty). Purple raiment was on kings (Judges 8:26). See also (Rev. 17:4, 18:12,16).

The Breastplate of Judgment

God gave Moses the instructions for making *holy garments* for the ministry of the priesthood in the 28th chapter of Exodus. These garments have a deep *spiritual significance* as we shall see. Starting in verse four of (Exodus 28) we read:

> **(Vs. 4) And these are the garments which they shall make; a *breastplate*, and an *ephod*, and a *robe*, and a *broidered coat*, a *mitre*, and holy garments for Aaron thy brother, and his sons, that he may minister unto me in the *priests' office*.**

> **(Vs. 15) And thou shalt make the *breastplate of judgment* with cunning work...(vs. 17) And thou shalt set in it settings of stones, even four rows of stones: the first row shall be a sardius [margin-ruby], a topaz, and a carbuncle: this shall be the first row. (Vs. 18) and the second row shall be an emerald, a sapphire, and a diamond (margin-sardonyx).**

> **(Vs. 19) And the third row a ligure [jacinth], an agate, and an amethyst. (Vs. 20) And the fourth row a beryl [margin-chalcedony], and an onyx, and a jasper: they shall be set in gold in their inclosings. (Vs. 21)** *And the stones shall be with the names of the children of Israel,* **twelve according to their names (or sequence of birth)...**

Clearly these 12 stones were "birth stones" of the 12 sons of Jacob or Israel respectively! Rueben being the oldest would be *represented* by the sardius—and Benjamin being the youngest would be *represented* by the jasper etc.

Twelve precious stones were selected for the high priests' breastplate. These stones were arranged in four rows of threes, one directly under the other. The following was their sequence from top to bottom, and left to right (Ex. 28:17-20). Sardius, Topaz, Carbuncle, Emerald, Sapphire, Diamond, Amber, Agate, Amethyst, Beryl, Onyx and Jasper.

The Arrangement of the Stones

Understanding the arrangement of the 12 tribes of Israel in the camp and their corresponding Zodiac sign—we can now assign their "birth stone" respectively.

However, we must realize that these stones were to be arranged in the breastplate of the high priest according to the *birth* of these twelve brothers, *not* according to their Zodiac sequence, notice:

> **And thou shalt take *two onyx stones* and grave on them the names of the children of Israel. Six of their names on one stone, and the other six names of the rest on the other stone, *according to their birth*. With the work of an engraver in stone, like the engravings of a *signet*, shalt thou engrave the two stones with the names of the children of Israel: Thou shalt make them to be set in ouches of gold (Ex. 28:9-11).**

Besides these two onyx stones engraved with the names of the tribes according to their birth—twelve stones were to be engraved individually in the same sequence.

Continuing God's instructions to Moses concerning the "stones of the breastplate", we read:

> **And the stones shall be with the names of the children of Israel, *twelve*, according to their names [birth], like the engravings of a *signet*; every one with his name shall they be according to the twelve tribes (vs. 21).**

To find the sequence of birth concerning Israel's twelve children we must turn to the book of Genesis.

Leah, Jacob's first wife found favor in God's eyes and bore Rueben [*See! a son!*]. Simeon [*God heard*]: Levi [*Added*] and

GOD'S RECREATIONS

Judah [*Praise*] were all born to Leah (29:31-35).

Rachel's desire for a son became impetuous and she gave her maid Bilhah to Jacob who conceived Dan [*Judge*] and Naphthali [*Wrestling*]—(30:1-8]

Impatient to conceive more sons, Leah turned and gave her maid Zilpah to Jacob who bore Gad [*Troop]*) and Asher [*Gladness*]—(30:11-13).

Leah then conceived Issachar [*Pay for hire*], and Zebulon [*Abiding*] (30:18-20).

Rachel finally conceived two sons—Joseph [*Adding*]— 30:22-27) and Benjamin [*son of my sorrow*] in her dying agony (35:18).

From this outline of the children's births, we can now assign their corresponding "birth stone" color to each tribe on the breastplate.

Israel's Corresponding Birth Stones

1 Reuben Sardis	2 Simeon Topaz	3 Levi Carbuncle
4 Judah Emerald	5 Dan Sapphire	6 Napthali Diamond
7 Gad Ligure	8 Assher Agate	9 Issacher Amethyst
10 Zebulon Beryl	11 Joseph Onyx	12 Benjamin Jasper

The Precious Stones
Their Tribe and Zodiac Sign

- **Sardius** [Heb. *odem*]—Rueben—brownish red to blood red.

   A red variety of chalcedony. This same Hebrew word is used for *Adam* in describing the first man coming from "red earth." The Zodiac sign *Aquarius* is attached to Reuben designating the *firstborn man.*

   Adam was the first physical man even as Christ the 2nd Adam is the firstborn spiritual man. This same Hebrew word is also used to describe the face of man in the four headed "living creature" in (Ezek. 1:5,10, 10:14,21). Take note of this for it has deep spiritual implication and will be explained shortly.

   The Zodiac sign Aquarius or man or *waterpourer* is also suggestive of Reuben as prophesied in (Genesis 49). In prophetic characteristic, his father labeled him as "unstable as water" [margin-bubbling over with water] as indicative of the "waterpourer." This sign connotates man's reward. Sardius is the first stone of the breastplate and the sixth in the spiritual Holy City (Rev. 21:20).

- **Topaz** [Heb. *pitdah*]—Simeon—yellowish-red to a pale green with a mixture of yellow.

   The second stone of the breastplate is related to the Zodiac sign *Pisces* and points to *Redemption,* or Christian deliverance as its root word *peted* means "to set free" or "to open." Topaz is the ninth stone of the Holy city (Rev. 21:20).

- **Carbuncle** [Heb. *bareket*]—Levi—red garnet to a deep red color with a mixture of scarlet.

   The third stone of the breastplate is associated with the Zodiac sign *Libra*. Its root word *barek* means "to couch, lie down, as a beast on its knees." It has the *symbolic* meaning of "Judgment" over the earth—even as Levi judged Israel as priests.

- **Emerald** [Heb. *napbech*]—Judah—green to a bright green color without any other mixture.

   A transparent deep green form of beryl. The root word *nephah* means "to scatter" and is highly relevant to the prophetic "scattering" of Judah (Isa. 11:12). The Zodiac sign *Leo* [lion] is attributed to Judah in Christ—the lion who destroys Satan. The

GOD'S RECREATIONS

fourth stone of the breastplate and fourth gem in the Holy city (Rev. 21:19).

- **Sapphire** [Heb. *saphir*]—Dan—dark blue to a clear blue being next to the diamond in hardness.

   The root word *sepher* means "a scroll, cipher, writing." The Zodiac sign *Scorpio* is linked with the tribe of Dan, and depicts the Church's conflict with Satan. It is the fifth stone of the Holy city (Rev. 21:19).

- **Diamond** [Heb. *yahalam*]—Naphthali—white to a clear sparkling gem. The most valuable of the precious stones.

   The root word *halam* means "to beat, smite, strike upon."

The Zodiac sign *Capricornus* [the goat] characterizes this stone and represents the "beating" Christ took for all of us. It *pictures* Christ's birth and resurrection.

- **Ligure** [Heb. *leshem*]—Gad—bright yellow to a dull red or cinnamon color with a mixture of yellow.

   The seventh stone of the breastplate is ligure, translated jacinth in the RVS. Some have thought this stone to be a blue stone. The Zodiac sign *Aries* has been attached to this stone. This sign has to do with the returning Christ for His Bride. It is the eleventh foundation stone of the Holy city (Rev. 21:20).

- **Agate** [Heb. *shebo*]—Asher—light blue to a white, reddish, yellowish, and greenish stone of the flint variety. The cheapest of all the precious stones.

   The root word of *shebo* means "to return," "time of returning to the earth." The Zodiac sign *Sagittarius* pictures the returning and triumphant Christ to the earth. This event is appropriately represented by the agate stone. Asher [happy] is also *symbolic* of this event as Christ restores the government of God on earth.

- **Amethyst** [Heb. *achelamah*]—Essacher—violet to a deep red and strong blue color which give it a purple hue.

   The root word is *chalam* and means "grief" or "afflict" "to wound" "or pierce through." The Zodiac sign associated with Issacher is *Cancer* which depicts Christ's Church ruling. This stone is the twelfth foundation stone of the New Jerusalem (Rev. 21:20).

- **Beryl** [Heb. *tarshish*]—Zebulon—green, yellow to a bluish green.

    The root word means "oxen" and is translated *taurus* in Latin. Some may think this sign best fits *Taurus* in the Zodiac, yet this is not possible based on the sequence of birth. Instead, *Virgo* representing Christ the promised seed is represented. It is the eighth stone in the Holy city (Rev. 21:20).

- **Onyx** [Heb. *shoham*]—Joseph—bright yellow to a stone of various colors. Like Joseph's multicolored embroidery [most likely 12 colors representing each tribe], this stone may have had 12 hues.

    The root word *shoh* means "lamb" and is used for the Passover lamb in (Exodus 12:3,5). It is no wonder that "the two stones upon the shoulders of the ephod," on which the names of the Children of Israel were graven, were *shoham* stones.

    These stones were *emblematic* of Christ's Passover as Redeemer of Israel. The Zodiac sign *Taurus* [the Bull] is appropriately assigned to this stone as a *symbol* of Christ's sacrifice. It is also fitting that Joseph be associated with these emblems—since it was through his seed that the Birthright be fulfilled.

- **Jasper** [Heb. *yashpeh*]—Benjamin—clear or opaque to a bright green, sometimes clouded with white and spotted with red and yellow. Mineralogists list 15 varieties of jasper.

    The root means "to gather" or "collect" "save" "salvation." The Zodiac sign *Gemini*, symbolic of Christ, the Prince of Peace is *emblematic* of Benjamin. Jasper is the last stone of the breastplate and the first foundation stone of the Holy city (Rev. 21:19).

Types of Heavenly Stones

As already noted, physical semblances are merely *types* or *patterns* of spiritual realities. But what could these 12 stones of the breastplate of the high priest of Israel possibly represent in God's heavenly throne? Through the world of color, the Word of God enlightens us like a prism that breaks up the white light of truth into a beautiful rainbow.

These stones were merely "shadows" of the heavenly fragments of ancient Paradise—they are the remnant of the *glory* contained in the garden of Eden.

The stones of the priest's breastplate appear to contain the same *symbolic* meaning as those of the great Cherub Lucifer who carried out God's government on earth prior to man.

Speaking of Lucifer's authority in the garden of Eden, God speaks:

Thou hast been in Eden the garden of God; every precious stone was thy covering, the sardius, topaz, and the diamond, the beryl, the onyx, and the jasper, the sapphire, the emerald, and the carbuncle, and gold...(Ezek. 28:13).

In the Septuagint Version [Hebrew translated into Greek], all twelve of these precious stones are listed. These "birth stones" then, represent God's heavenly throne! This is made clearer in the first chapter of Ezekiel. Notice how the "living creatures" who transport God's heavenly throne have the identical Zodiac signs as the four head tribes of Israel (vs. 10).

These creatures have four faces [Man, Lion, Ox, Eagle], just as the standards Reuben [Aquarius], Judah [Leo], Ephraim [Taurus] and Dan [Aquila] represented! When these tribes marched, these *four* leading tribes went in the vanguard with their standards bearing the emblems of the "living creatures."

When these four leading tribes were camped, these four emblems formed a square with the Tabernacle in the center. The Tabernacle of course was *symbolic* of God's heavenly throne!

The very throne of God these "living creatures" transport, is envisioned as a rainbow! Notice,

As the appearance of the *bow* that is in the cloud in the day of rain, so was the appearance of the brightness round about. This was the appearance of the likeness of the *glory* of God... (Ezek. 1:28).

Clearly, the stones of the high priest's breastplate are

emblematic of the very THRONE OF GOD in heaven!

The account in Ezekiel describes Lucifer as being an "anointed Cherub" set upon the mountain [government] of God (Ezek. 28:14). Could Lucifer have been the original "high priest" of God?

Further proof that the stones of the high priest's breastplate were *symbolic* of God's heavenly throne—is the fact that two formed the breastplate stones [beryl—vs. 12, and sapphire—vs. 26], are mentioned here in connection with God's throne!

In conjunction with God's spiritual city "New Jerusalem", we read of these very same stones again (Rev. 21:19-20). These stones represent the 12 TRIBES OF ISRAEL who will be in God's "New Heaven" and "New Earth" (vs. 12).

The whole of this *imagery* shadow the "image and likeness" of Jesus Christ as *pictured* by the characteristics of the lion, the ox, the man and the eagle.

Christ's unconquerable majesty, and might is *pictured* by the lion, and His willingness to carry our heavy burdens is *envisioned* by the ox's abilities. Christ came as the "Son of Man" or the perfected man in body and spirit. The completed spiritual man is *pictured* by the eagle—as His resurrected spiritual life soars from the earth and ascends into the heavens in glory and honor to the Great God!

Here we see how once again, the *earthly type* is a shadow of the *heavenly reality,* as God's final THRONE is set up to GOVERN the entire universe!

The Urim and Thummim

Regarding the "urim and thummim" stones, we read in Exodus 28:30:

> **And thou shalt put in the breastplate of judgment the Urim and the Thummim; and they shall be upon's Aaron's heart, when he goeth in before the LORD: and Aaron shall bear the judgment of the children of Israel upon his heart before the LORD continually.**

Josephus says according to the Hebrew, these stones literally signify "lights" and "perfections" or the "shining and the perfect." When questions regarding the will of the Eternal God were brought to the high priest for a decision, a halo of light encircled the precious stone on the right side of the breastplate, indicative of the Eternal's approval, while a cloud shadowing the stone on the left side of the breastplate was acknowledgement of God's disapproval.

Dakes Bible Commentary on "Notes on Exodus" states of these stones of "light":

> **Heb. *Uwriym*, plural of *uwr*, light; flame; fire. *Uwr* is from the root word *owr*, to be or make luminous; break of day; to give or show light; be enlightened; shine; set on fire. *Urim* literally means *lights*. The Heb. *Tummiym*, is the plural of *tom*, completeness; innocence; integrity; perfect; uprightness. *Tom* is from the root word *tamam*, to complete in a good or bad sense; be perfect. *Thummim* literally means *perfections* or *complete truth*.**

These stones representitive of "light" and "truth" were separate from the breastplate pouch and stones in the breastplate—and worn in or attached to the breastplate of the high priest when inquiring of God.

These "sacred" guiding stones of Israel were used in obtaining an answer from God when needed—regarding any problem which concerned the nation of Israel.

They were used in dividing the land to the tribes (Num. 34:17; Josh. 17:4). The order of the priesthood was settled by this means (1 Chron. 24:5-7; 25:9). Joshua was guided by them in leading Israel into Canaan (Num. 27:18-24). Saul was chosen through them. Saul enquired of God through them in war (1 Sam. 14:36-46).

Clearly, the Urim and Thummim were "enlighteners" or the "eyes" for the nation of Israel!

But what of today's spiritual Israel?

Who *guides* God's Church today as the *antitype* of the Urim and Thummim? Yes, ultimately Jesus Christ guides and heads the Church—but how does He do this?

Let's let the apostle Paul explain how God has called, "... some [to be] apostles; and some, prophets; and some, evangelists; and some, pastors and teachers: For the perfecting of the saints, for the work of the ministry, for the edifying of the body of Christ: till we all come in the unity of the faith..." (Eph. 4:11-12).

Today, God's Holy Spirit works through His ministry to "enlighten" and "guide" the Church—in making doctrinal and administrative decisions concerning the preaching of the gospel.

Most thankfully, God's ministry are today's modern Urim and Thummim! Through these two precious stones, the presence of our Savior Jesus Christ was present with the ancient priesthood in guiding the nation of Israel. It is indeed significant that these two stones representing two Hebrew terms that began with the first and last letters of the Hebrew Alphabet, even as the Alpha and Omega guides the New Testament Church of God (Rev. 1:8).

Chapter Four

GOD'S PLAN REVEALED BY HIS PROFESSIONS

God—The All Wise
Financial Adviser

There are countless examples and scriptures in the Bible concerning money—is it an evil? And what do you do with it if you have it? God uses money in a physical sense to show us many spiritual principles.

Our heavenly Father shows us that in the last days that rich men would heap treasures of gold and silver on the earth, but it would not help them (Jas. 5:1 7).

The parable of *Lazarus and the Rich Man* is a stern warning to all of us. The "Rich Man" in this account would not give any of his wealth away and therefore supposedly would burn in the lake of fire (Lk. 16).

The "Rich Man" in (Matthew 19:16) would not give away his money for an apostleship. He didn't trust that God would provide his needs and instead TRUSTED in his own wealth which Jesus

Christ knew was his sin.

Jesus warns us that it is harder for a rich man to enter the Kingdom, than for a camel to pass through the eyehole of a needle in (Matthew 19:24). That it would be equally as hard for a rich man to enter the Kingdom of God.

Some people have thought therefore that God's government would be more like a communist government, in which the people share everything as it is owned by the state from (Acts 2:45).

Here the apostles sold all their possessions and shared them with each other. Furthermore, the parable of the Vineyard in (Matthew 20:2) shows that—no matter when you started work, early or late in the day [an analogy to when a Christian is called] you get the same reward.

However, the parable of the Talents in (Matthew 25:14) relates the principle of the free enterprise system to make more money with the money you have—even if we put it in the bank to get interest (vs. 27). This parable relates *symbolically* to the Christian's spiritual growth of using his spiritual gifts with God's Holy Spirit and growing in Godly Character.

Ananias and his wife were put to death because they lied in regard to money as recorded in (Act. 5:1).

Jesus spares not when He says no man can serve two masters, God or mammon [money] (Matt. 6:24).

Christians are supposed to give to them that ask—and to them that would borrow not to turn away (Matt. 5:42).

Jesus uses the analogy of forgiving monetary debts to that of forgiving spiritual debts [sins], in (Matthew 18:23).

Realize the whole earth is owned by God and He will distribute it as He sees fit (Ps. 50:10).

Our Savior cautions us in (Luke 12:15-40) that a man's life consists not of physical possessions—and the man who wanted to build bigger barns to make more money was very foolish.

Judas received 30 pieces of silver for betraying Christ in (Mark 14:11).

Jesus incites Christians to be content with our wages and give to the person who doesn't have a coat if we have two, and meat also (Lk. 3:8-14).

Jesus states in (Luke 6:38) that what measure we meet, it shall be measured to us.

Wisdom is found in (Proverbs 22:7) where the borrower is

servant to the lender.

Psalm 49:16, 17 tells us not to worry about riches because you can't take them with you when you die.

Cause of Poverty

Prov. 19:15;	"Love not sleep lest thou come to poverty." Cross ref: (20:4-13).
Prov. 13 18	"Poverty and shame to him that refuseth instruction."
Prov. 23:21	"The glutton and the drunkard shall come to poverty."
Prov. 28:19	"He that follows after vain persons shall have poverty."
Prov. 10:4	"He that deals with a slack hand shall become poor: but the hand of the diligent maketh rich."
11 Thess. 3:10-13	"If you don't work, you don't eat."
Eccl. 9:10	"Whatsoever your hand finds to do, do it with all your might."
1 Sam. 2:7	"The Lord maketh poor, and maketh rich. He raises up the poor out of the dust, and lifteth up the beggar out of the dunghole."
Prov. 21:17	"He that loves pleasure shall be a poor man."

Have Mercy on the Poor

Prov. 14:21	"He that despiseth his neighbor sinneth: but he that hath mercy on the poor, happy he is."

Prov. 17:5	"Whoso mocketh the poor reproacheth his maker, and he that is glad in calamities shall not be unpunished."
Prov. 21:13	"Whoso stoppeth his ears at the cry of the poor, he shall cry himself, but shall not be heard."
Prov. 29:7	"The Righteous considereth the cause of the poor: but the unrighteous doth sing and rejoice."
Zech. 7:10	"Oppress not the widow or the poor."
Lk. 10:27-37	"Love your neighbor as yourself."
Lk. 10:7	"The labourer is worthy of his hire."
Acts 11:34	"God is no respecter of persons and we should follow God's example."
Ps. 41:1-3	"Blessed is he that considers the poor, the Lord will deliver him in time of trouble. The Lord will keep him alive, and shall bless him upon the earth. Heal him in sickness."
.Prov. 19:17	"He that hath pity upon the poor lendeth unto the LORD: and that which he hath given will he pay him again."
Prov. 19:9	Give some of your field to the poor. God's Word absolutely commands that we consider the needs of the poor! Do we have mercy? Show pity? Give help?
Prov. 3:27-28	"Withhold not good from them to whom it is due, when it is in the

GOD'S PROFESSIONS

	power of thine hand to do it. Say not unto thy neighbor, Go, and come again and tomorrow I will give; when thou hast by thee."
Jas. 2:15	"If a brother or sister be naked, and destitute of daily food, feed him."

Lending

Ps. 37:21	"The wicked borroweth and payeth not again:but the righteous shows mercy and giveth."
Matt. 18:23	The parable of forgiving physical debts to spiritual debts (sins).
Lk. 7:41-43	"Forgive us our debts" (spiritual sins).
Lk. 6:34	Christ tells us not to expect anything back after we lend to someone: "for sinners also lend to sinners to receive as much again."
Duet. 23:20	Christians are not to collect usury [interest] from their brother, but they can from Gentiles [non-believers]. Cross reference Lev. 25:36; Prov. 28:8; Ezek. 18:8).
Rom. 13:7 8	"Owe no man anything."
Psalm. 112:5	"A good man shows favor and lends: he will guide his affairs with disscretion."
Ps. 15:2	"Works of righteousness does no evil to his neighbor, takes no interest."

Giving Offerings

11 Cor. 9:6-7	"God loves a cheerful giver; whosoever sows Sparingly shall reap sparingly: he that sows bountifully shall reap bountifully."
Acts 20:35	"It is more blessed to give than to receive."
Prov. 11:25	If you give generously, God will make you grow fat (spiritually).
Lk. 12:47-48	"Much is required of him that much is given."
Duet. 16:16	Give as you can afford, don't give as the average person but as an expression of your blessings.
1 Cor. 8:1-5	The poor Churches gave beyond their means to the Church at Jerusalem.
Gal. 6:10	"As we have therefore opportunity, let us do good unto all men, especially unto them who are of the household of faith."
Matt. 13:22	If we as Christians become unfruitful in giving, we can choke the Word from going out to others.
Lk. 16:1	The unjust steward couldn't handle his boss' money wisely. Christians should be able to manage God's money wisely to give offerings so the gospel can be preached and to the needy or poor.
Matt. 12:42	The Widow's mite. She gave what she didn't have.

Acts 10:2	Cornelius, an Italian [Gentile] gave much money to the poor [very wealthy]—his prayers were heard even though only Israel was being called.

Is it wrong to have Riches?

John 10:10 declares that Jesus came to give life more abundantly. That it is God's will that we should prosper (111 Jn. 2).

It is God's will that our joy might be full (Jn. 15:11).

The Bible tells us that the hand of the diligent maketh rich (Prov. 10:4). God encourages us to enjoy the fruit of our labor (Eccl. 5:18; 2:24; 3:13;22; 9:10,11).

Joseph was very wealthy (Gen. 39:2), as well as Job (Job 1:3) and Abraham (Gen, 13:2; 24:35). Zebedee's children had hired servants (Mk. 1:20).

These are all positive scriptures showing that it is *not* wrong to have riches. But there are many scriptures which show that money is an evil in certain people's lives. Let's read them:

Lk. 16	The "rich man" would not feed Lazarus.
Matt 19	The young "rich man" would not give up his riches.
Acts 5	Money destroyed Ananias and Sapphria.
Eccl. 2	Solomon had everything money could buy, yet he was not happy.
Lk. 12:15	"A man's life consisteth not in the abundance of things."
Mk. 8:36	"For what does it profit a man if he gain the whole world and lose his soul?"

Ps. 62:10	If riches increase, set your heart not upon them.
Col. 3:2	Set your affection [mind] on things above, not on things on the earth.
Prov. 22:4	"By humility and the fear of the Lord are riches, and honor and life." Labor not to be [just] rich (Prov. 23:4).
Eph. 3:8	We have the riches of God—His truths!
Prov. 13:7	Some people are rich and yet are poor—others are poor and rich (spiritually). J. Paul Getty said he would give all his millions away if he could have one happy marriage!
Jas. 1:9-11	Let the brother of low degree rejoice in that he is exalted: But the rich, in that he is made low: because as the flower of the grass he shall pass away. For the sun is no sooner risen with a burning heat, but it withereth the grass, and the flower thereof falleth, and the grace of the fashion of it perisheth: so also shall the rich man fade away in his ways.
Prov. 3:13-14	"Happy is the man that finds wisdom and understanding, these are better than gold and silver."
Prov. 22:1	"A good name is rather to be chosen than great riches, and loving favour rather than silver and gold."
Prov. 14:30	Envy or covetness is rotteness of the bones.

GOD'S PROFESSIONS

Lk. 8:14	Those that fell among thorns were *choked* by riches and pleasures of this world! Riches are deceitful. Satan tempted Christ with riches (Lk. 4:5). God's people sinned more as blessings were increased (Jer. 5:7; Hosea 4:7). People who were blessed thought it was from God (Tim. 6:3 6).
1 Tim. 6:5-10	"Godliness with contentment is great gain: For we brought nothing into this world and it is certain we will carry nothing out. And to have food and clothing let us be content, but they that will be rich fall into temptation and a snare, and into lusts; for the love of money is [a root] of all evil."
Matt. 6:31-33	"Seek first the Kingdom of God and all these things will be added unto you."
Prov. 10:6	Blessings are upon the head of the just.
1 Tim. 6:3-11	Seek faith, love, patience, meekness instead of wealth.
Prov. 8:10,11,19	Seek wisdom rather than gold and silver or rubies.
Ps. 37:16	A little that the righteous man has is better than the riches of the wicked.
Ps 112:1-3	Blessed is the man that delights greatly in His Commandments and fears God. Wealth and riches shall be in his house.
Phil. 4:11	Paul learned to be content no matter what state he was in.
Job 31:24	We should not make gold our

confidence; but rather trust God. The rich man *trusted* in his own riches instead of God.

1 Tim. 6:17-19   "Charge them that are rich in this world that they be not highminded, *nor trust in uncertain riches*, but in the living God who gives us richly all things to enjoy."

Lk. 18:8   God says it is harder [not impossible] for a rich man to enter the Kingdom of God than a camel to pass through the eye-hole of a needle.

Rev. 3:17   The Laodiceans will be rich in physical goods—but blind spiritually!

Lk. 18:22-25   Jesus told the rich man to sell everything and give to the poor.

Matt. 19:27   Peter and the apostles forsook all they had.

Acts 2:45;4:34   The apostles and disciples sold their possessions, goods and lands. Although this scripture seems to indicate the apostles sold everything they had, this is not necessarily true. It was the Day of Pentecost and they were sharing with everyone who had need.

Acts 3:6   Peter said, "silver and gold have I none."

Lk. 19:8   Zacchaeus gave half his goods to the poor. Christ said it was a good thing this wealthy man did and that salvation had now come to his house. Jesus then proceeded to explain the *parable of the*

GOD'S PROFESSIONS

	Pounds. He explained that wise man would use money discretely and more would be given to him. On the other hand, if money was used foolishly it would be taken away and given to a wise man.
Acts 28:30-31	The apostle Paul had a house.
Mk. 1:29	Peter had a house.
Matt. 13:57	Jesus had a house (Mk. 6:4).
Jn. 19:27	John had a house.
1 Cor. 11:22	The early Church had houses.
Mk. 10:28-30	Jesus said that no man would have to leave houses or lands for His sake or the gospels, but rather they would have houses and lands NOW and in the world to come eternal life.
Matt. 26:7	When a pound of expensive ointment was poured on Christ's head, He did not say it was a foolish way to spend money instead of giving it to the poor like Judas wanted. This ointment was worth 300 pense. It's not that Christ wasn't concerned about the poor, He was rather addressing the apostle's needs at that particular moment! They could help the poor for the rest of their lives, but Christ would not always be there to educate them. It was a matter of priority!
Prov. 13:22	A good man leaves an inheritance to his children.
Matt. 13:44	The parable of *"The Kingdom of*

Heaven being like a treasure hid in a field; which when a man hath found, he hideth and for joy thereof, goeth and sells all he has and buys that field." This parable is about a person who is not seeking God's truth but *stumbles* on it and is called of God.

Matt. 13:45-46 The parable of *"The Kingdom of Heaven* being like a merchant man, seeking goodly pearls, who, when he had found one pearl of great price, went and sold all that he had, and bought it." This parable is about a person who is *seeking* God's truth and then God calls him.

Lk. 14:26-33 Jesus warns us that we must be willing to forsake all that we have or we cannot be His disciple. We have to be willing to give up everything to achieve salvation!

Lk. 12:33 Jesus said to sell that ye have and give alms.

Lk. 9:58 Jesus said: "Foxes have holes but the son of man hath no where to lay His head." Some may hink from this scripture that Jesus was a poor man. But in fact, Jesus was on His way to Jerusalem (vs.51), and His messengers were sent ahead to find a place to stay for the night (vs.52). However, the Samaritans wouldn't give Jesus a place to stay (vs. 53). The Samaritans had a bone of contention with the Jews over the Temple site (Jn. 4:20). So, Jesus being a Jew, had no home to lay His head temporarily that night!

Mal. 3:8	If you don't tithe you have robbed God.
Matt. 23:23	But tithing is not enough. Jesus said we must keep the weightier matters of the law, judgment, mercy, faith; etc.
1 Cor. 13:3	The apostle Paul wrote; "Though one gives to the poor and have not charity [Godly love] he is nothing."
Prov. 31:10	A virtuous woman's price is far above rubies.
Prov. 8:10,11,19	Wisdom is better than gold and rubies.
Prov. 13:11	"Wealth gathered by labour shall increase, wealth gathered by vanity shall be diminished."
Eccl. 5:10-15	Silver nor abundance will ever satisfy anyone in this life. The rich cannot sleep for fear of someone stealing from them. We came into this world with nothing and we will leave naked!

Clearly, from these many scriptures it is definitely not wrong to have wealth or riches. But one should be content with what he has, and should use what he has wisely—by giving to the poor and for God's work.

One should not set his heart on wealth in this life—but rather on wisdom, understanding, a good name, faith, love, patience, meekness, virtuousness and purity!

Insurance

Many Christians have wondered if they should take out life insurance policies on themselves—or just have complete *faith* that God will take care of them—even as He takes care of the birds of the air or the lilies of the field (Matt. 6:26-31). These are valid questions, so let's read some additional scriptures to get a better understanding of this subject.

Solomon, one of the wisest men who ever lived explained insurance from an ants perspective as the the ant prepares it's meat in the summer [for the winter]: **"Go to the Ant, thou sluggard; consider her ways, and *be wise;* who provideth her meat in the summer, and gathereth her food in the harvest"** (Prov. 30:24; 6:6-8).

Joseph was told by God to prepare for the future by storing food up for seven years (Gen. 41:15 43).

Solomon also wrote that a good man saves for his children (Prov. 13:22).

Paul tells us that a man who does not provide for his wife is called worse than an infidel (1 Tim. 5:8).

Based on these additional scriptures—it appears evident that the principle of saving for the future is *definitely* a wise thing to do.

Summary

As we have just read, money can be used for both good and evil. It is not necessarily wrong to have it—if it is used properly and the spiritual is not neglected as a result of having it. God's tithing system really works. But ever since man wanted to change God's system and replace it with his own (1 Sam. 8:10) we have had nothing but higher taxation.

Under the Old Covenant, if Israel didn't give tithes, God says they have robbed Him (Mal. 3:8). The nation of Israel was a theocratic Nation of Church and State. We are not, but God does expect us to give offerings to support His Ministry. God expects us to give offerings with a good heart willingly (1 Jn. 3:2). Cain's tithes were not acceptable to God for he had a bad attitude (Gen. 4:4-5).

God—The Benevolent Physician

There is a very clear teaching in regard to Christ having paid the physical penalty as well as the spiritual penalty of death in connection with Passover service instruction.

In (1 Corinthians 11:23-30) we read of the New Testament *symbols* given, the bread [representing Christ's body] which was broken for us and the wine [representing His blood] shed for us to forgive our spiritual sins that we may have eternal life.

There is a prophecy in (Isaiah 53:4-5), concerning Jesus Christ that says, **"By His wounds we are healed."** Matthew 8:16-17 records that Jesus **"...took our infirmities, and bore our sicknesses."**

This promise is confirmed again in (1 Peter 2:24) **"...who his own self bore our sins in His own body on the tree, that we, being dead to sins, should live unto righteousness: by whose stripes ye are healed."**

God has paid the penalty for our sins by sending His son Jesus to suffer the penalty of sin in our place. The penalty for physical transgression of God's health laws may be physical sickness or disease, physical impairment, pain and suffering or physical death.

Healing does not mean that God suspends the penalty so that the penalty is paid. Instead Jesus has already paid it for us.

Therefore, God may legally remove the penalty from the human sufferer now.

The Greek word for *heal* in (1 Peter 2:24) is "Iaomi" which is used most often in reference to a physical healing "now" rather than "future." Peter's mother-in-law was healed to fulfill this prophecy (Matt. 8:14-17).

By the scourging and beating that broke open Jesus' flesh represented now *symbolically* by the broken bread at communion service— are we now able to be healed!

The *Revised Standard Version* of (Isaiah 52 and 53) reads, **"As many were astonished at him—His appearance was so marred, beyond human semblance, and His form beyond that of the sons of men..."**

The apostle Paul writes in (1 Corinthians 11:27-30) that many Christians die because of "sin" and are not healed now because they don't appreciate the "wounds" that Christ our Communion Bread took for us (1 Cor. 5:7).

That by taking the Passover unworthily [not repenting of sin] Christ's wounds would not cover their sin and therefore they would not be healed and die.

The *Revised Standard Version* translates, **"That is why many of you are weak and ill, and some have died"**—not realizing Jesus himself paid the penalty for physical transgression of the laws of the human body—by allowing His body to be broken open by many stripes, and not relying on the living Christ for their healing!

It is God's Will to Heal

Many have wondered if it was God's will to heal them. If we stop to realize that God himself, through Christ, paid a tremendous price that we may partake of the MIRACLE OF HEALING, we will have to believe this is God's will. He is so willing—indeed so anxious to relieve us from pain, suffering or affliction that He gave His only begotten Son—the One who is our very Maker—to be beaten, to suffer in our place, so that, without violating any principle of His Law, we may be healed!

Let's read some additonal scriptures that embellish the meaning of *healing* in the Bible:

Psalm 147:3:	"He healeth the broken heart [mind] and binds up their wound [body]."
11 Chron. 7:14	God said He will "...heal their land."
Jer. 6:14:	"They have healed the hurt of my people."
Hosea 7:1:	God says, "When I would have healed Israel."
Isa. 19:22:	God says, "He shall smite and heal Egypt" as well as Babylon (Jer. 51:9).
Psalm 60:2:	God said He will heal the Earth.
Matt. 13:15:	God gives reference to healing the spirit or mind.
Ex. 15:26:	God says, "I am the Eternal ["Yahweh-Rapha"] that healeth thee."

The Hebrew word for "heal" in these scriptures is "rapha" and means simply to "make better" or "restore". This same Hebrew word is used in (11 Kings 18:30) for "repair" where Elijah repaired *'rapha'* the altar of the Lord that was broken down.

This same word is used in (Ex. 21:18-19) where a man was to heal "rapha" a man that he struck down or *restore* to that man a payment for the time he lost from work.

Thus, we see that the Hebrew word for "heal" means to "restore" or "make better."

There are two ways in which God has chosen to "heal" or "restore"or "make better" as recorded in the Bible, in regard to human beings. Many cases of sickness involved divine instantaneous miraculous supernatural intervention, while others experienced a slower, more natural healing.

Miraculous Divine Healing

Jesus said that His body was given for us (Lk. 22:19). By the physical beating He took, Christians can be healed (Isa. 53:4-5; 1 Pet. 2:24).

Christ healed Palsy (Lk. 5:18), Leprosy (Matt. 8:1), and the blind (Matt. 9:20). The apostles had power to heal (Matt. 10:6-7).

A lame man was healed by Peter (Acts 3:1). The apostles healed many (Acts 5:12). Peter raised a dead man (Acts 9:36-42). Elijah raised a man from the dead (1 Kings 17:17-23).

All these were instantaneous divine miracles!

Natural Healing

King Hezekiah was dying from a diseased condition of the body which terminated in a boil. His life was saved when the Lord answered his prayers through the prophet Isaiah. And Isaiah said, **"Take a lump of figs, and they took and laid it on the boil, and he recovered" (11 Kings 20:7).**

God's prophet Elisha appears to have given mouth to mouth resuscitation to a child, to bring him back to life (11 Kings 4:32-34). God Himself performed the first case of mouth to mouth resuscitation when He breathed into Adam (Gen. 2:7).

Daniel ate "pulse" and water to make his face appear fairer in flesh than all the children of the Babylonians who ate meat (Dan. 1:10-17). Here is a Bible facial that Webster defines as edible seeds of leguminous crops such as peas and beans.

In (Genesis 30: 14-17), God allowed Leah to conceive by using the aphrodisiac "mandrake", a member of the potato family.

The apostle Paul left Timothy sick (11 Tim. 4:20) and told him to take a little wine for his stomach (1 Tim. 5:23).

We read in (Jeremiah 51:8), where Balm, a herb, is used allegorically to help heal the pain of the nation of Babylon, acknowledging its healing value.

There must have been many known remedies since (Jeremiah 30:13) says "thou hast no healing medicines."

God shows allegorically in (Ezekiel 30:21-22) that a broken arm could be healed by placing it in a bandage to heal or restore itself naturally.

During the Millennium, God will use natural remedies of trees to heal the nations (Rev. 22:2).

Thus, we see that there is a much slower and natural way that God uses to heal or restore an individual's health.

God does not always heal miraculously, but rather through revealed natural laws such as He gave to the high priest and Moses in dealing with Israel's diseases.

Conditions for Healing

James 5:14-16 states:

> **If any sick is among you let him call for the elders of the church, and let them pray over him, anointing him with oil in the name of the LORD: And the prayer of faith shall save the sick, and the Lord shall raise him up; and if he has committed sins, they shall be forgiven him. Confess your faults one to another, that ye may be healed. The effectual fervent prayer of a righteous man availeth much.**

The apostle James gave Christian's instruction to go in *faith* to the elders of the Church to be anointed with oil. This is a ceremony recognizing God's authority. The ceremony, like baptism and the laying on of hands—does nothing spiritually or physically of and by itself. Rather it is a *symbol* of recognizing God's power!

Definition of Faith—"faith is the substance [assurance] of things hoped for, the evidence of things not seen" (Heb. 11:1).

How to get Faith—"Faith comes by hearing" (Rom. 10:17). We learn *faith* by other's experiences (Heb. 11:8-13). Faith is a gift of God (Eph. 2:8). Faith is a fruit of God's Holy Spirit (Gal. 5:22).

Faith without works is dead, as James records (Jas. 2:11-20). The Just shall live by *faith* (Gal. 3:11). Without *faith* it is impossible to please God (Heb.11:6). We must have faith that we will receive an answer (Jas. 1:5-7).

It must be pointed out here that it is not a sin if a person does not have *faith*. The scripture that says **"...whatsoever is not of faith is sin" (Rom. 14:23)**, is referring to people who already have *faith* and fail to utilize it, not to someone who never had it.

However, *faith* is not the only criteria that God goes by in considering healing. The apostle Paul had *faith* to move mountains (1 Cor. 13:2). Paul's *faith* healed a deadly serpent's bite (Acts 28:3-6).

Yet the apostle Paul could not stop a ship from pounding waves (Acts 27). He could not heal Trophimus at Miletum sick (11 Tim. 4:20). He could not heal Epaphroditus who was sick (Phil. 2:25-27). Paul left Timothy sick (11 Tim. 4:20). Yet Timothy himself had *faith* (Phil.2:20), but was sick frequently (vs. 20, 11 Tim. 4).

Steven was given power to perform great miracles, and had much *faith*—yet he died an early martyr (Acts 6:8). On the other hand, Christ healed a man with palsy without necessarily knowing how long he was a Christian, or how long he studied the Bible. The Centurion's *faith* was greater than any found in Israel (Matt. 8:5-10). Elisha got sick and died, yet his bones healed a man (11 Kings 13:14,21).

These many scriptures only prove that healing is not solely dependent upon our spirituality, but is conditional of yet other factors.

Prayer

After seeing Jesus perform many miracles, our Lord's brother James wrote, **"...the effectual fervent prayer of the righteous availeth much."** The apostle Paul prayed three times that God would remove his thorn in the flesh, but failed to receive God's mercy (11 Cor. 12:8-10). On the other hand, God healed Abimelech because of Abraham's prayer (Gen. 20:17).

David, a man after God's own heart, prayed three times a day (Ps. 55:17). Yet he could not save his child's life even after fasting to God (11 Sam. 12:15-23). However, God heard Hezekiah's prayers, and changed His mind concerning Hezekiah's death, and because of his tears of repentance granted him an additional 15 years even though he sinned during those additional years! (1 Kings 20:1-7).

Prayer is dependent on many factors. **"The Lord is far from the wicked; but he heareth the prayer of the righteous" (Prov. 15:29).** "...God heareth not sinners" (Jn. 9:31; 1 Pet. 3:12). At least not until they repent! We have to get sin out of our lives before we can draw close to God (Jas.4:8). Isaiah declares the Eternal's answer to the reason He doesn't heal sinners:

> **Behold, the Lord's hand is not shortened, that it cannot save: neither his ear heavy, that it cannot hear: But your iniquities [sins] have separated between you and your God, and your sins have hid His face from you, that He will not hear (Isa. 59:1-2).**

The Proverbs also declare this truth: **"He that turneth away his ear from hearing the law, even his prayer shall be an abomination" (Prov. 28:9).** Your prayer can be hindered if you don't treat your wife right (1 Pet. 3:7). David knew God would not hear him if he was a sinner (Ps. 66: 18-20). God did answer the prayer of the wicked King Ahab, who married Jezebel, once he repented. God gave him MERCY (1 Kings 21: 25-29).

Mercy

Why did God choose to heal Hezekiah and not Paul? Why did Christ heal the Centurion's servant, and not the child David asked God to heal?

We cannot say that the apostle Paul and David did not have as much *faith*. Nor can we say God did not hear their prayer because they were worse sinners.

Clearly, healing is dependent upon God's MERCY. However, God's *mercy* is dependent upon many factors. God blesses the man that considers the poor, and will heal him in sickness (Ps. 41:1-3). **"For he shall have judgment without mercy, that hath shewed no mercy..." (Jas. 2:13). "For God resisteth the proud and gives grace to the humble " (1 Pet. 5:5).**

But we cannot say that the apostle Paul or King David were not merciful in giving to the poor, or weren't humble men. Why then, weren't their prayers answered in healings? There are yet other factors to consider; but basically, God says, **"I will have mercy on whom I will have mercy, and I will have compassion on whom I will have compassion" (Rom 9:15).**

God healed Epaphroditus only because of His mercy (Phil. 2:27). There is no mention of faith, prayer, or any other obligation. It is simply because of God's Sovereignty and He has the power to heal or not depending upon His will!

In chapter nine of John, we read the story of the man who was blind from birth. Jesus said he did not sin, nor His parents—but it was done to show the power of God and to teach an object lesson.

To Convince

Throughout the Bible miracles were done for many reasons. Many were to convince people of God's power. This was done mostly for the spiritually weak. God showed Moses a miracle in the burning bush so he would *believe* (Ex. 3:1-2).

God performed the plagues in Egypt to *convince* the skeptical Israelites of His power as well as the Egyptians. We read that speaking in tongues was not for them that *believe,* but for them that believe not (1 Cor. 14:22).

In (John 9:3) God predestined a man to be blind from birth—so He could heal him, and show His greatness to the unbelieving Jews, whose eyes had become closed or blind spiritually.

Lazarus was raised from the dead so that the people would *believe* Christ was the Messiah (Jn. 11:4, 15,42).

Matthew 8:16-17 tells us Christ healed the sick in order to fulfill the prophecies. No question was asked as to one's *faith* or attitude.

Jesus wanted the people to know what His Kingdom was going to be like. The Kingdom will be a *restoring* of all things [earth, air, water, etc,] including the restoring of people's bodies or lives! (Acts 3:21).

As Christ did these miracles His fame spread (Matt. 4:23-25). They were a great *witness* of God's power to the world (Matt. 15:30-31). The resurrection from the dead is the ultimate in healing!

Naaman was healed when his attitude was changed (11 Kings 5:1-27). The same Hebrew word "rapha" is used in (vs. 3) for "recover" as "heal" in other places.

Why God doesn't Heal

Sometimes God allows our weaknesses to exist to show His strength, and make us *humble* to realize our total dependence upon Him. The apostle Paul said that if God had healed his "thorn in the flesh" he might have been exalted above measure (11 Cor. 12:7). God said to him, **"My grace is sufficient for thee: for my strength is made perfect in weakness" (vs. 9).**

Paul therefore took pleasure in his affliction realizing that when he was weak, he was strong (vs. 10). Paul realized that he might become too vain, if he would not need God for something. But God gave him just enough strength to get the job done. **"He gives power to the faint; and to them that have no might He increaseth strength" (Isa. 40:29).**

God did not always perform miracles, for He knew that miracles brought persecution along with them. If Jesus had performed miracles any sooner than He did, God's purpose for Him would have been thwarted.

A Conditional Promise

There are three Greek words used in the New Testament for "heal" or "healing."

- *theraperio*—"to care for," "treat," "restore," "heal."
- *iami*—"to cure or deliver," "heal physically now."
- *sozo*—"to save from death," "free from disease," "make whole," "to save from eternal death or salvation." This word is used in (Matt. 5:23 and Acts 14:9) in relationship with

physical healing although it is used approximately one hundred times in reference to a future spiritual healing—salvation!

In (James 5:14) where the question is asked, **"Is any sick among you?"**—We have already seen where *faith* and prayer, although necessary, are not the only criteria for healing; but rather God's *mercy*.

However, it should be understood that the Greek word for "save" in (James 5:15) is *'sozo'*, and in most instances it refers to "spiritual salvation" rather than a physical salvation of healing now.

In other words, even though the words **"if it be God's will"** are not included in James' context—it was understood by the early Church what was meant.

To further show that James meant a healing of the future, the Greek word "egeiro" is used in (vs. 15) for "raise him up." This same Greek word is used in (Matt. 11:5, 4:2, 16:21; Acts 3:15; and Rom. 6:4) all referring to the *resurrection* from the dead—at which time God will heal. James is here confirming the condition of healing in the resurrection.

God will follow through on His promise to heal us because of the stripes [wounds] Jesus took for us (1 Pet. 2:24)—the only question is when. Some will be healed *now*, others at the *resurrection* when we will have a new body (1 Cor. 15). As the prophet said, there is a time to heal (Eccl. 3:3).

Is God against Physicians?

The first chapter of (11 Kings) states that King Ahaziah, king of Israel at Samaria, son of evil Ahab, became sick and sent his messengers to go and inquire of Baalzebub—the god of Ekron whether he would recover. But God's angel told Elijah that King Ahaziah would die because he went to Baalzebub for advice. Baalzebub, the god of Ekron, was the patron deity of medicine.

In (11 Chronicles 16:12) we read of the account where Asa went to the physicians and died. On the other hand as we have already shown, King Hezekiah went to God and was *healed* and given 15 additional years to live (1 Kings 20:1-7).

What then can we learn from these ancient examples?

Does this mean that God is against physicians? We must realize the Hebrew word for physician in the Bible may mean a magician or witch—and we know God is definitely against these (Deut. 18:9-14).

However, physicians were recognized in the Bible as people who treated with herbs and natural remedies. Luke was called the beloved physician, not ex-physician (Col. 4:14). They embalmed the dead (Gen. 50:2).

Jesus recognized that these students of herbology could help the sick also. Matthew 9:12 reads: **"They that are whole need not a physician, but they that are sick."** However, the physicians could not help a woman that had suffered many ailments and spent all she had on them (Mk. 5:25-26).

In any event, the lesson to be learned from Asa and Ahaziah is to go to God for help. They chose to go to pagan gods instead the true God. James records for our admonition: **"Faith without works is dead" (James 2:20).**

Christians should consult physicians for advice as to what physical law they are breaking: **"...for where no counsel is the people fall! But, in the multitude of counsellors, there is safety" (Prov. 11:14).**

Doctors cannot heal, they can only work within the framework of God's laws. Only God can heal! Breaking physical laws has a bearing on whether we are sick or not, not on whether we will be healed or not.

God may heal us by instant miraculous means or by slower more natural means using revealed knowledge of health laws—but healing is dependent on God's mercy and purpose! Jesus gave no condemnation to physicians as pagans, charlatans or being incompetent. In fact, the scriptures show a positive effect of medicines [herbs] and other natural remedies figuratively, literally and metaphorically.

Disease—Types of Sin

Jesus performed countless miracles throughout His 3 1/2 year public ministry. Among them were the raising of the dead, healing of the deaf and mute, blind and palsy.

Each of these diseases are *types* of "sin" that Jesus will conquer in His triumph over Satan and sin!

The wages of sin is death (Rom. 6:23), yet Jesus proved His

power over sin and death by raising three individuals back to life!

Jesus healed the blind man to relate the *spiritual blindness* of the Jews (Jn. 9:14). To these BLIND Pharisees Jesus exhorted: **"...If ye were blind, ye should have no sin: but now ye say, we see; therefore your sin remaineth" (verse 41).**

To non believers, Jesus likened their condition to DEAFNESS: **"Therefore speak I to them in parables: because they seeing see not; and hearing they hear not, neither do they understand" (Matt. 13:13).**

Leprosy had the connotation to the sin of rebellion through DEFILEMENT of God's governmental structure.

Moses' sister Miriam was stricken with leprosy as a result of rebellion [murmuring] against God's chosen servant Moses— because he had married an Ethiopian woman (Num. 12:1,10-11).

King Uzziah of Judah was also smitten with the plague of leprosy when he *transgressed* against God's instructions and burned incense in the Temple (11 Chron. 26).

His sin was similar to that of Uzzah who was struck down for touching the Holy Ark and not following due order. These men tried to fulfill holy ordained offices of the priesthood in which they were not called.

What was Uzziah's fate for usurping God's holy office? **"And Uzziah the king was a leper unto the day of his death, and dwelt in a several house, a leper: for he was cut off from the house of the Lord..." (verse 21).**

Job was smitten with boils from the sole of his foot to his head until he learned not to be so SELF-RIGHTEOUS (Job 2:7).

As a result of Korah's rebellion, the plague broke out among the people, for their *murmuring* hearts had caught the infection of Korah's sin (Num. 16). Thus, the plague's spreading action impressed upon them the infectiousness of HERESY!

All of these examples were written to teach us vital spiritual lessons! Let us not become spiritually blind!

God—The Magnificent Army Officer

From the *analogy* of a soldier's uniform, God tells us through the apostle Paul to:

> **Put on the whole *armour* of God, that we may be able to stand against the wiles of the devil...stand therefore, having your loins *girt* about with truth, and having on the *breastplate* of righteousness and your feet *shod* with the preparation of the gospel of peace; above all, taking the *shield* of faith, wherewith ye shall be able to quench all the fiery darts of the wicked (one). And take the *helmet* of salvation, and the *sword* of the Spirit, which is the Word of God (Eph. 6:11-17).**

Paul continues this *analogy* of a Christian's "spiritual battle" with evil as he told Timothy:

> **Therefore, endure hardness, as *a good soldier of Jesus Christ*. No man that wars entangles himself with the affairs of this life: that he may please him who has chosen him to be a soldier (11 Tim. 2:3-4, paraphrased).**

Most definitely, a Christian is in a spiritual BATTLE against Satan the devil—and this spiritual armour is absolutely essential to attain victory! The Christian's victory, of course, is attainment of God's Kingdom.

As in any physical army, a Christian must also go through *basic training* so he will not become a spiritual casualty along the way.

Exercising our minds *daily* in the Word of God will ensure a strong and determined mind to overcome Satan's sharp attacks. Like any adversary, Satan has a battle plan and he is using highly advanced weaponry to bombard our minds.

Satan tries to sabotage new Christians before they even enter into God's *boot camp*—by luring them with wealth and riches and other things of this world!

Christians who have been in God's army for many years must also be very careful never to take their armour off [though it may become heavy at times], lest they become *battle fatigued*. This is exactly what Satan desires, and he tries to get you interested in other things to lose your concentration. By succumbing to the "wicked ones" tactics we will eventually become AWOL [absent without leave] and eventually leave God's Church!

It is therefore imperative to keep up our spiritual health by staying on a proper combat diet of Bible study—which includes both *milk* and *meat*. This will take DISCIPLINE and daily exercise even as in any physical army.

Daily prayer is also essential in maintaining spiritually strong minds to fight against Satan's battalions. It has been said that an army moves on it's stomach—but the Church of the living God moves on it's knees!

Taking orders from those higher up is a lesson every army officer must learn. The officers in God's army of course are His ministers—and we should listen to their advice, realizing they have rule [are guides] over us (11 Cor. 10:8,12,13; Heb. 13:7).

Before Christians can give orders—they must learn to take orders! This will take COURAGE and FAITH in the government of God. Our heavenly Officer once said to ancient Israel concerning fighting a battle:

> **When you go out to the battle against your enemies, and you see horses, and chariots, and a people more than you, be not afraid of them: for the Lord your God is with you, who brought you up out of the land of Egypt (Deuteronomy 20:1, paraphrased).**

A Christian has many insurmountable battles to fight daily, but must trust God to hold up the walls of the waters around him as He did the ancient Israelites—so he will not drown in the spiritual battles of Babylon!

God continues to explain what a Christian's attitude should be toward spiritual battle:

> **And it shall be, when you come near unto the battle; that the priest shall approach and speak unto the people, And shall say unto them, Hear, O Israel, you approach this day unto battle against your enemies: let not your hearts faint, fear not, and do not tremble, neither be you terrified because of them; For the Lord your God is He who goes with you, to fight for you against your enemies, to save you...What man is**

THE FOOLISHNESS OF GOD

there who is fearful and fainthearted? Let him go and return unto his house lest his brother's [in war] heart faint as well as his heart (verse 2-8).

God the Father does not want anyone in His army who lacks *faith* in Him. He is our *Commander in Chief* and His Son Jesus Christ is our *Captain* (Heb. 2:10). We must take the shield of faith (which is complete trust in God). Then He stands by His promise to *never* forsake us in battle!

It has been said that "Knowing your enemy is half the battle"—every Christian should know that Satan wants to devour him before he reaches final victory. Though Satan may launch surprising attacks, we must never be caught completely off guard. He will try every diabolical trick in the book to wear us down—including implanting evil thoughts about our troops (brethren) and Officers (ministers).

Satan will try to convince us that we no longer need our armour and that we can survive without the help of the troops for protection.

Jesus Christ invites us to be in His army in the final battle of Armageddon to put down the demonic governments of this world (Rev. 19). But Satan would like nothing more than for us to remove our spiritual armour so his henchmen can remove our helmet of salvation from us—don't let this happen to you!

The weapons of a Christian Soldier are spiritual [prayer, Bible study, meditation, fasting, exercising God's Holy Spirit through fellowship] not physical (11 Cor. 10:3-4).

The first enemy of a Christian's warfare is himself. He must *conquer* vanity, lust, greed, jealousy, pride, self-righteousness, etc. Satan will attack us daily, working on our particular weaknesses, trying to wear us down, and make us quit.

He wants us to give up from being a member of God's family and be out of the Kingdom of God! But like the apostle Paul, we must fight the good fight and endure to the end (11 Tim. 4:6).

Don't remove your Armor

The word for *armor* in (Ephesians 6:13-18) refers to any body covering designed for protection in combat. In this case, it is protection for our spiritual lives! But Satan, through his subtle influence, can convince us to take off God's armor, a piece at a time, until we are completely spiritually naked and unprotected!

For the sake of those who are in danger of believing it is easier to fight with less of the spiritual weight of God's armor, consider the following scenario:

The devil is like a military general, eagerly plotting the demise of his enemy—in this case, you and me. He deals in subtleties, launching surprise attacks here and there until we're caught off guard.

His plan begins by inspiring discouragement and doubt among God's troops about the Church, about its leaders and about our calling, hoping eventually to convince us that we can no longer have faith even in Christ's leadership and protection.

Once that happens, it is so easy for us to unfasten the support of *truth* that God has fastened to our loins (vs. 14), thereby becoming a little more vulnerable to attack.

Later in the battle, without that girdle of truth to protect our vital organs, it becomes more natural to agree that the weight of our armor is quite heavy. That is when the weary soldier takes off another piece of equipment, the *breastplate of righteousness* (vs. 14).

Only partially protected now, the soldier searches more desperately for an effective battle plan, listening to any "foolish saying" (Isa. 30:10), but is led ever closer toward the inevitable ambush.

Removing his boots for speed, he runs to and fro in the midst of battle with *feet that are no longer shod* with the preparation of the Gospel of peace (vs. 15). He loses sight of the Church's commission to preach the Gospel and to prepare a people for the Lord.

Satan's attack nears its apex. After a barrage of manipulation and disorientation, the Christian lays aside His *shield of faith.* Now he or she can no longer quench the fiery darts of the wicked (vs. 16). Another casualty is recorded in the great conflict.

After the Christian is down, his blood poured out over the field, Satan's henchmen remove his *helmet of salvation* (vs. 17, the last gesture that seals his fate.

We must never let this come true in our life!

God—The King of Kings

When Pilate asked Jesus if He was King of the Jews, Jesus replied, "Thou sayest it" (Lk. 23:3). The apostle Paul called Jesus the King eternal (1 Tim. 1:17). He is also referred to as, "The King of Kings" (1 Tim. 6:16, Rev. 17:14, 19:16).

Jesus will be King over other Kings in the world tomorrow. Resurrected Christians are to RULE with Christ as Kings (Rev. 1:6, 5:10, 1 Pet. 2:5,9).

Our most righteous Judge shows this future time through the parable of the Kingdom being like a king [Himself] who will take account of his servants (Matt. 18:23).

The parable of the marriage to a king [Christ] and the Bride [the Church] is given in (Matthew 22).

The parable of a man [Christ the King] traveling into a far country [heaven] to return [to earth] is given in (Matthew 25). Notice: **"Then shall the King say unto them on his right hand, come, ye blessed of my father, inherit the kingdom prepared for you from the foundation of the world" (Matt. 25:34).**

The book of Hebrews envisions Jesus as *crowned* with glory, who will bring many sons unto glory, being the captain of their salvation (Heb. 2:9-10).

When our Savior and King returns to the earth, He will have a gold crown on His head (Rev. 14:14), and will RULE with a rod of iron as the King of the earth (Rev. 2:27, 12:5).

There is a "crown of righteousness" which the Lord, the righteous judge, shall give all Christians at His appearing (11 Tim. 4:8). But only if we are faithful! (Rev. 2:10). Like the captain of our salvation, Christians are destined to be Kings—therefore, let no man take your crown! (Rev. 3:11).

Chapter Five

GOD'S PLAN REVEALED BY THE GALILEAN PARABLES

One of the most fascinating means by which the All-wise God has chosen to reveal His GREAT PLAN, is that of *parable*s.

A parable is simply a colorful story of everyday life that portrays an important SPIRITUAL LESSON to the listener. It may be in the form of a comparison, riddle, proverb, metaphor, allegory, fable or type. Oftentimes it is a "folk story" in nature describing the surrounding environment or geography. In essence, a parable is "an earthly story with a heavenly meaning."

During Jesus' 3 1/2 year ministry, He spoke nearly forty parables which contained examples of everyday life in ancient Judea and its surrounding areas. These parables contained many *symbols* of the populous' occupations such as farming (field, fig tree, sower, seed, mustard seed, etc.) and fishing (sea, fish, net, etc.). Practically His entire ministry was *painted* with *graphic colors* for: **"Without a parable spake He not unto them" (Matt. 13:34).**

Through parable of everyday life, Jesus uses *hieroglyphics to* explain *higher truths*. By understanding common everyday life—we can comprehend spiritual life! Physical objects are used to explain spiritual truths, or as the apostle Paul wrote: **"For the invisible things of him from the creation of the world are clearly seen, being understood by the things that are made, even His eternal power and Godhead; so they are without excuse" (Rom. 1:20).**

It is not surprising that Jesus chose to speak in parables, as this was a common method of teaching for the time. The noted scholar Alfred Edersheim writes in his book: "Perhaps no other mode of teaching was so common among the Jews as that by parables...Every ancient Rabbinic work is literally full of parables" (*The Life and Times of Jesus the Messiah*, Grand Rapids, Mich.: William B. Eerdmans Pub. Co; 1972, p. 580).

This fact is also demonstrated by several accounts of parables in the old Testament—See (Ezek. 17:2; ll Sam. 12; Isa. 5:1-6).

As already stated—parables were spoken to convey a profound spiritual lesson. Each parable is like a nugget of gold that we must dig and search for with diligence, if we wish to find its true vein.

However, this was not always the case with Jesus! When the disciples of Jesus asked Him why He spoke in parables, the MASTER STORY TELLER replied:

> **Because *it is given unto you* to know the mysteries of the kingdom of heaven, but to them *it is not given*. For whosoever hath, to him shall be given, and he shall have more abundance: but whosoever hath not, from him shall be taken away even that he hath. Therefore, speak I to them in parables: because they seeing see not; and hearing they hear not, neither do they understand (Matt. 13:10-13).**

In Jesus' own words, He says He spoke in parables to the general public to *cloud* the meaning rather than to make it vivid! Why? Because Jesus knew the general populous was not yet ready to *obey* the deep spiritual truths of a Christian life!

Oftentimes God veils Himself, for His brightness would destroy us! So, it is with His glorious truth. Sometimes He veils it, other times He unveils it. Only God knows what we can bear during certain dispensations.

GALILEAN PARABLES

Jesus did however, explain the meaning of each parable to His 12 disciples privately, whom He was grooming for the Kingdom of God. On other occasions, He did expect the Pharisees to understand—and addressed them accordingly. Jesus held the scribes and Pharisees ACCOUNTABLE for what they heard and understood, based on the scripture in James: **"Therefore to him that knoweth to do good, and doeth it not, to him it is sin" (Jas. 4:17).**

Six Themes of Parables

There are six clearly defined groups of parables given—each having its own theme or message. Each theme or group of parables were given at a *precise time* for a *specific lesson*. It is very important to understand this and the circumstances that led up to *where* and *when* each theme was presented.

The six themes of Jesus' parables portray WHEN the Kingdom of God would start, WHO and HOW to enter in, WHERE it will be and WHY it will eventually rule over the entire earth!

The six themes can be categorized as follows:

- **The Galilean Parables**—Theme: *The Kingdom of God*. There were 10 given in all, *portraying* HOW to enter and grow in the Kingdom of God. Four were given solely for the benefit of Jesus' disciples.

- **Parables of Israel's History**—Theme: *The Change of Administration* from Jew to Gentile. This can only be understood by comprehending the parables of Israel's history as a nation. Not only can God's plan for the *present* dispensation be clearly defined from these parables—but also His plan for the *future* of the world and Israel's part in it.

- **Evangelistic Parables**—Theme: *God's Mercy* to those who have strayed from the truth, and have *repented*! Our heavenly Father eagerly awaits those who have forsaken the right way with endless mercy. He stands ready to forget and forgive by His infinite grace and power—those that have stumbled along the straight and narrow path to salvation—but have now repented of their sins!

- **Prophetic Parables**—Theme: *Prophetic events* of the future about to explode on the world scene. Unbeknown to the world, but as sure as the sun will set tomorrow—mind boggling events are about to appear on the horizon. Prior to the Messiah's intervention to restore the government of God on earth—earth shaking news will sweep this globe as definite *signs* of Christ's return occur!

- **Parables of Christian Admonition**—Theme: *Service and reward* parables based upon the *way of life* a Christian has lived. Stern warnings are given to those who fail to live in accordance with God's WAY OF LIFE!

- **The Futility of Riches**—Theme: *Earthly possessions are only temporary* and can destroy Christians if they are not careful. Riches have been a stumbling block to those unaware of Satan's tactics to *choke* their spiritual development.

The first set of parables are termed the "Galilean Parables" because of the environment in which they were given. They set a precedent for the other themes.

The **Galilean Parables** consists of 10 parables. Six were given by Jesus sitting on a small boat near the shore of Galilee to the people, and four were given *privately* to His disciples. You will recall that Jesus was born in Bethlehem, grew up in Nazareth and later moved to the town of Capernaum which was near the Sea of Galilee.

As the crowds gathered on the hillside to hear Jesus speak—His voice echoed across the water which acted like a natural amphi-theater, since there were no electronic amplification in those days.

The ten Galilean parables are recorded in (Matthew 13, Mark 4 and Luke 8). The following is a list of the ten Galilean parables:

- **The Parable of the Sower** (Matt. 13:3-9).

GALILEAN PARABLES

- **The Wheat and the Tares** (Matt. 13:24-30).

- **The Lamp Under the Bushel** (Mk. 4:21- 25).

- **The Grain of Mustard Seed** (Matt. 13:31-32).

- **The Kingdom Like Leaven** (Matt. 13:33).

- **The Seed Cast into the Ground** (Mk. 4:26-29).

- **The Hidden Treasure** (Matt. 13:44).

- **The Merchant Seeking Pearls** (Matt. 13:45,46).

- **The Net Cast into the Sea** (Matt. 13:47-50).

- **The Householder and His Treasure** (Matt. 13:52).

Doctrinal in Nature

The meaning of the first six parables were *not* explained to the general populous, but Jesus did explain them privately in a house to His disciples, notice:

> **All these things spake Jesus *unto the multitude* in parables; and without a parable spake he not unto them: That it might be fulfilled which was spoken by the prophet, saying, 'I will open my mouth in parables; I will utter things which have been kept secret from the foundation of the world.'**
>
> **Then Jesus sent the multitude away, and went into the house: and his disciples came unto him, saying, *Declare unto us* the parable of the tares of the field (Matt. 13:34-36).**

In addition to explaining the first six parables to His disciples, Jesus gave them four additional parables. These last four parables contained deep *spiritual lessons* that only applied to the disciples and were doctrinal in nature: **"And he taught** them many things by parables, and said unto them in his doctrine..." (Mk. 4:2).

The definition of a Church doctrine is: "A biblical teaching of Jesus Christ that contains truths or principles that a Christian should live by."

The Parable of The Sower

Hearken; Behold, there went out a sower to sow: And it came to pass, as he sowed, some fell by the way side, and the fowls of the air came and devoured it up. And some fell on stony ground, where it had not much earth; and immediately it sprang up, because it had no depth of earth:

But when the sun was up, it was scorched; and because it had no root, it withered away. And some fell among thorns and the thorns grew up, and choked it, and it yielded no fruit. And other fell on good ground, and did yield fruit that sprang up and increased; and brought forth, some thirty, and some sixty, and some an hundred (Mk. 4:3-8).

The parable of *The Sower* is the first word painting that Jesus gave and sets a *precedent* for the method of understanding the rest of the parables. Jesus said to His disciples concerning the parable of *The Sower*. **"...know ye not this parable? And *how then will ye know all parables?*"** (Mk. 4:13).

Jesus Explains

The parable of *The Sower* was very easy for the general populous to relate as many of them were farmers—"a sower went out to sow grain in his field." Those listening could all comprehend how the seed could fall on four different types of soil, 1) the wayside, 2) stony ground, 3) among thorns, and 4) good ground.

But the spiritual meaning of how each of these categories represented a kind of person that God is CALLING was not understood. Jesus, our great Teacher had to expound the spiritual intent to His disciples later in private.

Jesus confided to them that, "...the sower soweth *the word"* which represented God's Word in which they were now going to preach (verse 14). Jesus, of course, is the ultimate Sower, but now His disciples were to follow in His footsteps.

The *seed* represented the Word or *gospel message* which the apostles and their followers throughout the ages would preach. This is the "incorruptible seed" of the Word of God (1 Pet. 1:22-25; Matt. 5:19). The ground or earth represents the world.

The four types of ground on which the seed fell, represents 4 categories of people that would respond to the gospel message—some with *lethargy* others with zeal!

- **The Seed by the Wayside:** Those individuals classified as "falling by the wayside" are people who allow God's truth to fall on deaf ears. They have a closed mind. These people *never* allow God's truths to take deep root in their life due to Satan's subtilty, **"Satan cometh immediately, and taketh away the word that was sown in their hearts" (vs. 15).**

Such people are EASILY OFFENDED by practically anything from a minor doctrinal point to harsh rumors about the Church and individual ministers. Sudden changes of personal circumstances, such as being laid-off, or a marital problem, is all it will take to set off their sensitive time-bomb. Their transient time in the church is very short.

Individuals in this category reject the truth for a myriad of reasons—but the end result is tantamount to REJECTING the gospel message of God's coming Kingdom, before it is allowed to take root.

- **The Seed on Stony Ground:** Individuals in this category allow more roots to take hold than the ones "by the wayside" and even become members of God's Church: **"Then they that gladly received His word were *baptized...*"**

These potential servants are happy in the faith as long as things remain placid with work, family or neighbors. Those in this category: **"...have no root in themselves, and so endure** but for a time: afterward, when *affliction* or **PERSECUTION ariseth for the word's sake, immediately they are** *offended*" **(Mk. 4:17)**. This group has "no root in themselves"—they are faithful as long as they don't receive any ridicule or persecution about their beliefs. Such people are willing to acquiesce with God's Word rather than withstand scorn and suffering by outside pressures.

These people lack a deep abiding *faith* and are only irresolute ornaments taking up valuable chair space. Because the parable relates this type of person to "stony ground" or ground that is shallow of earth and plenteous of rock—these are people with stony hearts!

- **The Seed among Thorns:** The seed that was "sown among the thorns" is typical of individuals who have surpassed those in the previous categories spiritually. They have been *baptized* and began to bear "spiritual fruit" in that their lives were changing—but "the cares of materialism of this world" put a damper on any progress gained.

They begin to go back to their old carnal ways of thinking about the pleasures of this world! Notice what Jesus said of them: **"...the cares of the world, and the** *deceitfulness* **of riches and the** *lusts* **of things entering in,** *choke* **the word, and it becometh unfruitful" (Mk. 4:19)**.

These individuals begin to set their heart on physical MATERIALISTIC things and goals—they want to accrue bigger houses, better cars, more clothes, a desire to climb up the social ladder of success, etc. Entering into God's Kingdom and helping others is no longer their first love—wealth, money and power become their primary motivation in life.

The apostle Paul admonishes Christians not to choke God's Holy Spirit by thinking on the opulence of physical things, rather: **"set your affection on things above, not on things on the earth" (Col. 3:2)**, and that **"...to be carnally [materialistically] minded is death..." (Rom. 8:6)**.

- **The Seed on Good Ground:** The final category in which the seed of the gospel message fell is on "good ground." This is a classification of Christians who are continuously bearing "GOOD FRUIT" spiritually in their lives. But even within this category there is a difference as to how much fruit each Christian will bear.

The parables of the "Talents" and "Pounds" are two other parables that illustrate how much fruit each individual Christian can and will bear. The parable of *The Talents* informs us that we are not all born with the same amount of talent and therefore cannot all bear the same amount of fruit.

The parable of *The Pounds* graphically explains that some given an equal amount of talent will bear more fruit than others—because of more effort or *desire*. Of course, no one can bear any amount of fruit without the help of Jesus as He said: **"I am the Vine, ye are the branches: He that abideth in me, and I in him, the same bringeth forth *much fruit*: for without me ye can do nothing" (Jn. 15:5).**

The earth in which this seed germinates represents God's Church as "firstfruits out of the world" (Jas. 1:18). These "firstfruits" will grow in the earth only to be "offered" to God fulfilling the Day of Pentecost!

This unique parable also illustrates the need for a proper environment in which the seed can grow. The fowls devoured up the seed that fell in stony places, withered away because it didn't have much earth, and was therefore sun scorched because it had no root.

The seed that fell by the wayside, on stony ground, and among thorns did not produce fruit because of an improper environment. The seed that fell on good ground was the only seed that produced fruit because it had the proper conditions for growth.

Relating this parable to the proper climate for Christians to produce fruit, we must realize that we can wither away from God's Church because of a lack of Bible study and prayer.

The Parable of
The Wheat and Tares

Another parable put he forth unto them, saying, the kingdom of heaven is likened unto a man which sowed good seed in his field: But while men slept, his enemy came and sowed tares among the wheat,

> *and went his way. But when the blade was sprung up, and brought forth fruit, then appeared the tares also. So the servants of the householder came and said unto him, Sir, didst not thou sow good seed in thy field? from whence then hath it tares?*
>
> *He said unto them, An enemy hath done this. The servants said unto him, Wilt thou then that we go and gather them? But he said, Nay; lest while ye gather up the tares, ye root up also the wheat with them. Let both grow together until the harvest: and in the time of harvest I will say to the reapers, Gather ye together first the tares, and bind them in bundles to burn them: but gather the wheat into my barn (Matt. 13:24-30).*

Once again Jesus gave a very colorful parable relating everyday rural life to that of the Kingdom of God. Farmers knew very well that *tares* were weeds which grew along side of the *wheat*, only to be distinguishable when they came to maturity. But while in the blade stage they looked very much the same. Jesus explained the *spiritual* meaning of this parable to His disciples:

> **The field is the world; the good seed [true Christians] are the children of the Kingdom; but the tares are the children of the wicked one [Satan—compare Jn. 8:44; 1 Jn. 3:8]; the enemy that sowed them is the devil [the god of this society, 11 Cor. 4:4]; the harvest is the end of the world; and the reapers are the angels. As therefore the tares are gathered and burned in the fire; so shall it be in the end of this world [Greek: *aionos*, meaning *age*].**

Jesus is the sower in this parable of "good seed" while Satan is the sower of "bad seed". The *wheat* are synonymous of "the good seed" while "tares" represent the offspring of the *wicked one*.

Thus, Jesus illustrated very graphically the fate of all who are belligerent towards the government of God. These individuals refuse to *obey* God's authority and eventually will be discarded into the "lake of fire" and consumed into ashes as their final destiny (Mal. 4:3; Rev. 20:14-15).

Both believers [wheat] and nonbelievers [tares] will co-exist till that day of reckoning. Then will begin the separation of the wheat from the tares or sheep from goats! In the interim, God allows the Judas's to dwell with His true Church, even as He allowed the serpent to enter Paradise. Why? Because "an enemy has done this"!

The Parable of The Lamp Under A Bushel

And he said unto them, is a candle brought to be put under a bushel, or under a bed? and not to be set on a candlestick? For there is nothing hid, which shall not be manifested; neither was any thing kept secret, but that it should come abroad. If any man have ears to hear, let him hear (Mk. 4:21-23).

Ye are the light of the world. A city that is set on an hill cannot be hid. Neither do men light a candle, and put it under a bushel, but on a candlestick; and it giveth light unto all that are in the house (Matt. 5:14-16).

Several times throughout His 3 1/2 year public ministry—Jesus "enlightened" the apostles as to their commission. This *portrait* of their commission was given specifically to the Church to impress upon them and future Christian's that God's precious truths are *not* to be hidden—but shared!

Jesus said that Christians were to be "a light to the world" by their WAY OF LIFE and with their gospel message (Matt. 5:14-16).

Jesus articulates to His pupils:

Fear them [the people] not therefore: for there is nothing covered, that shall not be revealed; and hid, that shall not be known. What I tell in

darkness, that *speak ye* in light: and what ye hear in the ear, that *preach ye upon the housetops* **(Matt. 10:26-27).**

Even as Jesus was a "light to the world" in the flesh—His spiritual body [the Church] is to follow in His footsteps and preach the gospel of *light* to this world of *darkness* (Jn. 1:9). However, Christians can only shine in emulation of the "True Light" by having the Spirit of Light dwelling in them (Jn. 5:35).

A candle can only give light once it is lit—and we can only radiate love when we have received love through God's Spirit (Gal. 5:22). Once lighted, Christians must function as burning and SHINNING LIGHTS and not hide their spiritual light.

A bushel is usually emblematic of trade or work in the Bible—and therefore Christians should be a shining example of Christianity to those we come in contact with at work. One must be cautious, however, and realize "a light" is not "a bell", and therefore refrain from trying to convert others through words. Actions and deeds speak louder than words!

Good works result in a light reflecting the glory of God!

Palestine sits on a hill, and in the days of Christ it was surrounded by major trade routes that the existing world around them [Egypt, Assyria] partook.

God wanted the nation of Israel to be a "light" to the world about them showing "good works" in treating their slaves and keeping His commandments.

The *city* set on a hill is surely reminiscent of Jerusalem, the "apple of God's eye." Jerusalem was to be God's light to the world, and will be during the millennial Kingdom set up on earth! At this time, Jerusalem will be a *light* and the admiration of all nations!

Today, Jerusalem is still a darkened city spiritually, because of the veil of deception hanging over their eyes!

The Parable of
The Grain of Mustard Seed

Another parable put He forth unto them, saying, the Kingdom of heaven is like to a grain of mustard seed, which a man took, and sowed in his field: which indeed is the least of all seeds: but when it is grown, it is the greatest among herbs, and becometh a tree, so that the birds of the air come and lodge in the branches thereof (Matt. 13:31,32).

The parable of *The Grain of Mustard Seed* pictures the GROWTH of God's Church throughout the ages. As the previous parable depicted the spreading of the gospel message—this parable points to the growth of the Church as a result of that glorious message.

A mustard seed is one of the tiniest of seeds—but when it grows, it changes into a prodigious shrub thousands of times its own size. In Jewish idiom, a mustard seed was used to weigh what was considered the smallest measurable amount. The mustard is a plant that grows in one year from seed to a height of twenty to thirty feet.

The Church of the living God in the New Testament started out with 12 disciples, and wound up with only 120 followers at the culmination of Jesus' 3 1/2 year ministry (Acts 1:15).

But on the Day of Pentecost when the Holy Spirit was to descend, three thousand devotees were added to the Church (Acts 2:41-47). Since this very humble and early inception, God's Church has indeed grown like a mustard seed throughout the past centuries and will especially enlarge during Christ's millennial reign, observe:

> **And there was given Him [Christ] dominion, and glory, and a kingdom, that all people, nations, and languages, should serve Him: His dominion is an everlasting dominion, which shall not pass away, and His kingdom that which shall not be destroyed (Dan. 7:14).**

The prophet Isaiah wrote more of Christ's imminent government: **"For unto us a child is born, unto us a son is given: and the government shall be upon His shoulder: and His name shall be called Wonderful, Counsellor, The Mighty God, The Everlasting Father, The Prince of Peace.** *Of the increase of His government and peace there shall be no end..."* **(Isa. 9:6-7).**

In this present dispensation, God is calling many but only a few are chosen to be a part of His soon ruling Kingdom. That is why Jesus called His Church a "little flock" (Lk. 12:32). But ultimately, untold billions will be a part of His glorious family! This is all a result of one man [Christ] sowing a seed in His field! The birds that lodge in the mustard tree are *symbolic* of those who will inhabit the Kingdom!

The Parable of
The Kingdom Like Unto Leaven

Another parable spake He unto them; The kingdom of heaven is like unto leaven, which a woman took, and hid in three measures of meal, till the whole was leavened (Matt. 13:33).

This is a most *unique* parable that entertains two opposing and diametrically opposite schools of thought. The most common conception, spawned by Martin Luther in his *Exposition* and expounded by many of the Reformers—is that this parable has basically the same meaning as the parable of the kingdom like unto "A Grain of Mustard Seed."

These proponents believe this parable graphically *pictures* the "SPREADING" or "branching out" of God's Kingdom on earth. The reasoning being, leavening is an agent used to make dough *rise* or *expand*.

It is because of this "spreading action" of leaven that Jesus also described the Kingdom of God in which it will eventually permeate the entire earth! It is true that the Church [woman] has expanded like leaven in preaching the gospel into all the world.

The other concept is that this gospel message was *hidden* since the apostolic age for 1900 years only to fulfill prophecy in the last days (Matt. 24:14). Soon the "whole" world will be leavened by the "good news" of Christ's second advent.

The leaven in the meal stresses that the power in the kingdom will be internal and not external. By its internal power [God's Holy Spirit internalized] it will effect an external transformation of society. Thus, this parable stresses the power within the individual.

Its use in the sacrifices representing the perfection of the person and work of Christ, also shows a positive effect of leavening (Lev. 2:1-3).

The opposing view of this concept is that leavening, in almost every other passage of the Bible is used *metaphorically* or *figuratively* to describe SIN and its degeneracy power upon the individual or God's Church. In essence, it represents sin and apostasy! Let us examine this line of reasoning more carefully.

Had Jesus ever given any negative parables previously [parables that include sin, Satan or apostasy] in His proclamation of the Kingdom of God?

Yes, indeed!

Recall the parable of "The Sower" and "Wheat and Tares" given previously in the same chapter. Both parables accentuate the intrusion of "the wicked One" into God's Church! Jesus said, **"An enemy has done this!"** Satan plants wicked seeds of *heresy* and false brethren or "tares" in God's Church! Apostasy has occurred in all ages of the Church since apostolic times.

Now consider these interesting facts. Leavening in every other passage in the Bible is used *symbolically* or *metaphorically* to mean something sinful, evil or corrupt—*never* something good! The word *leaven* occurs 71 times in the Old Testament and 13 in the New Testament, and in each case, it refers to something corrupt!

Notice the following scripture references:

Ex. 12:15-20	"Seven days shall ye eat unleavened bread; even the first day ye shall put away leaven out of your houses; for whosoever eateth leavened bread from the first day until the seventh day, that Soul shall be cut off from Israel." This festival in which no leavening products such as yeast are to be used—*typifies* the removal of sin from the person's life *symbolically*.
Ex. 34:25	"Thou shalt offer the blood of my sacrifice with leaven."
Ex. 12:8-20	All sacrifices made by fire upon the brazen altar *symbolically* represented

the *sinless* offering of Jesus Christ. See also (Lev. 2:11; 6:14-18). Lev. 10:12; 23:17,18). Only unleavened cakes were permitted upon the holy altar. During the Feast of Pentecost, two loaves of bread, a *prefigure* of the Church on Pentecost—Acts 2), were baked with leaven. These loaves represented the *sinful* nature rather *sinless* nature still in the Church.

Lk. 12:1   Jesus admonished: "Beware ye of the *leaven* of the Pharisees, which is *hypocracy,*"

1 Cor. 5:5-8   Paul cautioned the brethren at Corinth: "A little leaven leaveneth the whole lump. Purge out therefore the old leaven, that ye may be a new lump, as ye are unleavened...the leaven of *malice* and *wickedness*...the unleavened bread of *sincerity* and *truth*." Paul thus describes the physical property of "puffing up" in leavening to describe a type of *sin* that vaunts its ugly head which is *vanity*.

The question arises, if all previous references to the use of leaven represented something evil—would Jesus use it in a parable to bewilder His disciples?

Being Jews, they understood its implication in "Unleavened Bread" and the hypocritical *leavening* of the Pharisees. How then, would they have interpreted the meaning of leavening in this parable? This is a matter of conjecture—but let us now consider an alternative rendition.

Take note that there are *two* important elements used in conjunction with leavening in this parable—namely "a woman" and "three measures of meal."

As we have observed so many times before, *everything* in God's Word is relevant—and the seemingly unimportant "number" or "element" has deep *spiritual* enlightenment.

What does a *woman* signify in the Bible spiritually? Either God's true Church or Satan's counterfeit false system! Could the *leaven* in this parable be referring then to Satan's false system encroaching throughout the world? Could this parable be a continuation of thought of the parable of *The Sower* and *Wheat and Tares* in which "an enemy has done this"?

The *Woman* or Church in this parable "hides" the leaven in the meal. If this *leavening* represents the gospel message spreading throughout the world—why hide it? Jesus told His disciples to preach the gospel from the housetop (Matt. 11:27).

Hiding has never been God's method of proclaiming His message. Instead, Christians are exhorted to **"let their lights shine"** not hide it under a bushel! Jesus Himself spoke openly and audaciously to the world (Jn. 18:19-21), and COMMANDED His apostles to do likewise (Mk. 16:15). The gospel is to be announced like a trumpet in all the world as a witness unto all nations (Isa. 58:1; Acts 19:8; 11 Cor. 5:20; Matt. 24:14).

Contrariwise, we know definitely that the early Church was penetrated by false brethren (Gal. 2:4). These "false teachers" brought in damnable heresies (11 Pet. 2:11,12), unbeknown to the early Church (Jude 4:5). What can we make of the "three measures of meal" in the parable? Why three measures instead of four or six? Was this a slip of the tongue by Jesus? Just a casual number?

Numbers are highly significant in the Word of God as already demonstrated. Is there a place in scripture that uses such terminology as "three measures of meal"? The answer is an astounding yes!

When the "law of the offerings" were given to Israel—the "Meat-offering" [a picture of Christ being offered as man's food], usually contained threetenths of an ephah. An omer [tenth part] of an ephah was the smallest amount acceptable for the Meat-offering (Ex. 16:36), but three-tenths was the usual amount (Num. 15:9; 28:12; 20, 28; 29:3, 9, 14).

If the meal in this parable is *symbolic* of a "Meat-offering" to God—this *woman* or false Church mingled leaven with it which was forbidden under Israelite law (Lev. 2:11). Because Christ was *pictured* as man's food for communion with God as the "Meat-offering"—this false Church [woman] corrupted Christ's doctrine by mixing false doctrine [leavening] with it.

Two concepts regarding the meaning to this parable have been presented here. Which one is correct? Can both be correct? Because Jesus did not explain the details of this parable openly, as He did the "Sower" and "Wheat and Tares", perhaps it would be wise if we did not become too dogmatic in propagating one view over the other. Instead, let us see the truth in both concepts and apply them in our lives accordingly.

The Parable of The Seed Growing of Itself

And He said, So is the kingdom of God, as if a man should cast seed into the ground; and should sleep, and rise night and day, and the seed should spring and grow up, he knoweth not how. For the earth bringeth forth fruit of herself; first the blade, then the ear, after that the full corn in the ear. But when the fruit is brought forth, immediately he putteth in the sickle, because the harvest is come (Mk. 4:26-29).

Right after Jesus gave the parable of *The Sower*, He proceeded to give the parable of *The Seed Growing of Itself*. This is not the same as the parable of *The Sower* and is unique to only Mark. Actually, it is complimentary to the conversion of the "good seed" in the parable of *The Sower*.

The story of "the seed growing of itself" is another beautiful *analogy* that Jesus gave to better understand a deep spiritual truth. This truth is—even though we are incapable of understanding the mechanics of conversion, it happens! The apostle Paul made mention of this miracle in 1 Corinthians 3:6-7: "**I have *planted*, Apollos *watered*; but *God gave the increase*. So then neither is he that planteth anything, neither he that watereth; but God that giveth the increase.**"

Even as the process of planting physical seed that brings forth fruit not completely understood—so it is with the spiritual process of bearing spiritual fruit! We know that God's Holy Spirit must have intercourse with our human spirit to produce spiritual thought—but the mechanics of this process is only understood by God (1 Cor. 2:9-16).

Only God knows and only He will reap in His fully ripened harvest at the conclusion of this age (Jn. 6:44; Acts 2:47; Jas. 1:18).

The "Blade" to "Ear" to "Full Corn" are all stages of development of physical seed to full *maturity.* Christians come to FULL MATURITY through a growth process as well.

Although many envision Jesus as *The Sower* in this parable—it is more applicable to His ministry. Jesus never slumbers or sleeps, and as our High Priest is *actively* engaged in our spiritual development daily!

It is God's ministry and his disciples responsibility to *plant* the seed and for God to make it *grow!* This is the natural order of conversion. But how God makes it grow is a *mystery* in certain respects to us humans, yet we see the results!

During the "blade" stage of a Christians development, he is *actively* drinking in the Word of God through prayer and Bible study. In the "ear" stage, he begins to take the *form* and shape of a Christian through *service*—yet he is not fully ripe or mature.

Finally, just as corn becomes "fully ripe"—the Christian has matured through time and experience and begun to help others carry their burdens as well. He produces succulent ripe fruit!

Although we can comprehend a great deal of the Christian growth process—there is much we do not understand. Understanding God's *will,* is one of the most difficult things for a Christian to encounter—yet God knows what He is doing, and must do in each of our lives to help us reach spiritual maturity.

In some cases, it will be a trial of health—others financial. Some may lose loved ones along the way—yet the end result of this Christian experience is a fully ripened delicious fruit!

However, if we fail to produce the kind of fruit expected, God will remove the *talent* from us and give it to someone more faithful. This is made crystal clear in (verse 25) of this chapter: **"For he that hath, to him shall be given: and he that hath not, from him shall be taken even that which he hath."** This is made vivid in the parable of *The Talents* which we shall explain shortly.

The Parable of
The Treasure Hid in The Field

Again, the kingdom of heaven is like unto a treasure hid in a field; the which when a man hath found, he hideth, and for joy thereof goeth and selleth all that he hath, and buyeth that field (Matt. 13:44).

Now we begin with the last four Galilean parables. These were spoken *only* to Jesus' 12 students privately in a house (Matt. 13:36). Recall how the first six parables were addressed to the people standing on the shore of the Sea of Galilee from a small boat. These last four parables all deal with vital DOCTRINAL issues in relation to God's soon coming Kingdom.

The parable of *The Treasure Hid in a Field* is reminiscent of a type of individual God is CALLING. This particular kind of disciple is one who was not necessarily searching for God's truth of salvation [the treasure]—but *stumbles* upon it. Ultimately, this is not accidental but providential, for no man can come to the truth, except the Father call him (Jn. 6:44). Yet, when it happens—this individual realizes he has found a precious jewel—the pot at the end of the rainbow!

He is now willing to forsake all of his worldly possessions in order to purchase this field or treasure. From the time this person sets his heart upon being a Christian—nothing, not the fear of losing his job, mate, friends or money will prevent him from attaining this prized treasure. He is willing to renounce *everything* to be a disciple of Jesus Christ (Lk. 14:28-33).

In a typical sense, Jesus fulfilled this parable. He was as a man which found a treasure [His Church] hid in a field (the world). Then out of joy, sold all he had [gave His life] to purchase the field.

The *field* in this parable can be compared to the *world* as the parable of the Sower enunciates! Clearly, all who are in the field [world]—both Jew and Gentile have been REDEEMED by the precious blood of Jesus Christ!

One cannot help but relate *the purchase of a field* to the incident in (Jeremiah 32) in reference to the people of Jerusalem. This was the year before Judah and Jerusalem's fall to

Nebuchadnezzar's Chaldean empire.

Amid the gloom and doom of Jeremiah's prophecy, Jeremiah was commanded to buy a field, in public ceremony, and put the deed away for safe keeping. This physical display *envisioned* the time when Jerusalem would be bought back again, and the captives would be allowed to return to cultivate their land once again after 70 years of captivity in exile! Undoubtedly this will be a dual event to when Christ returns.

May God help us to get the "wheels of our salvation" moving so we will desire to purchase the unsearchable riches of Christ!

The Parable of The Pearl of Great Price

And again, the kingdom of heaven is like unto a merchant man, seeking goodly pearls: who, when he had found one pearl of great price, went and sold all that he had, and bought it (Matt. 13:45-46).

Our heavenly Merchantman is seeking goodly pearls [righteous Christians] for His Church. The price Jesus paid for His Church was His very life! Jesus, gave His very life as a ransom for many (Matt. 20:28). Truly, we have been purchased with a great price (1 Cor. 6:20; 7:23).

As "purchased pearls" being prepared to fit in Christ's royal diadem—we will all fit into God's holy city of Jerusalem like a jewel in a beautiful setting (Rev, 21).

Observe, that the gates of this spiritual city are described as "Pearls" (verse 21), representing the tribes of the children of Israel, and are depicted as the foundations of the glorious city (verse 14).

In this present state however, Christians are not yet of pearl quality, but we will be made precious pearls of God through our Lord and Savior Jesus Christ. Notice the wording in Ephesians 2:1:7: **"Wherein in time past ye walked according to the course of this world, according to the prince of the power of the air...But God, who is rich in mercy, for his great love wherewith he loved us...That in the ages to come he might shew the exceeding riches of his grace in his kindness toward**

us through Christ Jesus"

We are truly His workmanship! What a wonderful opportunity awaits all who qualify to be a precious pearl of Christ's!

Lest there be any doubt that Jesus is the "pearl of great price" to be sought after, Notice Jeremiah 29:13-14: **"And ye shall seek me, and find me, when ye shall search for me with all your heart. And I will be found of you, saith the LORD..."** This was in reference to the nation of Israel's *repentance* and *return* to their Savior after captivity in the end-time.

This word *portrait* is also analogous to the way an individual is *called* into God's truth. Unlike the previous parable, this individual is SEEKING the truth (goodly pearls).

In reality, we can never truly seek the Eternal until He seeks us (Jn. 6:44). This person may have been a religious hobbyist—looking many years for the truth among Church denominations. Finally, one day—after a long search, God opens his mind to truths he never before understood! He is excited, ardent and determined never to let what he has found escape him. He too, is willing to abandon all he has in order to be one of God's chosen disciples.

The moral of this story is that *faith*, coupled with *patience* and *diligence,* is rewarded immensely! Here again, as in the parable of *The Treasure Hid in a Field*—Jesus fulfilled in a *typical* sense.

The Parable of The Net Cast Into The Sea

Again, the kingdom of heaven is like unto a net, that was cast into the sea, and gathered of every kind: which, when it was full, they drew to shore, and sat down, and gathered the good into vessels, but cast the bad away. So shall it be at the end of the world: the angels shall come forth, and sever the wicked from among the just, and shall cast them into the furnace of fire: there shall be wailing and gnashing of teeth (Matt. 13:47-50).

This particular gem of a parable had special significance to the disciples who were fisherman by trade. Jesus prophesied to Peter and the others that they were to become "fishers of men."

Being Fisherman, they understood the importance of proper bait to attract the various *kinds* of fish in the sea. Likewise, "fishers of men" must be capable of baiting the hook with the bait of the gospel. But not all the men they were to catch with the *lure* of the gospel net—would be fit for the Kingdom of God.

Peter later wrote of *false teachers* and false brethren that would enter into the flock (11 Pet. 2:1). These false brethren would eventually be sifted out.

This parable, like *The Wheat and the Tares; The Sheep and the Goats*; and *The Ten Virgins* all speak of a SEPARATION of the good from the bad as they exist side by side in life. The world in which they live is represented *symbolically* by the sea. Actually, all are bad that are caught in the net until they come to *repentance*.

The time of SEPARATION of the "good" and "bad" will ultimately come—then God's holy angels shall gather the "good" from the "bad." The good will live on forever while the bad will be *burned* in the "lake of fire"!

The Midnight Express is plummeting down the track of salvation—there is going to be a head on collision of the wicked and God. The sands in humankinds hourglass are running out—may God help us to see our fate!

The Parable of
The Householder's Treasure

> *Then said He unto them, Therefore, every scribe which he instructed unto the kingdom of heaven is like unto a man that is an householder, which bringeth forth out of his treasure things new and old (Matt. 13:52).*

The final Galilean parable was particularly aimed at the disciples whom Jesus had just admonished concerning conditions of entering the Kingdom of God.

The meaning of the things "new" and "old" in this parable is in reference to the teachings of the "Old" and "New" covenants. There is a prophecy in (Psalm 78:2) that Jesus was to fulfill, notice: **"That it might be fulfilled which was spoken by the prophet, saying I will open my mouth in parables; I will utter things which have been kept secret from the foundation of the world"** (Matt. 13:35).

Did Jesus fulfill this prophecy?

Truly, Jesus did utter things to His disciples that were not written in the Old Covenant! But His students were to teach the truths contained in the Old Covenant as well. That is why God's Church is "...built upon the foundation of the *apostles* and *prophets*, Jesus Christ Himself being the chief corner stone" (Eph. 2:20).

What is a Christian's FOUNDATION built upon? It is built upon the solid foundation of Jesus Christ and not upon spiritual quicksand! It is built upon the word's and teachings of Jesus who is our foundation Rock!

Chapter Six

PARABLES OF ISRAEL'S HISTORY

THE PARABLE OF THE WICKED HUSBANDMEN

There was a certain householder, which planted a vineyard, and hedged it round about, and digged a winepress in it, and built a tower, and let it out to husbandmen, and went into a far country: And when the time of fruit drew near, he sent his servants to the husbandmen, that they might receive the fruits of it.

And the husbandmen took his servants, and beat one, and killed another, and stoned another. Again, he sent other servants more than the first: and they did unto them likewise. But last of all he sent unto them his son, saying, They will reverence my son. But when the husbandmen saw the son, they said among themselves, This is the heir; come, let us kill him, and let us seize on his inheritance.

And they caught him, and cast him out of the vineyard, and slew him. When the lord therefore of the vineyard cometh, what will he do unto those husbandmen? (Matt. 21:3344).

The parables of Israel's history demonstrate the common theme: "The Change of Administration" from Jew to Gentile.

This can only be understood by comprehending the parables of Israel's history as a nation. Not only can God's plan for the *present* dispensation be clearly defined from these parables—but also His plan for the future of the world and Israel's part in it.

The parable of *The Wicked Husbandmen* is an extension of the parable of *Two Sons.* The householder in this parable is Christ who went away to a far country (heaven).

The husbandmen in this parable is *symbolic* of the nation of Israel—who has continuously REJECTED God's chosen *servants* throughout history—as well as their own transcendental purpose. They have *killed* God's servants, the prophets through *beatings* and *stonings!*

Ancient Israel stoned Jeremiah; cut Isaiah in two; clubbed Amos to death; allowed the head of John the Baptist to be a gift on a silver platter; and stoned Steven! See (Jer. 20:1,2; 37:15; 38:6; 26:20-23; 1 Kings 18:13; 22:24; 11 Kings 6:22,31; Matt. 23:29-37; Acts 7:5; 11 Chron. 24:2; Heb. 11:36-38).

Jesus cries out because of these atrocities in Matthew 23:37: **"O Jerusalem, Jerusalem, thou that *killest* the prophets, and *stonest* them which are sent unto thee..."** How Jesus would have loved to see His chosen people repent, so He could take them under His wing—even as a mother hen gathering her chicks (vs. 37).

It was this same stiff-necked nation through the leadership of the Pharisees that killed the householders son (Jesus Christ). When Jesus returns as lord of the vineyard, He will destroy those who have rejected Him (vs. 41-42).

Ironically, the Pharisees failed to perceive this parable was directed at them personally, and unwittingly pronounced their own condemnation. When they realized Jesus spoke of them—they wanted to kill Him then and there (vs. 46). There was venom in their hearts and minds!

Therefore, *the Kingdom of God* was *temporarily* taken from them and given to other nations [Gentiles] that will bring forth fruit (vs. 43). Paul mentions the transfer of the Vineyard [rulership over His goods] to include Gentiles in Romans 11:15-23). Here Gentiles are envisioned as "a wild olive tree" grafted into God's Vineyard which originally only included Israelites.

Now, a *holy nation* is being prepared by God which includes converted Jews and Gentiles to rule over His Vineyard (1 Pet. 2:9; Rev. 1:6). This will be a nation of people consisting of many different nationalities—yet all with the same willing heart of faithfulness.

They will be eager to accept Jesus as their Savior and *repent* of their sins. These servants will not desire to crucify their Master, rather they will want to help Him cultivate His Vineyard and implement His plans for making the Vineyard fruitful!

Though these be few in number as "...the harvest is great, but the laborers are few," they will be desirous in helping God convert the world!

Incidently, this is the *only* parable that vividly describes our Lord's death!

For further proof that this parable referred to Israel's past history, all we need do is turn to (Isaiah 5) where it is evident that this is almost identical wording. If there be any doubt as to the interpretation of the Vineyard's identity through *symbolism*—Isaiah explains: **"For the *vineyard* of the LORD of hosts *is the house of Israel*, and the men of *Judah* his pleasant plant..." (Isa. 5:7).** See also (Hosea 10:1; Ps. 80; 81).

Ironside sums up Israel's past and future history:

> **By and by, the vine is going to be replanted in Palestine. In fact, we may go further and say, The vine is being replanted in Palestine. The Jews are going back to their own land; it stirs one's soul as Scripture is being fulfilled before our eyes. They are being replanted in their own vineyard, but replanted for what? For the vintage of the wrath of God. A remnant will be gathered out, separated to the Lord, but the rest will be given up to unsparing judgment in the time of Jacob's trouble. Fleshly Israel, the vine of the earth, can produce no fruit for God. But, in that day of distress, the clusters of the vine of the earth will be cast into the great winepress of**

the wrath of God (*Lectures on the Revelation*, p. 267).

The cultivation of God's Vineyard, or Israel's early history began when the Vineyard was transplanted from Egypt to the fertile soil of Palestine. Further, the tiling or removal of Israel's enemies from the land to enhance rapid growth are all outlined in the eightieth Psalm.

All through the Word of God, the nation of Israel is *figuratively* labeled as God's Vine! Sometimes Israel is called an olive tree, sometimes a fig tree. See (Hosea 10:1; Joel 1:7).

The Eternal is now in the process of *restoring* His Vineyard back to "the house of Israel." This process began in 1948 when the nation of Israel became a nation once again!

THE PARABLE OF THE TWO SONS

But what think ye? A certain man had two sons; and he came to the first, and said, Son, go work to day in my vineyard. He answered and said, I will not: but afterward he repented, and went.
And he came to the second, and said likewise. And he answered and said, I go, sir: and went not. Whether of them twain did the will of his father? They say unto him, The first. Jesus saith unto them, Verily I say unto you, That the publicans and the harlots go into the kingdom of God before you.

For John came unto you in the way of righteousness, and ye believed him not: but the publicans and the harlots believed him: and ye, when ye had seen it, repented not afterward, that ye might believe him (Matt. 21:28-32).

This true to life story struck deep in the heart of the Pharisees who rejected Jesus' teachings. It is aimed at all religious leaders garbed in HYPOCRISY who reject the message of Christ. Like the parable of *The Wicked Husbandmen*, it gives hope to the common people who accept Him joyfully!

The second son is a *portrait* of all kinds of super sanctimonious religious types—who worship God through lip service—but deny Him in works of repentance! The first son depicts the worst of sinners who at first defiantly *refuse* to repent of their heinous sins, but later in life accept this calling. These are the penitent sinners [publicans and harlots] that Jesus referred to and delighted in their works of repentance.

Contrariwise, the Pharisees openly mutinied against the proclamation of repentance by John the Baptist, but the common sinners believed in his message. To those who *repent* like the first son, will be granted the Kingdom of God. Those who rebel like the second son will be thrust out of the Kingdom and there will be "weeping and gnashing of teeth."

The deeper implication of the "two sons" in this parable are *types* of the nation of Israel and the New Testament Church—composed of repentant Gentile sinners (publicans and harlots).

Notice the wording of Jesus to His Old Testament wife: **"For John came unto you [Israel] in the way of righteousness and ye believed him not."**

Each of us must daily slay the deadly dragons of sin in our lives—before they destroy us!

THE PARABLE OF THE BARREN FIG TREE ACCURSED

And on the morrow, when they were come from Bethany, He was hungry: And seeing a fig tree afar off having leaves, He came, if haply He might find any thing thereon: and when He came to it; He found nothing but leaves; for the time of figs was not yet. And Jesus answered and said unto it, No man eat fruit of thee hereafter forever. And His disciples heard it. (Mk. 11:12-14).

The question we want to answer here is WHY did Jesus curse the fig tree? Did He have something against barren fig trees? Now this is a very interesting parable and *portrays* three very important spiritual lessons for us today. Therefore, let's scrutinize this parable very carefully.

- The first point to be gleaned from this parable is that Jesus DID expect this tree to have fruit upon it even though it was *not* the season for figs. Why was this?

Well, certainly the Creator of heaven and earth, (including fig trees), must have felt there would be some figs upon this tree if it had leaves! So, the first point we can learn from this parable is yes—Jesus did expect fruit from this tree even though it was not yet the season for figs. The reason being, this tree had leaves on it prematurely.

Jesus, the Great Botanist knew that leaves were a sign that fruit should bear, as He used this analogy in discerning the *signs* of the times in (Matthew 24). There, Jesus said: **"Now learn a parable of the fig tree, when his branch is yet tender, and putteth forth leaves, ye know that summer is nigh: So likewise ye, when ye shall see all these things, know that it is near, even at the doors" (Matt. 24:33-34).**

The parable of *The Barren Fig Tree* is an illustration of God's enduring patience with sinners to come to REPENTANCE! God is not willing that ANY should perish but that ALL should come to repentance (1Tim. 2:3-9; 11Pet. 3:8-10)!

That is why Jesus said of the tree He cursed, **"No man eat fruit of thee hereafter forever"**—that is speaking of ETERNAL LIFE!

The first lesson we can learn from this parable is that no Christian who fails to produce fruit in his life will live *forever* (have eternal life). This is made crystal clear from several parables as just quoted.

- Let us now read on to understand the next object lesson of this obscure parable. In (verse 15 of Mark 11) Jesus says:

And they come to Jerusalem: and Jesus went into the temple, and began to *cast out* them that sold and bought in the temple, and overthrew the tables of the money changers, and the seats of them that sold doves; And would not suffer [permit] that any man should carry any vessel through the temple. And He taught, saying unto them, Is it not written, My house shall be called of all nations the house of prayer? but ye have

made it a den of thieves.

Like the parable of *the Wicked Husbandmen*, this parable was especially aimed at the Pharisees and stood as a stern WARNING to the nation of Israel. Immediately after Jesus cursed the fig tree, He stormed into the Temple and threw out the hypocritical Pharisees!

These disciples of Satan were turning God's House into a religious carnival. Jesus had warned these Pharisees on several occasions, that the Kingdom would be taken from them and they would be *cast* into outer darkness.

He said there would be "weeping and gnashing of teeth" (Matt. 8:12). Jesus asked them, **"Ye serpents, ye generation of vipers, how can ye escape the damnation of hell?" (Matt. 23:33).**

As we have read, the nation of Israel is pictured as a *fig tree* in the Bible. Jesus' physical hunger in this parable was only *superficial* of a deeper spiritual hunger He had for Israel's refusal to repent as a nation.

Israel showed outward leaves of piety, but inwardly they did not bear the fruit of *faith* in God!

The Barren Fig Tree in Luke's account is also a direct reference to the FRUITLESS nation of Israel. Notice the "three years" in which the Lord [God] gave the fig tree [Israel] to produce fruit. This is the approximate time of Jesus' ministry—after which Israel was still spiritually barren!

Christ cursed the fig tree [Israel] to bear no more fruit forever [for the age] in (Mark 11:12-14), as He declared Israel's infertility for the remainder of this age. Then after Israel's 2520 years punishment, God will begin to restore her as far as producing fruit in converting other nations!

During the Millennium, Israel will once again bring forth fruit for other nations to emulate and enjoy!

- Finally, the lesson of FAITH is to emerge from this parable as the champion of the people. When Peter recalled how Christ had cursed the fig tree and it had become *barren*, he asked his Master the meaning of it (verse 20). This was Jesus' reply:

> **Have *faith* in God. For verily I say unto you, that whosoever shall say unto this mountain, Be thou removed, and be thou cast into the sea; and shall not doubt in his heart, but shall believe that those things which he saith shall come to pass; he shall have whatsoever he saith. Therefore, I say unto you, that what things soever you desire, when ye *pray*, believe that ye receive them, and ye shall have them.**

The morning after Jesus had said to the barren fig tree: **"...no man eat fruit of thee hereafter for ever"**—it was found dead from root to branch by the disciples. The future apostles then recalled how Jesus had *cursed* the barren fig tree the previous day. What is the spiritual significance to this strange occurrence?

Positively, Jesus associates *the barren fig tree* with *faith*. If we desire to move a mountain—it will take a great deal of *faith*. The object lesson is that no physical obstacle should stand in our way of entry into God's Kingdom. Only spiritual obstacles such as a lack of faith, can hinder this spiritual process from producing ripe, luscious fruit!

Incidently, this was the only miracle that Jesus performed that was not a *blessing* but a *cursing!* The lesson for us should be obvious. If we want to enter the Kingdom of God, we must have a deep abiding faith in our Maker. Notice also that PRAYER is a vital *key* to faith. Faith being a fruit of the Holy Spirit (Gal. 5:22), and the Holy Spirit must be stirred up daily by *prayer* (11 Tim. 1:6). Faith is also tied to righteous *works* (Jas. 2:17-26).

In summary, the parable of *The Barren Fig Tree* that Jesus cursed teaches us (3) object lessons:

- Christians must *produce* fruit in their lives in the form of repentance and love. If they don't—they stand to be "burned" in the lake of fire!

- The nation of Israel must *repent* of being hypocritical in its religious worship, or else they will be cast out of God's spiritual temple and into "outer darkness."

- Faith is absolutely essential to making it into God's

kingdom—without it we are doomed! With it we can *remove* every physical obstacle in our path!

Let us take heed of the parable of *The Barren Fig Tree* lest Jesus CURSES us for not bearing fruit and we wither away forever! There is very interesting wording found in (Isaiah 65:20) concerning those who are brought up in the Great White Throne resurrection to Judgement.

God's Word thunders to those who are still *unrepentant* at the end of a period called the Great White Throne Judgement, notice: they **"...shall be accursed"**—burned up in the Lake of fire!

As Christians, let us remember the lessons contained in the Parable of the Barren Fig Tree that Jesus cursed!

THE PARABLE OF THE BARREN FIG TREE

He spake also this parable; A certain man had a fig tree planted in his vineyard; and he came and sought fruit thereon, and found none. Then said he unto the dresser of his vineyard, Behold, these three years I come seeking fruit on this fig tree, and find none: cut it down: why cumbereth it the ground? And he answering said unto him, Lord, let it alone this year also, till I shall dig about it, and dung [fertilize] it: And if it bear fruit, well: and if not, then after that thou shalt cut it down (Lk. 13:6).

Jesus describes in this parable what will happen to fig trees that do not bear fruit. This is the *third* time in which Jesus used a fig tree to describe an object spiritual lesson. Each account speaks of a different fig tree.

It takes time for spiritual fruit to be born in most peoples lives. Our just and loving Father gives us plenty of time to change. He even *cultivates* us with special care [fertilizer] so we have no excuse not to grow. God gives us every advantage!

But when we fail to produce spiritual fruit after sufficient time—God will cut us down like a barren fig tree! Turn your

Bible to (John 15:1-6) to see the fate of those who fail to grow spiritually!

There, Jesus confers:

> **I AM the true vine, and my Father is the husbandman. Every branch in me that beareth not fruit He taketh away: and every branch that beareth fruit, He purgeth it, that it may bring forth more fruit. Now ye are clean through the word which I have spoken unto you. Abide in me, and I in you. As the branch cannot bear fruit of itself, except it abide in the vine, ye are the branches: He that abideth in me, and I in him, the same bringeth forth much fruit: for without me ye can do nothing. If a man abide not in me, he is cast forth as a branch, and is *withered*; and men gather them, and *cast them into the fire*, and they are burned.**

The *fire* Jesus is referring to—is "the lake of fire" that will CONSUME rebellious and sinful beings like a dead fig tree at the end of the age. See also (Jn. 3:9; Matt. 7:16-19; Heb. 6:7-9). God makes no bones about our fate if we *neglect* our Christian calling!

Christians who become *sterile* spiritually in the form of *love* and *repentance* stand in danger of the death penalty! Any Christian who does not grow spiritually and OVERCOME sin in this life, will be thrown into the lake of fire like a dead tree!

The Barren Fig Tree in Luke's account is also a direct reference to the *fruitless* nation of Israel. Notice the "three years" in which the Lord [God] gave the fig tree [Israel] to produce fruit. This is the approximate time of Jesus' ministry, after which Israel was still spiritually barren!

THE PARABLE OF
THE WINESKINS AND RENT GARMENT

> *And he spake also a parable unto them; No man putteth a piece of a new garment upon an old; if otherwise, then both the new maketh a rent, and the piece that was taken out of the new agreeth not with the old. And no man putteth new wine into old bottles; else the new wine will burst the bottles, and be spilled, and the bottles shall perish. But new wine must be put into new bottles; and both are preserved. No man also having drunk old wine straightway desireth new for he saith, The old is better (Lk. 5:36-39).*

The common people had just asked Jesus why the disciples of John the Baptist and the Pharisees *fasted*—but that His disciples did not (vs. 18).

Jesus responded to them in this parable through three separate metaphors. *The Bridegroom, The Rent Garment* and *The Old Wineskins,* all pertain to *when* and *why* one should FAST, and *how* to enter the Kingdom of God.

Through this colorful imagery, Jesus is showing that there is indeed a right and proper time to fast. While Jesus was here in the flesh, His disciples were very close to Him personally, and therefore spiritually. But after He returned to heaven in glorified form, fasting became a method to *maintain* this intimate relationship with God.

However, there is a right and wrong way to fast. Jesus condemned the hypocritical and superfluous Pharisees for their frequent sanctimonious fasts "to be seen of men" (Matt. 6:16-18).

The mended garments and wine bottles [wineskins] are used by Jesus in this parable to teach us how to enter His Kingdom.

The parable of *The Wedding Feast* indicates that proper attire by the guests of the wedding, is absolutely essential to be at the marriage to the Lamb. When Jesus miraculously changed the water into wine at the wedding-feast at Canna—there were all classes of people present, including publicans and sinners.

Undoubtedly, many of them had on torn and tattered clothing. Using this wedding-feast as an illustration of a higher spiritual principle, Jesus expounds on the Kingdom of God.

Trying to mend a new patch on an old garment is virtually impossible, for the old material will weaken the new. The same principle applies to putting new wine in old bottles (wineskins). It simply will not work! The fermentation produced by "new wine" will literally explode these bottles!

These two metaphors graphically portray the putting away of *our old life* and starting a *new life* in Christ. The two LIFE STYLES will not go together—even as *old* and *new* garments or *new* wine in *old* bottles! When one is filled with new wine, he is filled with new energies and gifts of the Holy Spirit (Acts 2:13).

Our old garment [symbolic of our old sinful nature] cannot be mended by mixing the new garment of truth. Jesus said we cannot mix the two ways of life, for: **"No man can serve two masters..." (Matt. 6:24).** We must all put on the new garment of righteousness and serve God with all of our being. The "old garment" represents the old *outward nature* now changed by the "new wine" or Holy Spirit that regenerates from within.

Upon receiving God's Holy Spirit one starts to develop a new creature. If the old bottle [wineskin] will not stretch to accept this newly fermented truth—it will burst! This analogy can be applied to Christians whose old *unyielding* nature prevents them from growing spiritually.

Jesus explains in (verse 39), the carnal attitude towards His new way of life: **"No man also having drunk old wine straightway desireth new: for he saith, the old is better."** True, *old wine* tastes better temporarily—but the *new wine* is more lively or zesty!

Fasting is a vital tool for the people of God while the Bridegroom tarrys. This is one method by which we can have a continual supply of God's Holy Spirit [new wine] flowing into us while the Bridegroom is away!

Undoubtedly this parable also has connotations to the changing of the Old and New Testaments. Jesus was explaining in metaphor that the old Jewish dispensation was now passing away (the old garment). Israel is referred to as a "rough garment" in (Zechariah 14:4).

The old garment of Israel had a rent in it and was worn out! By dying on the cross at Calgary—Jesus rent the old Testament garment in two! Recall how the curtain separating the holy place from the Holy of Holies in the Temple was torn in two when Jesus died (Matt. 27:51).

But the Jews thought the old way of life was better with their ceremonial fasts—and still do! They thought the old wine was better than the new! This parable also reminds us of the marriage feast at Cana when Jesus performed His first miracle by turning water into "good wine" (Jn. 2).

A new wineskin has some "give" to it, and allows for the expansion, but old, used skins have lost their elasticity. They would burst! The wine would be spilled and the wineskin ruined.

Now, what most of us do—is try to fit this new truth into our old way of life. That is only natural, because it is hard to change, and no one likes to admit having been wrong. The old way of life is familiar and comfortable, and we want to hang on to as much of it as possible.

As Christians take the plunge and follow God's way of life, we will begin to miss the "old wine" less and less. We will see it for what it is—a hollow counterfeit of the real thing!

Using another metaphor, putting the gospel of grace into the law, will bust open new wineskins!

THE CHANGING OF ADMINISTRATION

Paul explained very graphically in (Romans 11) that the Gentiles [wild olive branches] could be grafted into the Jewish olive tree! God's Vineyard or work had now been entrusted to them temporarily!

The witness-bearing and fruit-bearing were now given to the Gentiles primarily—although some of the natural branches [Jews of the early Church] would remain!

However, just prior to our Lord's return, the Vineyard will once again be given to the nation of Israel—for an end-time witness upon the earth to all nations! This is made vivid in Paul's exhortation of the dispensational change in Romans 11:1-2: **"I say then, Hath God cast away His people? God forbid..*God hath not cast away His people* which He foreknew"**!

J. Dwight Pentecost explains this transformation to the Church:

The fact that God was going to form Jews and Gentiles alike into one body was never revealed in the Old Testament and forms the mystery of which Paul speaks in Ephesians 3:1-7; Romans 16:25-27; Colossians 1:26-29. This whole mystery program was not revealed until after the rejection of Christ by Israel. It was after the rejection of Matthew 12:23-24 that the Lord first makes a prophecy of the coming church in Matthew 16:18. It is after the rejection of the Cross that the church had its inception in Acts 2. It was after the final rejection by Israel that God called out Paul to be the Apostle of the Gentiles through whom this mystery of the nature of the church is revealed.

The church is manifestly an interruption of God's program for Israel, which was not brought into being until Israel's rejection of the offer of the Kingdom. It must logically follow that this mystery program must itself be brought to a conclusion before God can resume His dealing with the nation of Israel, as has been shown previously He will do. The mystery program, which was so distinct in its inception, will certainly be separate at its conclusion. This program must be concluded before God resumes and culminates His program for Israel (*Pretribulation Rapture Theory*, p. 201).

Now a quotation from Alva J. Mclain's book entitled *Daniel's Prophecy of the Seventy Weeks*, p. 8:

More than one expositor has stumbled over the ultimatum of Christ, 'I was not sent but unto the lost sheep of the house of Israel.' The only adequate explanation is to see, what our Lord understood clearly, the contingent nature of His message of the Kingdom. To put the matter in a word: *the immediate and complete establishment of His Kingdom depended upon the attitude of the nation of Israel*, **to whom pertained the divine promises and covenants...**

Peters offers this rendition of the mission of Christ:

> The Kingdom was offered to the nation in good faith, i.e. it would have been bestowed *provided* the nation had repented. The foreknown result made no difference in the tender of it, so far as the free agency of the nation is concerned; that result flowed from *a voluntary choice.* The national belief did not change God's faithfulness, Rom. 3:3. It would be derogatory to the mission of Christ to take any other view of it, and *the sincerity and desire* of Jesus that the nation might accept it, is witnessed in His tears over Jerusalem, in His address to it, in His unceasing labors, in sending out the twelve and the seventy, and in His works of mercy and love. It follows, then, that the Jews had *the privilege* accorded to them of accepting the Kingdom, and if the condition annexed to it had been complied with, *then* the Kingdom of David would have been most gloriously re-established under the Messiah (*The Theocratic Kingdom*, I, 377).

Israel in Tribulation

There is going to come a time when the Great God of heaven will once again intervene in the course of human affairs—and restore again His Kingdom to the nation of Israel.

Jeremiah's prophecy describes this time setting as "Jacob's trouble" (Jer. 30:7), and Stanton explains the Jewish attitude during this crucial period:

> **The tribulation is primarily Jewish. This fact is borne out by Old Testament Scriptures (Deut. 4:30; Jer. 30:7; Ezek. 20:37; Dan. 12:1; Zech. 13:8-9), by the Olivet Discourse of Christ (Matt. 24:9-26), and by the book of Revelation itself**

> (Rev. 7:4-8; 12:1-2; 17, etc). It concerns 'Daniel's people,' the coming of the 'false Messiah,' the preaching of the 'gospel of the kingdom,' flight on the 'sabbath,' the temple and the 'holy place,' the land of Judea, the city of Jerusalem, the twelve 'tribes of the children of Israel,' the 'song of Moses,' 'signs' in the heavens, the 'covenant' with the Beast, the 'sanctuary,' the 'sacrifice and the oblation' of the temple ritual—these all speak of Israel and prove that the tribulation is largely a time when God deals with His ancient people prior to their entrance into the promised kingdom. The many Old Testament prophecies yet to be fulfilled for Israel further indicate a future time when God will deal with this nation [Deut. 30:1-6; Jer. 30:8-10, etc.] (*Kept From the Hour*, p. 30-31).

From these multitude of very definite scriptures, it is very clear that the main intention of the Great Tribulation is to bring about the conversion of a multitude of Jews and Israelites.

During this very dreaded time, they will be told by the "Two Witnesses" that they are about to enter into the blessings of the kingdom and experience the fulfillment of all Israel's covenants. The "Two Witnesses" will preach the "good news" that the Messiah is about to return and deliver them and restore the Kingdom of God to them (Matt. 24:14).

One walking in the spiritual footsteps of John the Baptist will declare the identical message, and prepare Israel for the return of their Messiah. Spiritual Elijah will proclaim this truth to Israel in preparation of Christ's return, even as John prepared them for Christ's first coming, notice:

> Behold, I will send you Elijah the prophet before the coming of the great and terrible day of the Lord: And he shall turn the heart of the fathers to the children, and the heart of the children to their fathers, lest I come and spite the earth with a curse (Mal. 4:5-6).

Pentecost writes of this prophetic announcement:

> **This witness is seen to be effective in that multitudes of Jews are converted during the tribulation period and are waiting for the Messiah (Rev. 7:1-8) and the wise virgins of Matt. 25:1-13). It is also God's purpose to populate the millennium with a multitude of saved Gentiles, who are redeemed through the preaching of the believing remnant. This is accomplished in the multitude from "all nations, and kindreds, and people, and tongues" (Rev. 7:9) and in the "sheep" (Matt. 25:31-46) that enter the millennial age. God's purpose, then, is to populate the millennial kingdom by bringing a host from among Israel and Gentile nations to Himself (*Things To Come* p. 237-238).**

The Barren Fig Tree to bear fruit

God will start His plan with a *remnant* of physical Israelites according to His grace (Rom. 11:5). It is highly probable that this remnant will consist of 144,000 physical *firstfruits* of Israel (Rev. 7), as well as those brought back out of captivity. However, these are most likely different than the 144,000 *firstfruits* in (Revelation 14:1,4) who appear to represent the Gentile Church in *duality* and are Tribulation Saints!

It will be at this moment that *the barren fig tree of Israel* will once again become a *fruitful Vineyard* of the Lord! These "firstfruits" of Israel will be the start of God's refurbishing the nation of Israel for His Kingdom's glory!

Consequently, during this present dispensation—God has taken the fruitfulness of His Kingdom from Israel! This is made explicit from the striking words of our Lord in the parable of the Wicked Husbandmen: **"Therefore say I unto you, the kingdom of God shall be *taken* from you, and *given* to a nation bringing forth the fruits thereof" (Matt. 21:43).**

Israel is *pictured* as the Father's Vineyard in the parable of *The Wicked Husbandmen*. He entrusted Israel to produce luscious fruit as His earthly witness—but they neglected His Vineyard!

Then the Father sent His Son to be the Husbandman over His Vineyard. There is a prophecy in (Zechariah 13:5) in which the Messiah is described as "an husbandman"! Christ, as keeper of His Father's Vineyard, tried to promote spiritual growth in Israel for 3 years—but to no avail! (Lk. 13:7).

Finally, Jesus became the Vine Himself and the source of *all* fruit-bearing (Jn. 15). Jesus had been sent to the lost sheep of the house of Israel (Matt. 15:24). His commission to His disciples was: **"...Go not into the way of the Gentiles...But go rather to the lost sheep of the house of Israel" (Matt. 10:5-6).**

But from the time Israel rejected her King—the call became: **"Go not to the lost sheep of the house of Israel—but into the highways of the Gentile world" (Matt. 22:9-10; Acts 13:46).**

The parables of the *Marriage Supper* and *Great Feast*, clearly distinguish between those who were bidden [Israel] because of their refusal, and those now invited. This new invitation was the start of a new dispensation of grace to the Gentile!

Along with a change of administration came the blessings of the first-born as Paul clarifies: **"As he saith also in Osee, [Hosea] I will call them my people; and her beloved, which was not beloved. And it shall come to pass, that in the place were it was said unto them, Ye are not my people: there shall they be called the children of the living God" (Rom. 9:25-26).** This was a quote from (Hosea 1:10).

This was the promise to Israel which Paul now reiterates and claims for the Church! Paul now shows us the change in dispensations carries with it the same blessings!

To assume that these were only privileges and blessings to Old Testament Israel is a blatant mistake. For now these blessings have been engrafted into the new dispensation which includes Gentiles! The Church now takes on the responsibilities of Israel as "light bearer" and also the *blessings* that go along with it!

The prophets spoke of Israel's captivity and respite of sacrifice (Hosea 3:4); of the desolation of their land, and divinely imposed blindness (Isa. 6:9-12; Jn. 12:38-41).

There are also references to the times of blessings of Gentiles, of tribulation in the last days, and of Christ's imminent return to establish His Kingdom in Israel. But we look in vain for any light on Israel's fate during the present dispensation!

The New Testament establishes God's purpose for the Church—both Jew and Gentile alike. However, the purpose for the Gentiles was NOT known previously by the prophets! But God shall yet have mercy on Jacob, and will yet choose Israel, and set them in their own land (Isa. 14:1). He **"shall choose Jerusalem again" (Zech. 2:12).** For the present, God is making no distinction between Jew and Gentile (Rom. 10:12).

The present age, unannounced by the prophets, must be completed before God resumes His plans for His ancient people. There is a distinct break in the text between the "cutting off" of the Messiah, and the events to transpire during the last seven years of Israel's history—such as the setting up of the "abomination of desolation" (Dan. 9:26-27).

When Jesus began His public ministry, He read the Messianic prophecy of Isaiah which declared **"…the acceptable year of the Lord, and the day of vengeance of our God" (Isa. 61:1-2; Lk. 4:16-21).**

After reading only the first part of the scripture, Jesus stopped reading at the comma between the two phrases. The reason is that He had come to proclaim **"…the acceptable year of the Lord"** during which time the Gentiles could come to God [as well as the Jews]—but not the day of vengeance. This must await the end of the age, plainly showing that Jesus recognized the time element by the correct punctuation. This is a good illustration of how dispensations of prophecy are divided by a simple comma.

However, during this current dispensation, the Church of God is a chosen generation—as God inspired Peter to write: **"But *ye* are a chosen generation, a royal priesthood, an holy nation…which in time past were *not* a people, but now *the* [not a] people of God" (1 Pet. 2:9-10).** Thanks be to God for His marvelous truths and wonderful plan—that allows for all of humankind to become a part of His family!

Chapter Seven

EVANGELISTIC PARABLES

THE PARABLE OF THE TEN VIRGINS

Then shall the kingdom of heaven be likened unto ten virgins, which took their lamps, and went forth to meet the bridegroom. And five of them were wise, and five were foolish. They that were foolish took their lamps, and took no oil with them: But the wise took oil in their vessels with their lamps.

While the bridegroom tarried, they all slumbered and slept. And at midnight there was a cry made, Behold, the bridegroom cometh; go ye out to meet him. Then all those virgins arose, and trimmed their lamps. And the foolish said unto the wise, Give us of your oil; for our lamps are gone out.

But the wise answered, saying, Not so; lest there be not enough for us and you: but go ye rather to them that sell, and buy for yourselves. And while they went to buy, the bridegroom came; and they that were ready went in with him to the marriage: and the door was shut. Afterward came also the other virgins, saying, Lord, Lord, open to us, but he answered and said, Verily I say unto you, I know you not. Watch therefore, for ye know neither the day nor the hour wherein the Son of man cometh (Matt. 25:1-13).

The ten Virgins in this parable most likely represent the TRIBULATION SAINTS being made ready for the Bridegroom [Jesus Christ]. Oil in the Bible is *analogous* to God's Holy Spirit as we have read under the *types*.

Here then are 50 percent of the last era of God's Church on earth unprepared for the returning Jesus Christ! Why? Because they were "lukewarm" in applying and utilizing God's Holy Spirit which must be *stirred up day by day!* In the second and third chapters of the book of Revelation, God's seven Church eras are given.

These have existed since apostolic times down unto the end of the age. Jesus said the gates of hell [Greek, *hades*, meaning the grave] would never prevail against His Church. In other words, it [Christ's Church] would *never* die out!

However, this is not to say the Church would always remain "unspotted" in character. The last two eras of God's Church in *type* at the end time are the Philadelphia and Laodicean. The Philadelphians will be granted PROTECTION from the Great Tribulation because of their *faithfulness* in applying God's way of life (Rev. 3:10).

However, this is not evident with the Laodiceans who are "lukewarm" in religious observance and will therefore have to be *tried in fire* [Great Tribulation] to learn some very bitter lessons (Rev. 3:18). These individuals have let the cares of this world [riches, etc. vs. 17], *choke* God's Word to the point they have become unfruitful! They will be slumbering spiritually—but 50 percent of them (5 of 10) will wake up in time to meet the Bridegroom!

Jesus incites the Laodiceans to *repent* and wake up out of their slumber: **"Behold, I stand at the door, and *knock:* if any man hear my voice, and open the door, I will come in to him, and will *sup* with him, and he with me" (Rev. 3:20).** Those who fail to hear this call will not make it to the marriage supper of the Lamb, and possibly into the Kingdom of God!

Satan's spiritual sharks are constantly circling about to

devour us—and we must ward them off so we won't find ourselves in a "Laodicean attitude"?

THE PARABLE OF THE ROYAL MARRIAGE FEAST FOR THE KING'S SON

The kingdom of heaven is like unto a certain king, which made a marriage for his son, And sent forth his servants to call them that were bidden to the wedding: and they would not come. Again, he sent forth other servants, saying, Tell them which are bidden, Behold, I have prepared my dinner: my oxen and my fatlings are killed, and all things are ready: come unto the marriage.

But they made light of it, and went their ways, one to his farm, another to his merchandise: And the remnant took his servants, and entreated them spitefully, and slew them. But when the king heard thereof, he was wroth: and he sent forth his armies, and destroyed those murderers, and burned up their city. Then saith he to his servants, The wedding is ready, but they which were bidden were not worthy. Go ye therefore into the highways, and as many as ye shall find, bid to the marriage (Matt. 22:1-14).

This graphic illustration entails the principles of *The Great Supper; The Wicked Husbandmen; and The Ten Virgins* all rolled up into one.

Our magnanimous Dad is preparing a SPOTLESS BRIDE for His Son Jesus Christ through the Church. God the Father is featured in this parable as a King preparing a *royal wedding feast* for His son whom He loves.

Throughout the ages, our heavenly King has bidden [invited] many guests through His *servants* to the wedding feast. Israel, of old, refused their invitation from God's Old Testament prophets and instead killed them. Once again God bid for guests to fill His marriage feast chambers through the invitation of New

Testament servants whom they also killed!

This was too much for the King to bear, so He sent forth *armies* to destroy those wicked murderers and *burned* their city (vs. 7). In A.D. 70, Roman soldiers under General Titus stormed and completely ransacked the city of Jerusalem, destroying the Temple and fulfilling this prophecy.

When the nation of Israel failed to respond to God's generous invitation to the marriage of His Son—He called Gentile nations (from the *highways* of the world). It was the nation of Israel that *slew* God's servants the prophets, who bid them to be the first ones in the Kingdom of God (Jer. 37:15; 38:6, 26:20-23; 11 Chron. 24:21; Matt. 23:37). When Christ returns in full glory, He will destroy those who have rejected Him and His servants (vs. 7).

What a rude awakening!

But now there is a stern warning to those newcomers invited to the marriage feast to be diligent, lest they meet this same fate. Like the parable of *The Ten Virgins*—Christ warns those who would not take their calling seriously. If anyone thinks he can make it to the marriage feast of the Lamb [and hence into the Kingdom] without developing GODLY CHARACTER by utilizing God's Holy Spirit—he has been bamboozled! This is depicted by the 5 *foolish* Virgins in (Matthew 25) who had insufficient oil [Holy Spirit] in their lamps [lives], and by the proper wedding apparel required in this parable.

God the King, began inviting Gentiles as His wedding guests after Israel refused their calling. But observe, these guests included both *good* and *bad*—distinguishable only by their garments. Those who do not have on the *garments of righteousness* spiritually, shall be cast into outer darkness—for truly there shall be **"weeping and gnashing of teeth"** (vs. 13).

Marriage or Marriage feast?

The first part of this parable is straight forward and easy to decipher. The Jewish people received the first and second invitation to God's MARRIAGE FEAST. This invitation was given under Moses and the Old Covenant and before the crucifixion!!

Although the actual marriage feast was well into the future

EVANGELISTIC PARABLES

[the Millennium], the Jews were offered a part in the first resurrection beginning the Millennium [and beginning the 1,000 year marriage feast!].

But they rejected Christ's message!

The beginning of the *marriage feast* is announced by an angel in (Revelation 19). This announcement is followed by a description of Christ's Bride arrayed in white linen ready for the battle of Armageddon.

A major problem in trying to make some sense as to *who* is "Christ's Bride", the "wedding guests" and *when* "the marriage will occur"—is due to a biblical mistranslation!

When the translators deciphered the Greek into English, they decided to interpret the Greek word *gamos* (Strong's #1062, nuptials, marriage, wedding) as "marriage" in (Revelation 19:7). But they translated this identical word *gamos* as "marriage supper" in (Revelation 19:9). This same Greek word is used to describe the *marriage feast* for the King's Son in the parable of (Matthew 22) and the *marriage feast* of the 10 Virgins in (Matthew 25).

Conclusively, the Greek word *gamos* means "marriage feast" and should have been translated as such in (Revelation 19). Consequently, this scripture should read: **"Let us be glad and rejoice, and give honour to him: for the *marriage feast* of the Lamb is come..." (Rev. 19:7).**

But what is this marriage feast *for* and *who* will be the Bride? To better understand, we must comprehend the physical espousal period. This *spiritual* marital relationship with Christ is *pictured* by the *physical* Hebrew custom of marriage.

Concerning this Millennial marriage feast, Pentecost writes:

> **The wedding supper, then, becomes the parabolic picture of the entire millennial age, to which Israel will be invited during the tribulation period, which invitation many will reject and so they will be cast out, and many will accept and they will be received in. Because of the rejection, the invitation will likewise go to the Gentiles so that many of them will be included. Israel, at the second advent, will be**

> waiting for the Bridegroom to come from the wedding ceremony and invite them to that supper, at which the Bridegroom will introduce His bride to His friends..(*Things To Come*, p, 227-228).

As to the interpretation of the "marriage feast" and "marriage supper," Pentecost has this to say:

> Inasmuch as the Greek text does not distinguish between marriage supper and marriage feast, but uses the same word for both, and since the marriage supper consistently is used in reference to Israel on earth, it may be best to take the latter view and view the marriage of the Lamb as that event in the heavens in which the church is eternally united to Christ and the marriage feast or supper as the millennium, to which Jews and Gentiles will be invited, which takes place on the earth, during which time the bridegroom is honored through the display of the bride to all His friends who are assembled there (*Things to Come*, p. 228).

A lesson in Hebrew espousal

In Biblical times, the Hebrews had lengthy engagements of a different character than our engagements of today. The announced intention to become husband and wife began a period in which legal authority of the coming union was already in force.

Before the couple became man and wife, there was a "day long" marriage feast! This was evident in the marriage of Jacob and Leah (see Gen. 29:22). Jacob did not know that the bride was Leah until the next morning! If Leah had been there during the entire wedding feast, surely Jacob would have known she was not Rachel!

There was actually three stages a prospective bride and groom encountered. Oftentimes the parents of the future couple pre-arranged a marriage contract [covenant] while they were still children. A payment of a suitable dowry was also included as part of the agreement. For all intent and purpose, the couple was legally married at this point.

When the couple reached adulthood—the marriage ceremony took place, following a "wedding feast" in which the *friends* of the bride and groom were invited. This wedding feast was similar to the one Christ attended at Cana (Jn. 2:1-12).

Biblical weddings—types of the Church

Perhaps you have not given it much thought before—but did you ever stop and think *where* today's modern marriage customs originated? Biblical weddings were quite different from the elaborate white gown ecclesiastical ceremonies performed by a priest or rabbi of today! In fact, there is no Biblical evidence that any such type of ceremony was ever performed by an Old Testament [Levite] or New Testament [minister] priest of God!

When Adam and Eve were united in marriage—there is no Biblical evidence that they recited any vows to God as an officiating minister! Eve did not wear a white gown and there is no evidence of a "big splash" of a wedding reception afterwards!

Now, we are not suggesting for one moment that it is wrong to have a minister perform a marriage ceremony—on the contrary, for their counsel and advice beforehand is encouraged by Paul in (1 Corinthians 7). This should be done by every Christian couple to better understand their Christian roles (Eph. 5).

During Patriarchal times we know that marriages were oftentimes pre-arranged by parents, as was the case of Isaac. Because Isaac and his wife Rebekah are a *type* of the marriage between Christ and His Church—perhaps we can learn more about the marriage of the Church through them.

Recall, Abraham is a *type* of God the Father who chose Isaac's wife for him (Gen. 24:3-4). After having his servant seek out a proper wife for Isaac from his household, a wedding gift [Heb. *mohar*] was given to Rebekah's parents (vss. 10-24).

A suitable "dowry" was then negotiated between the two consenting parents which became a part of the wedding contract or agreement (vss. 28-50). Upon consulting with the bride-to-be [in some cases], and after she consented to the conditions of the contract—she and her parents were given a *mohar* (type of dowry—vss. 53-58).

The marriage was finally consummated when Rebekah was taken to Isaac's home (tent—vss. 61-67).

Concerning the marriage ceremony, the *Expository Times* contributes:

> **When we hear of a wedding today, certain questions immediately occur to us. Where did the marriage ceremony take place? Was it held in a church or at a registry office? If the former, in what church, and who was the officiating minister?...To the Jew of Biblical times these questions would have been meaningless. No marriage occurred in a 'place of worship', except in so far as the Jews regarded all their customary practices as shot through and through with religious significance...There was no officiating minister...** (*Expository Times* April, 1975, Vol. LXXXVI, No. 7).

The basic wedding pattern

As time passed, the Hebrew wedding ceremonies became more elaborate and formalized from that of Isaac and Rebekah. However, the general format remained the same, namely:

- The bride was generally chosen by the groom's parents, without the groom's prior knowledge.
- A suitable dowry was negotiated between the parents of the bride and groom which became a formal contract.
- The groom and his friends took a wedding gift *[mohar]* to the house of the bride, and presented it to her parents. Then a celebration took place in the home of the bride.
- The wedding procession composed of the bride and groom's friends marched to the house of the groom. This was often done in the evening accompanied with lit torches.
- Upon arriving at the home of the groom, the bride was formally accepted into the groom's family, and a wedding feast began. The wedding celebration would last anywhere from a day to a week.
- Finally, the marriage was consummated when the groom

took the bride to his home.

On page 271 of his book, *The Revelation of Jesus Christ*, John F. Walvoord explains the three phases of the Eastern marriage customs:

> **Though marriage customs varied in the ancient world, usually there were three major aspects:**
>
> - **The marriage contract was often consummated by the parents when the parties to the marriage were still children and not ready to assume adult responsibility. The payment of a suitable dowry was often a feature of the contract. When consummated, the contract meant that the couple were legally married.**
>
> - **At a later time when a couple had reached a suitable age, the second step in the wedding took place. This was a ceremony in which the bridegroom accompanied by his friends would go to the house of the bride and escort her to his home. This is the background of the parable of the virgins in Matthew 25:1-13.**
>
> - **Then the bridegroom would bring his bride to his home and the marriage supper, to which guests were invited, would take place. It was such a wedding feast that Christ attended at Cana as recorded in John 2:1-12. The marriage symbolism is beautifully fulfilled in the relationship of Christ to His church. The wedding contract is consummated at the time the church is redeemed. Every true Christian is joined to Christ in a legal marriage. When Christ comes for His church at the rapture [Christ's second Advent, *emphasis mine*], the second phase of the wedding is fulfilled, namely, the Bridegroom goes to receive His bride. The third phase then follows, that is, the wedding feast.**

The Betrothal

The BETROTHAL period is designated as that period of time between the giving of the *mohar* and the actual marriage union. This generally took a whole year. Actually, negotiations over the terms of the contract was the most difficult part to resolve, and oftentimes took a year or longer to come to an agreement (Hastings, *Dictionary of Christ and the Gospels),* article, "Betrothal." This is evident from the seven year agreement Jacob made with Laban over Rachel (Gen. 29:20).

However, the Hebrew *betrothal* period was quite different from our modern-day engagement period. For all practical purposes, the couple was legally married at this point.

Should a betrothed person die prior to the consummation, the remaining partner was labeled a "widow" or "widower." Divorce proceedings were necessary, should one party decide to back out prior to the consummation.

You will recall how Joseph wanted to put Mary away [divorce her] before they were actually married, when he suspected sexual impropriety (Matt. 1:19). This only proves that the Hebrew marriage custom, was a *covenant* or contract between two consenting parties prior to actual sexual relations!

Sexual copulation is what actually bound the marriage or made the two "one flesh" (1 Cor. 6:16; Matt. 19:5). On the night of consummation, hymeneal blood was collected by the groom on a cloth to prove the bride's virginity. The mother-in-law of the groom waited in an adjoining room, to make sure there was no "hanky-panky" by the groom in the event he wanted to conspire against her for prior sexual misconduct (Deut. 22:15-20). This momentous event was humorously portrayed in the movie "Yentl" starring Barbara Streisand.

Clearly, the legality of the marriage was binding prior to the actual coming together in sexual relations!

The *Encyclopedia Biblica* offers this in regards to the act of betrothal:

> **Legally considered, the marriage relation was formed by the act of betrothal that is to say, by the payment, on the bridegroom's part, of the *mohar* to the parent or guardian of the bride, with this she passed into the possession of her**

> **husband. To betroth a wife to oneself, meant simply to acquire possession of her by payment of the purchase money...The girl's consent is unnecessary... the arrangements about the marriage, and especially about the *mohar*, belonged to the province of the father or guardian [Gen. 24:50 ff; 29:23; 34:2]** (*Encyclopedia Biblica,* 1914 edition, Vol. 1, Cheyne & J.S. Black, London).

The Betrothal of the Church

Plainly, there is a difference between the betrothal, feast and marriage! The Church is now BETROTHED to Christ! According to the understanding of the Hebrew custom, after Christ returns with His Bride, the marriage feast could take place spiritually for 1,000 years!

Jesus made this abundantly evident when He prophesied to His disciples: **"But I say unto you, I will not drink henceforth of this fruit of the vine, until that day [at the marriage feast], when I drink it new with you in my Father's kingdom" (Matt. 26:29).**

Do you suppose God would have a WEDDING FEAST without any wine? The final proof that this feast will occur on earth after Christ returns, is because that is where God's Kingdom will be! How clear!

At the present time, the Church is in the betrothal stage. Next, in sequence with the Hebrew custom, she will enjoy the one thousand year wedding feast ruling with Christ in His Kingdom. Finally, the Church is to be "joined in one" to Christ *after* the Millennium as "bone of His bone and flesh of His flesh."

Now, we are not disputing the fact that Israel will also be the Bride in the future (Jer. 3:1,8,14,20). Both history and geography have been determined by God's purposes towards Israel (Deut. 32:8-9).

While it is quite apparent that the Church is not *synonymous* with Old Testament Israel, we must not assume there is no connection! Jesus is not God the Father—but to say they are not both God is a fallacy!

It might just as well be said that the Church is not Old

Testament Israel—but to say it is only Gentile because of this privileged Gentile dispensation would also be a grave fallacy!

The Millennial Banquet

The MARRIAGE FEAST could be another way of describing the millennial reign of Jesus Christ with His *espoused* Bride on earth! This entire one thousand year courtship period of Jesus and His Bride will culminate in marriage! But the marriage will be at the *end* of the Millennium! Remember, an espoused Bride is not yet a wife!

It is only then that we see "New Jerusalem" descending as the Lamb's Wife! This will come *after* the 1,000 year [day-long feast] of the Millennium! Recall how God's days are a thousand years (11 Pet. 3:8).

"New Jerusalem" is a part of a new creation—and far more glorious than the present "Jerusalem Above"! But it comes down to earth out of heaven *after* the Millennium is finished!

Jesus is coming back to present to Himself a glorious Church without spot or wrinkle! But this will happen *after* the Millennium when *New Jerusalem* becomes His Wife!

Who are the Wedding Guests?

Ah! Now we come to the nitty gritty! Granted, we have a Bride in the New Testament Church. Granted, that the wedding supper occurs on earth at Christ's return!

But where does Israel fit into the picture, and *who* are the wedding guests mentioned in the parable of The Royal Marriage Feast?

There is no contest that Israel was the Bride of Christ through a previous marriage. But this marriage ended in divorce (Jer. 3:1,8,14,20). There is also no question about the fact that Christ will one day remarry His former wife—the only question is when? The remarriage of Israel need not correspond to the marriage of the New Testament Church in time!

Could it possibly be that those invited as wedding guests of the Bride, will be tribulation Saints as well as Old Testament Israel? Let's read Revelation 19:9: **"And he saith unto me, write, Blessed are they which are called unto the marriage supper of the Lamb [as guests, emphasis mine]."**

It should be apparent that the "Ten Virgins" of (Matthew 25) are not the same group as form the Bride during the feast! Christ comes for a Bride (singular) not virgins (plural). How can they be Bridesmaids and the Bride at the same time?

In view of the *types* and double *symbolism* running throughout God's Word—it is quite likely that the wedding guests who are called to the marriage supper (Rev. 19), the wise virgins (Matt. 25), and the Bride herself—will include both Israelites and the New Testament Church of God!

To say that the Levites were priests who administered service to God in the Temple would be an absolute truth. But to say that they were not a part of the nation of Israel would be a misnomer! Each tribe had a specific function—yet all were Israelites! In other words, all Levites were Israelites, but not all Israelites were Levites!

This concept may also parallel the two Church dispensations! There may be different groups such as Old Testament Saints, New Testament Saints, Tribulation Saints, Millennial Saints, etc. all under the banner of "Church" forming the eventual Wife of Christ!

All will comprise the Wife of Christ at the Millennium's conclusion—but in the interim they are distinctly classified!

Summary

The ancient Hebrew wedding ceremony is a *picture* of the relationship of Christ to His Church. There were three phases of courtship.

First, there was the lengthy engagement period which outlined the legality of the marriage. This is similar to the contract [New Testament] the Church is currently under during its *espousal* period.

Next, a "day-long" *marriage feast* preceded the actual coming together as man and wife. This corresponds to the Millennial reign of Jesus Christ ruling with His Bride.

During the Millennium, both houses of Israel will be reunited into one fold in preparation of the marriage (Jn. 10:16). Judah and Israel will be one during the Millennium, with one Shepherd [Christ] ruling over them (Ezek. 37:22-26). This will be the time the New Covenant will be made with them (Heb. 8:8; Jer. 31:31-33).

Finally, at the Millennium's conclusion, "New Jerusalem", that holy spiritual city composed of all overcomers during all ages—will be joined with Christ as "bone of His bone" and "flesh of His flesh" forevermore!

THE PARABLE OF THE LOST SHEEP

And he spake this parable unto them, saying, What man of you, having an hundred sheep, if he lose one of them, doth not leave the ninety and nine in the wilderness, and go after that which is lost, until he find it? And when he hath found it, he layeth it on his shoulders, rejoicing. And when he cometh home, he calleth together his friends and neighbors, saying unto them, Rejoice with me; for I have found my sheep which was lost. I say unto you, that likewise joy shall be in heaven over one sinner that repenteth, more than over ninety and nine just persons, which need no repentance (Lk. 15:3 7).

Once we have willingly undertaken the journey towards salvation, Jesus will do everything in His power to keep us on that straight and narrow path. At times we may wander and stumble along the way—but as long as we continue to pick ourselves up, *forgiveness* will be given time and time again!

This is parabolically illustrated by the three parables of *The Lost Sheep, Recovery of the Lost Coin,* and *Return of the Prodigal Son.* This chapter is a companion to *The Sinful Woman* of (Luke 7:36-50) and *The Adulterous Woman* in (John 8:1-11).

In the parable of *The Lost Sheep,* God shows how very precious each Christian is to Him as our "Good Shepherd." Through the analogy of a shepherd caring for the one stray in 100—God demonstrates His concern for us and will do everything possible to recover strayed sinners from His flock. When sinners return—our loving God is exuberant with joy and wants the faithful to rejoice with Him!

This parable also describes the time when the nation of Israel will be brought back into God's fold. Christ said of this event: **"And other sheep I have which are not of this fold: them also I must bring, and they shall hear my voice; and** there shall be one fold, and one shepherd" (Jn. 10:16).

Jesus had been sent to the lost sheep of the house of Israel (Matt. 15:24). His commission to His disciples was: **"...Go not into the way of the Gentiles...But go rather to the lost sheep of the house of Israel" (Matt. 10:5-6).**

Christ had come to His own nation of Judah (Jn. 1:11), but they had rejected Him! Israel and Judah had both rejected the gospel message and the commission then became: **"Go not to the lost sheep of the house of Israel—but into the highways of the Gentile world" (Matt. 22:9-10; Acts 13:46).**

But there is coming a time when a new covenant will be made with the houses of Israel and Judah when God will write His laws in their hearts (Jer. 31:31-33; Heb. 8:8). At this time both houses will be reunited under Christ the Chief Shepherd! (Ezek. 37:22-26). Thus the "other sheep" of Israel will be brought back into the "fold" of Judah!

The restoring of God's "fold" began in 1948 when the Jews once again were restored in their homeland. Soon God will begin pouring out His Holy Spirit on Jerusalem and begin the conversion process of Israel. A few sheep will return to His fold at this time (144,000)—later during the Millennium, the entire flock will be brought back into God's fold!

THE PARABLE OF THE LOST COIN

Either what woman having ten pieces of silver, if she lose one piece, doth not light a candle, and sweep the house, and seek diligently till she find it? And when she hath found it, she calleth her friends and her neighbors together, saying, Rejoice with me; for I have found the piece which I had lost. Likewise, I say unto you, there is joy in the presence of the angels of God over one sinner that repenteth (Lk. 15:8-10).

This parable, like *The Lost Sheep*—declares God's JOY for recovering His lost property. Just as one finds a lost coin and rejoices with his friends—so God in His iridescent joy rejoices with His friends [the host of angels in heaven] for the restoration of one repentant sinner.

The truth contained in this parable, *parallels* that of the "lost sheep" and "prodigal son" in that our heavenly Father delights in the retrieving of a strayed sinner. However, this parable explains another aspect of this vital truth. Unlike the "lost sheep" [Christians] who stray from the flock [Church] because of their own choice—the coin in this parable is lost at *home* because of *negligence* of the owner!

Could the *woman* in this parable be analogous to the Church or individual Christians composing that Church, who are careless in edifying new members? How many times do we hear of neophyte Christians becoming "turned off" or "offended" because of something that should not have been said by an older member?

If the coin in this parable is representative of Christians being lost because of inattentiveness by the Church—it also shows the *earnestness* in which the woman [Church] seeks to find and recover that coin through painstaking diligence.

THE PARABLE OF THE PRODIGAL SON

And he said, A certain man had two sons: And the younger of them said to his father, Father give me the portion of goods that falleth to me. And he divided unto them his living. And not many days after the younger son gathered all together, and took his journey into a far country, and there wasted his substance with riotous living. And when he had spent all, there arose a mighty famine in that land; and he began to be in want. And he went and joined himself to a citizen of that country; and he sent him into his fields to feed swine.

And he would fain have filled his belly with the husks that the swine did eat: and no man gave unto him. And when he came to himself, he said, How many hired servants of my father's have bread enough and to spare, and I perish with hunger! I will arise and go to my father, and will say unto him, Father, I have sinned against heaven, and before thee...And he arose, and came to his father. But when he was yet a great way off his father saw

> *him, and had compassion, and ran, and fell on his neck and kissed him... (Lk. 15:11-32).*

The parable of *The Prodigal Son* completes the *Evangelistic* parables. The younger son in this parable *pictures* all those in a general sense who have been ENLIGHTENED with God's truth—but are entertained by the riotous living of the world.

They feel that God's way of life is too stringent and they must have a taste of the world. While in the world, they become entangled with the filth and slop of wrong living habits.

Like the prodigal son, sometimes these people wake up from their dream world and return home. They begin to perceive their new found freedom is a cruel taskmaster compared to the light yoke of God's way of life. This particular individual was joined with the "harlots" of the world (vs. 30). Many have forsaken God's truths today, and have committed *spiritual adultery* with the "harlots" of false doctrines.

After this seditious son had spent several years in the mire of contemptuous living, his "eyes were opened" to recognize this futility. Finally, "he came to himself" [came to his senses] (vs. 17) and returned home. His father was *overwhelmed* to greet him and welcome him back with open arms and a kiss of *compassion* (vs. 20).

In a more specific sense, this parable necessitates the arraignment and judgment of the sinful but repentant nation of Israel. Once the nation of Israel repents of its heinous sins—the Eternal will restore and exhalt His chosen son [prodigal nation] to Himself! The elder son can be represented of the nation of Israel who thought that "works of the law" would earn you favor in the Father's eyes, but rejected the gospel of grace.

This is a *cameo* representation of our just and loving Father in heaven, who stands willing to forgive and welcome back repentant sinners [and nations] with overwhelming joy! God will then remove those sins and make that individual an equal with all the faithful. This is indicated by the Father's removal of *filthy garments* [sins] and replacing them with the best robe [symbolic of *righteousness*] (vs. 22).

Then the Father supplies the forgiven son with a ring (symbolic of the Holy Spirit), and shoes (symbolic of the gospel) and a feast (symbolic of heavenly food). Then the son no longer felt unworthy because of the Father's grace (vs. 19).

There is nothing more pleasing to our heavenly Dad than to see those who have sunk so deep into the cesspools of this world, recover in genuine REPENTANCE. Such joy is not the portion of those who have been faithful for years, like the eldest son. To those that have been faithful—they must believe their benevolent Father has reserved something special for them because of their deep abiding fidelity!

This parable also has implications to those in the Church as the elder son was laboring in his "father's harvest." He can be compared to a Church member who snubs his nose at other "lowlier members" in the congregation. Perhaps he even has an office in the Church such as minister, deacon or elder. He wears his badge of authority with unmerciful impatience with others.

This individual doesn't realize it, but his conscience tells him he is "holier than thou." He has forgotten the prophet Isaiah's admonition: **"But we are all as an unclean thing, and all our righteousness are as filthy rags; and we all do fade as a leaf; and our iniquities, like the wind, have taken us away" (Isa. 64:6).**

Job, and the self-righteous Pharisee also had this deadly sin of self-righteousness! We Christians must not let this attitude hold us in its sinister clutches!

Chapter Eight

PROPHETIC PARABLES

THE PARABLE OF THE FIG TREE

Now learn a parable of the fig tree; When his branch is yet tender, and putteth forth leaves, ye know that summer is nigh: So likewise ye when ye shall see all these things, know that it is near, even at the doors. verily I say unto you, This generation shall not pass, till all these things be fulfilled (Matt. 24: 32-34).

The disciples of Jesus had just asked Him what would be the *signs* that the end of this hell-bent age is near (vs. 3). Then Jesus proceeded to give a *series* of events that would occur *simultaneously* prior to His second coming.

Jesus then gave an *outline* of future world conditions including, false prophets, wars, rumors of wars, famines, pestilences, earthquakes, persecution, lawlessness, the preaching of the gospel for a witness unto all nations, the Great Tribulation, the sun and moon darkened, stars falling from heaven and the earth shaken—then shall the end come! (verses 4-31).

The parable of *The Fig Tree* was then given as an *analogy*, to illustrate, these SIGNS of the time. Just as a fig tree starts bearing leaves before summer—these signs would indicate that the return of Christ was imminent. Jesus further explained, **"So likewise ye, when ye shall see *all* these things, know that it [Christ's return] is near, even at the doors"** (vs. 33).

Such *signs* will be the shock waves that will shake the very foundation of our human race!

THE PARABLE OF THE WATCHFUL PORTER

> *For the Son of Man is as a man taking a far journey, who left his house, and gave authority to his servants, and to every man his work, and commanded the porter to watch. Watch ye therefore: for ye know not when the master of the house cometh, at even, or at midnight, or at the cock-crowing, or in the morning: Lest coming suddenly he find you sleeping. And what I say unto you I say unto all, Watch (Mk. 13:34-37).*

Right after Jesus gave the parable of *The Fig Tree*, describing the sequence of prophetic events that would trigger the end of this age—He gave the parable of *The Watchful Porter*.

This parable also dovetails the parable of *The Talents* in (Matthew 25:14). Jesus is the man who left His house [Church], and gave authority to His servants [the ministry], and to every man his work (individual responsibility to grow spiritually). As watchful porters, it is our Christian *liability* to make sure that the entrusted commission of preaching the gospel be accomplished! It is also our *obligation* to make sure we are growing and overcoming spiritually, so we will be ready when Christ returns.

Jesus warned: **"Watch ye therefore: for ye know not when the master of the house cometh...vs. 35)**. The question we must all ask ourselves, are we being FAITHFUL and *watchful* porters for Christ? Or are we letting the "fickle finger of fate" guide our destinies?

THE MARRIAGE SUPPER OF THE LAMB

> *Let us be glad and rejoice, and give honour to Him: for the marriage of the Lamb is come, and His wife hath made herself ready. And to her was granted that she should be arrayed in fine linen, clean and white: for the fine linen is the righteousness of saints. And He saith unto me, write, Blessed are they which are called unto the marriage supper of the Lamb (Rev. 19:7-9).*

We have already proven that the New Testament Church will comprise the Bride of Christ as well as the Old Testament prophets. Where this marriage supper will take place and how long it will last is anyone's guess.

Perhaps there may even be two pre-nuptial suppers, one heavenly, and one earthly. One representing the *heavenly* Church and one for *earthly* Old Testament Israel.

This concept may sound like spiritual polygamy to some—but this is only speaking in *figurative* language. As already noted, two entities can apply to the same figure even as the Church is both Christ's Body and Wife.

Because the Bible is loaded with *duality*—is it not conceivable to think that there could be two marriage suppers expressing two different glories of God?

Could it be that the marriage supper of the Lamb in heaven would be for the New Testament Church while there could also be one on earth with the ancient prophets and apostles representing ancient Israel? Remember, the apostles will be ruling over each of the 12 tribes (Matt.19:28). Christ said Himself that He would not drink of the fruit of the vine again until He drank it with the apostles in His Father's Kingdom (Matt. 26:29).

Symbolically, the New Testament Church would represent Christ's heavenly Bride while Israel His earthly Bride. Both being purchased with His precious blood—but each being a special treasure with a different glory!

CHRIST COMES WITH HIS ARMIES

And I saw heaven opened, and behold a white horse; and he that sat upon him was called Faithful and true, and in righteousness he doth judge and make war. His eyes were as a flame of fire, and on his head were many crowns: and he had a name written, that no man knew, but He himself. And he was clothed with a vesture dipped in blood; and his name is called The Word of God, And the armies which were in heaven followed him upon white horses, clothed in fine linen, white and clean.

And out of his mouth goeth a sharp sword, that with it he should smite the nations: and he shall rule them with a rod of iron: and he treadeth the winepress of the fierceness and wrath of Almighty God. And he hath on his vesture and on his thigh a name written, KING OF KINGS, AND LORD OF LORDS (Rev. 19:11-16).

The next event to follow the marriage supper of the Lamb—will be the coming of the Lord to the earth with His armies to smite the nations!

Obviously, the rider on the white horse is Jesus Christ who now comes as the champion of His people. The Prince of Peace now comes to RULE the world with a rod of iron, no longer a humble Lamb to be slaughtered. Now Jesus comes to take vengeance upon His enemies and to deliver His people from persecution. Faithful and True is His name—for He comes to execute righteous judgment of God's Word and to establish His Father's divine government on the earth.

Christ's army from heaven will comprise His holy angels (Mk. 8:38), along with the resurrected called, chosen and faithful Saints (Rev. 17:14).

All the kingdoms of the earth are to be His—the KING OF KINGS, AND LORD OF LORDS! This will be the fulfillment of Daniel 2:44-45.

THE HARVEST OF SOULS

And I looked, and behold a white cloud, and upon the cloud one sat like unto the Son of man, having on his head a golden crown, and in his hand a sharp sickle (Rev. 14:14).

When the Son of Man [Christ] returns to this earth the second time—He will REAP the earth with a sharp sickle! But surprisingly this reaping of souls on the earth is not for the Church!

This astounding truth is revealed in God's Word by several passages. But let's begin with the parable of *The Sower*, where Christ pictured the earth as His *field* to garner!

The *field* is not the *Church* as some believe in the parable of the Sower, but rather the *world* as interpreted by the Master story teller! Therefore, the *tares* are not as some suppose "Church members," but rather the "wicked" of the *earth* influenced by Satan (Matt. 13:38).

Both are to grow together in the world until the harvest when Christ will say to the reapers: **"Gather ye together *first* the tares, and bind them in bundles to burn them; but gather the wheat [Church] into my barn" (Matt. 13:30).**

The same sequence of end-time events is demonstrated through the parable of *"The Kingdom of Heaven likened unto a Net* that was cast into the Sea," notice:

> **Again, the kingdom of heaven is like unto a net, that was cast into the sea, and gathered of every *kind*: which, when it was full, they drew to shore, and sat down, and gathered the good into vessels, but cast the bad away. So shall it be at the end of the world [age]: the angels shall come forth, and *sever* the wicked from among the just, and shall cast them into *the furnace of fire*: there shall be wailing and gnashing of teeth (Matt. 13:47-50).**

Notice this end-time scenario! The tares or wicked of the world are to be gathered first!

At the end of the age, God's angels will gather the tares to be burned *before* He garners His people to inherit the Kingdom (Matt. 13:39-42). This will most likely occur during the 1290 and 1335 day period of time *after* Christ returns (Dan. 12). We will read this prophecy shortly.

The sequence of these events also brings to mind the parable of **"One shall be *taken*, and the other left,"** which we will also cover shortly. So, notice again, first, the tares will be taken to be BURNED—and the righteous shall be *left* to "shine forth as the sun in the kingdom of their Father..." (Matt. 13:43).

This time sequence is illuminated by what occurred in the days of Noah! Concerning this *parallel* time, Christ said:

> **But the same day that Lot went out of Sodom it rained fire and brimstone from heaven and destroyed them *all*. Even thus shall it be in the day when the Son of man is revealed (Lk. 17:29:30).**

As already demonstrated, the lives of Noah and Lot are clearly *types* of what will happen in the last days! Here, Jesus expressly compared the destruction by the flood to the annihilation of the wicked in the end of the age.

Therefore, if this was a *type* of what is to come—ALL UNBELIEVERS will be wiped off the face of the earth! Could Jesus mean what He says? **"Even thus shall it be in the days when the Son of man is revealed."**

Can we take our Savior literally?

Who will populate the Millennium?

Now we have a problem! If *all* the *wicked* are destroyed in the Great Tribulation—and if the righteous are changed into spiritual beings with eternal bodies upon Christ's return—who will be left to populate the Millennium?

Whoever this group is—they will have physical bodies! Why? Because the resurrected Christians will be kings and priests over physical human beings!

During the Tribulation, multitudes will accept Jesus as their personal Savior and repent! However, these individuals will not be changed into spiritual beings at that time. Instead, they will inherit the Millennium in their natural physical bodies!

PROPHETIC PARABLES

The *Companion Bible* has an Appendix describing the period of time Daniel spoke of as 1335 days and the *resurrection of Israel after* Christ returns (Dan. 12:11-12). This will be the gathering of the dispersed of Judah, which comes *after* the Tribulation at the end of the age—when the angels gather God's "elect" from the four corners of the earth (Isa. 11:12; Ezek. 5:10; Matt. 24:31).

The *Companion Bible* states that the word "stand" in (Daniel 12:13), means "resurrection" (see margin on Dan. 12:13). This will be a great harvest of souls as *pictured* by the Feast of Tabernacles! Israel is called God's "elect" in (Isaiah 45:4 and 65:9).

According to this speculative scenario, this enmasse resurrection and *gathering* of the souls of Israel will begin prior to the glorious 1,000 year reign of Jesus Christ. Therefore, there may be a 75 day interval between Christ's return and the resurrection of Israel. This is calculated by adding 1260 + 75 = 1335 (see *Companion Bible,* Ap 89 & 90). According to this concept, Christ's New Testament Bride is resurrected after the 1260 days, Israel 75 days later! Although this concept may be viewed as possible, we must realize that at best it is highly speculative, and we must proceed with due caution.

This gathering of God's "elect" [Israel] from the "four corners of the earth" will take place after Satan [Leviathan the piercing serpent] is bound and chained (Isa. 27:1; Rev. 20:1-3).

If only believers enter the Millennium, and all the incorrigible eradicated—someone is sure to ask, "what about the scripture in (Zechariah 14:16-19)?" This scripture reads:

> **And it shall come to pass, that every one that is left of all the nations which came against Jerusalem shall even go up from year to year to worship the King, the LORD of hosts, and to keep the feast of tabernacles. And it shall be, that whoso will not come up of all the families of the earth unto Jerusalem to worship the King, the LORD of hosts, even upon them shall be no rain.**
>
> **And if the family of Egypt go not up, and come not, that have no rain; there shall be the plague,**

> wherewith *the LORD will smite the heathen that come not up to keep the feast of tabernacles.* **This shall be the punishment of Egypt, and the punishment of all nations that come not up to keep the feast of tabernacles.**

How could this happen we might ask if all were believers at the beginning of the Millennium? The answer is that although believers entered the Millennium—some of their children will become rebellious after a while as has always happened! Witness the nation of Israel in the wilderness.

The difference under God's perfect administration is that *rebellion* will not be tolerated and will be crushed immediately!

As we have just proven, the *sickle* of the Lord is not for the righteous—but for the incorrigible of the earth! This sickle personifies a "cutting action" or *decision* making that will separate the righteous from the wicked—the Sheep from the Goats!

It is very possible that the separation of the Wheat from the Tares will take place *during* the 45 days (1290 + 45 = 1335) after Christ returns! Perhaps Satan will be bound and chained by the angel Gabriel 45 days after the 1290 days.

One shall be taken

> **I tell you, in that night there shall be two men in one bed;** *the one shall be taken, and the other left.* **Two women shall be grinding together;** *the one shall be taken,* **and** *the other left.* **Two men shall be in the field;** *the one shall be taken,* **and** *the other left.* **And they answered and said unto him, Where, Lord? And he said unto them, Wheresoever the body is, thither will** *the eagles be gathered together* **(Lk. 17:34-37).**

This parable has puzzled many—yet it is quite clear when viewing the entire context. Realize this! The taking of one and the leaving behind of one is in reference to *the days of Noah and Lot!* (see verses 26-33).

If we can understand what happened to Noah and Lot, we can understand the correct interpretation of this parable!

Both Noah and Lot are *types* of Tribulation Saints who will go through the Tribulation fires—not those who have been faithful!

Noah's family is *typical* of the 144,000 physical Israelites of Jacob's family who pass through the Tribulation under God's protection (Rev. 7).

Consider this!

If Noah's flood is a *type* of the Great Tribulation—"the flood took them ALL away!" Those that *remained* were saved, while those *taken* by the flood waters were destroyed!

As you will recall—*everyone* who was not aboard the Ark perished! Total annihilation of the wicked is *pictured* by this *duality* during the last days! This event is also a *foretaste* of Armageddon in which *all* the wicked will perish—rather than the Tribulation in which only partial destruction occurs!

Peter makes mention of the fact that Noah's flood was also a *type* of the "lake of fire" that will destroy the wicked at the Millennium's conclusion (2 Pet. 3). Both water and fire are *types* of cleansing agents! The old world of Noah was cleansed by water to prepare for a new world. Likewise, the earth will be cleansed by *fire* at the end of the Millennium before the new earth is made!

Lot's wife is a *type* of those individuals who neglect to "flee" during the Tribulation when the Abomination of desolation is set up!

Notice the wording in connection to "eagles" or vultures gathered together over dead bodies (vs. 37). This entire context is in reference to conditions of Noah's and Lot's day which were *types* of the Tribulation and Armageddon! Matthew gives the identical time setting as *prior* to the Tribulation (Matt. 24:28).

Matthew 24:27 places the chronology of the "eagles gathering" just *after* the Great Tribulation: **"For as the lightning cometh out of the east...so shall also the coming of the Son of man be."** This is the exact context of (Luke 17:24) which then proceeds to describe the days of Noah!

Luke 17 is in reference to the Tribulation and gathering of the wicked to be destroyed—but where? This is what the disciples asked Jesus! He explained: **"Wheresoever the body [corpse or carcass—Matt. 24:28] is, thither will the eagles [Gr. 'vultures' or 'birds of prey'], be gathered together"** (vs.

37). In other words, there are going to be a lot of vultures preying on the graveyard of dead bodies of the wicked or unrepentant of the earth.

The *King James Version* has the words *men* and *women* in italics which means it is not in the original Greek.

This verse is referring to the *prepared* and *unprepared* who have "mingled together" in the closest intercourse of everyday life!

The Winepress

Quickly turn to (Revelation 14:19,20) for more substantial proof of the end-time sequence of events:

> **And the angel thrust in his *sickle* into the earth, and gathered the vine of the earth ['the one shall be taken, and the other left'] and cast it ['Where, Lord?'] into the great winepress of the wrath of God. And the winepress was trodden without the city [Jerusalem], and *blood came out of the winepress,* even unto the horse bridles, by the space of a thousand and six hundred furlongs (180 miles).**

Here we begin to get all of the pieces to this end-time puzzle together. The "woman" has escaped to a place of safety for 1260 days or 3 1/2 years. The 144,000 physical Israelites (Rev. 7) and 144,000 Gentile Tribulation Saints (Rev. 14) are protected *during* the time of Satan's wrath! Millions will be converted as a result of the Tribulation!

At the end of this dreaded time—Christ returns to separate the "wicked from the righteous", the "wheat from the tares", the "sheep from the goats"!

The righteous will stay to inherit the Kingdom—but the wicked will be *taken* to be squashed into *human wine* whose blood would run 180 miles long, reaching the bridles of a horse!

Where?

The Supper of the great God

Wherever the *eagles* [vultures] are gathered together! (Lk.

17:37). Now turn to (Revelation 19) to find the incredible answer:

> **He treadeth the winepress of the fierceness and wrath of Almighty God...And I saw an angel standing in the sun; and he cried with a loud voice, saying to** *all the fowls that fly in the midst of heaven,* **Come and gather yourselves together unto the supper of the great God; that ye may eat the flesh of kings, and the flesh of captains, and the flesh of mighty men, and the flesh of horses, and of them that sit on them, and the flesh of all men, both free and bond, both small and great (Rev. 19:15-18).**

Now we come to the grand finale of God's feast—if you will, the dessert. This scene describes the destruction of the demonic led armies of the earth gathering for the final battle of Armageddon.

The "Beast" and his religious cohort "False Prophet" [Antichrist], scurry to combine the kings of the earth in one last desperate pursuit to destroy God's coming government. This will represent man's last effort to rule the earth before all unrighteousness is squelched.

However, these armies are completely smitten only to become food for the birds of prey.

Although this will be a gruesome sight—it will be filled with JUBILATION as God's ensuing utopia government will finally be ushered in—this will truly be "a feast fit for a king"!

According to (Zechariah 12:2,9) the location of the winepress will be just outside the city of Jerusalem. This will be where the armies of the earth will be gathered for the final battle of the earth.

The Valley of Decision

> **I will also gather all nations, and bring them down into the valley of Jehoshaphat, and will plead with them there...Let the heathen be wakened, and come up to the valley of Jehoshaphat: for there will I sit to judge all the**

heathen round about. Put ye in the *sickle*, for the harvest is ripe: come [tread], for the press is full, the [vats] overflow; for their wickedness is great. multitudes, multitudes in the valley of decision: for the day of the Lord is near in the valley of decision (Joel 3:2, 12-14).

Realize this is all *symbolic* language used to illustrate the destruction of the wicked at the end of the age!

The *sickle* the angel casts in is *symbolic* of the harvest of wicked souls—represented by the *vine!* The winepress is *symbolic* of Christ trampling on these human grapes to crush them or kill them!

But what about the 180 miles of blood mentioned in Revelation 14 that reaches the horses bridles—is this *symbolic* or real? If it is literal, this certainly would not entail just the armies of Armageddon—it would have to represent ALL of the wicked left on earth!

This prophecy will occur in the "Valley of Jehoshaphat" where the Lord will punish the wicked tares!

Good mixed with Bad

There is a *definite* and *distinctive* DIVISION between "good" and "bad" people as outlined in many of the parables. These "bad" cannot therefore refer to those who are "true" Christians—but rather those who are "professing" Christians! These people are in actuality infidels!

The parables of the "Wheat and Tares"; "Good and Bad Fish"; "Good and Evil Servants"; "Wise and Foolish Virgins"; "Sheep and the Goats"; "Profitable and Unprofitable Servants"; the "Guest without a Wedding Garment"; and "One Shall be Taken, One Shall be Left"—all characterize this same theme!

Several of these parables show that God's angels will be the agency to SEPARATE the "just" from the "unjust" the "righteous" from the "wicked" the "good" from the "bad"!

Our Lord and Savior makes it very clear as to when this event transpires from several parables! The parables of the "Wheat and the Tares" the "Good and Bad fish" and the "Winepress" all give the vital time element of this separation. In the dynamic words of Jesus Christ, the division of the wicked and just is thundered loud and clear! Christ said dogmatically: **"So shall it be at the end of the age"**!

Under the Old Testament, God made it abundantly clear that the Israelites were not to be "unequally yoked with unbelievers." The Almighty God gave vivid instructions concerning this in Deuteronomy 22:9-11: **"Thou shall not sow thy vineyard with divers seeds: lest the fruit of thy seed which thou hast sown, and the fruit of thy vineyard be defiled. Thou shall not plow with an ox and an ass together. Thou shalt not wear a garment of divers sorts, as of woolen and linen together."**

All these precepts refer to the *separation* of the *good* from the *bad* and therefore keeping the kind pure! The reason God instituted these laws, was to teach the Israelites a spiritual lesson from the physical things before them that they could understand. The lesson here was that the all-knowing God wanted to keep the races pure, and therefore forbade the Israelites to marry other nations (Deut. 7:3).

Christians are also exhorted to keep unspotted from the world, or as Paul put it: **"Wherefore come out from among them, and be ye separate, saith the Lord, and touch not the unclean thing; and I will receive you" (11 Cor. 6:17)**

When the New Testament will be made with Israel

Christians now form, spiritually the *true Israel* of the New Testament. A testament is a will that declares a person's will as to the disposal of his possessions after his death (Heb. 9:16). Upon the death of Christ—He left a will, or testament in which Christians may become beneficiaries of His goods. These heirs of salvation are now being perfected to be Christ's spotless Bride upon His return (Eph. 4:12,13).

Christians have now entered into the New Testament. After 2520 years of Gentile rule, the living Jesus Christ is soon coming to *restore* the ecclesiastical government of His Father to the nation of Israel. He will be the mediator of the New Testament which is based upon better promises (Heb. 8:6-10, 9:15).

The New Testament is not and will not be made with human mortals who fail to keep their word—but rather with individuals who have proven through *trial* and *test* that they desire to be faithful to the laws, authority and government of God! At the resurrection, the N.T. Church will become a perfect spiritual nation [a holy nation—1 Pet. 2:5,9] with a spiritual nature and power to keep God's law's perfectly!

The Old Covenant between Jesus and Israel was started by a marriage and the New Testament will also be started by a "marriage feast." So, if we can tell when the marriage feast takes place between Jesus and the converted nation of Israel—we will know when the New Testament begins for them! The "marriage feast" will take place only after the resurrection of the Church..

The preparation for the marriage feast of the Lamb, takes place just before Christ returns to smite the nations as recorded in (Revelation 19:7,9). This scripture also indicates that the preparation for the "marriage feast" will take place in heaven (vs. 1), and Christ's Bride, now resurrected, is spotless and receives white garments *symbolic* of this (vs. 8).

The Bride then comes with Christ's army (vs. 14), who comes to subdue the nations and help set up God's Kingdom on earth (vs. 15). Jude 14 states that Jesus will come *with*, not *for* 10,000's of His saints (Gr. "hagios", meaning "holy ones"). This verse undoubtedly refers to angels who will also be coming with Christ (11 Thess. 1:6), as well as the resurrected Saints (Rev. 17:14). Paul writes in (1 Thessalonians 3:12,13) that Jesus comes *with* not *for* the saints (see also Zech. 14:1,5).

The Dead rise First

The dead *in Christ* and those living on the earth who are Christians—will be resurrected to "meet" Christ in the air on the beginning of the last trumpet of the Seventh Seal, as recorded by Paul in (1 Corinthians 15:50-52 and 1 Thessalonians 4:16).

Although the Bible plainly says that **"...no man hath ascended up to heaven but he which came down from heaven..." (Jn. 3:13)**, and **"King David is not ascended into the heavens" (Acts 2:34)**—it does not mean that *no one will ever ascend into heaven!* But rather, no one had ascended into heaven at the time this prophecy was written—except Christ, the firstfruit! There are three heavens spoken of in the Bible. The clouds in our earthly atmosphere is the *heaven* where the resurrected Saints will meet Christ!

The "Two Witnesses" are taken up to heaven after the 2nd Woe—which is before the 3rd Woe or the 7th Seal even starts

(Rev. 11:14). It was a fellow servant [not an angel] who was telling John this vision from heaven (Rev. 19:10; 22:8-9). Revelation 14:1 states that there are 144,000 firstfruits (vs.4), [the Church or Bride] in heaven, redeemed from the earth (vss. 2,3), with Christ on Mt. Zion, which is in heaven (Heb. 12:22). They are before the throne of God (Rev. 14:5). This occurs before Babylon the Great is fallen (vs. 8) and occurs before Christ returns (vs. 14).

We read in (Revelation 7:9) that people are before God's throne before the 7th Seal even starts! The Seventh Seal consists of seven Trumpets. The Seventh Trumpet consists of seven Plagues. Christians are to be resurrected at the last Trumpet of the Seventh Seal. This is not to say that everyone who dies immediately goes to heaven! On the contrary! However, it does appear that certain groups will be resurrected just before the Seventh Seal starts!

Jesus pictures the Church—His new Bride as a "crown of glory" in (Isaiah 62). Notice the analogy of a *virgin* marrying a bridegroom in (verse 5). This Bride will have a new name (vs. 2) when glorified and be a "crown of glory" (vs. 3). In (Zechariah 9:16), God describes His Church as "stones of a crown", and in (Malachi 3:17) we find that the Lord will make up His "jewels"—spiritual crown of glory—the Bride now resurrected who shall return [from heaven or "the clouds"] and discern between the righteous and the wicked (vs. 18).

John reveals the "new name" of God's Church in Revelation 3:12, and the name of "New Jerusalem" which is the holy city in glorified form—or the Church (Rev. 21:2).

And so we see that the preparation for the "marriage feast" will most likely occur in heaven, after the Church is resurrected, just before Christ returns to conquer the nations! It will be at this time that the New Covenant will most likely be made with the nation of Israel!

Resurrections to occur in stages?

It is interesting to note that there are 7 weeks, each followed by a Sabbath of rest during Pentecost, and there are 7 Churches or as some believe eras of God's Church (Rev. 1:4). Since Pentecost represents the Church dispensation—it follows that each week may be representative of a Church era throughout history.

Therefore, it is very possible that each Church era will be resurrected [in it's own *order*—1 Cor. 15:23] during the Jubilee year on the 50th day, or the actual day of Pentecost in the future. The number "50" you will recall, denotes a release from bondage, even as the Jubilee year released the Israelites from all their debts every 50th year!

The word *order* [Gr. *tagma*], according to Robertson and Plummer, "is a military metaphor; 'company,' 'troop,' 'band,' or 'rank.' We are to think of each 'corps' or body of troops coming on in its proper position and order..." (*First Epistle to the Corinthians*, p. 354).

It seems as though each Church era is represented by a "week"! Jesus described His Coming for the Church in "watches" or "stages" in (Luke 12:36-40). This could mean that each Church era would be resurrected at a separate time (each man or era in his own order). The Marriage Supper parable in (Matthew 22:1-14) suggests that while the marriage supper is going on, more Christians would be resurrected to make it to the marriage supper after it had started.

The parable of the 10 Virgins in (Matthew 25) shows that of those that are called to the marriage feast [and therefore into the Kingdom]—only 50% make it! These would be those qualifying for the last Church era or Laodicean.

If "the last shall be first", then the natural order of the resurrections would be as follows: 1)Laodicean, 2) Philadelphia, 3) Sardis, 4) Thyatira, 5) Pergamos, 6) Symrna, 7) Ephesus. These would occur practically *instantaneously,* yet each in their own order!

Some have seen the "Two Witnesses" represented by the "two wave loaves" during Pentecost as being the first ones accepted unto God—remember these loaves had leaven in them and had something to do with Pentecost—the firstfruits—the Church! The assumption is that they are the "Two Witnesses", and they will most likely represent the last two eras of God's Church—Laodicea and Philadelphia. It follows then that the other eras will be resurrected after them (in their own order).

However, what does God's Word say they represent? God's Word indicates the "two wave loaves" represent the two covenant *firstfruits!* God Himself interprets their meaning in Leviticus 23:17: **"...they are the *firstfruits* unto the Lord."**

PROPHETIC PARABLES

Here then is a possible scenario of what could happen. The Church eras could be resurrected fulfilling Pentecost during a Jubilee year (the 1260 day resurrection).

The "marriage supper" could take place in heaven, starting the New Covenant before Christ returns with His new Bride to smite the nations (Rev. 19).

Those Saints who were killed during the Great Tribulation and those who are still alive will be caught up to meet Christ in the air to fight in the final battle of Armageddon.

Then 144,000 *firstfruits* of Israel (Rev. 7) and 144,000 Gentile Tribulation *firstfruits* (Rev. 14) could be resurrected 30 days later (the 1290 day resurrection).

The subject of the "resurrections" is a very technical and confusing one—so let's not be too dogmatic. But note this—the apostle Paul uses *three* different Greek words for "resurrection" in the New Testament in reference to the resurrection—why? Could it be because Paul knew there would be more than one resurrection prior to the Millennium?

The Greek word for "resurrection" in (Philippians 3:11) is a different word than any other place. Concerning the rising of the dead in Christ, Paul writes in 1 Thessalonians 4:16-17:

> **For the Lord himself shall descend from the heaven with a shout, with the voice of the archangel, and with the trump of God: and *the dead in Christ* shall rise first: Then we which are alive and remain shall be caught up together with them in the clouds, to meet the Lord in the air: and so shall we ever be with the Lord.**

The first point to realize is that Paul does not call this event *a resurrection*—and this word "first" may not have any connection with the "first resurrection" of (Revelation 20:5-6) whatsoever! Two EVENTS are spoken of, not necessarily two RESURRECTIONS! First, "the dead in Christ shall rise"—and second, the living who remain shall be caught up in the clouds together, with them.

That this is a separate event from the "first resurrection" is also indicated from the new revelation given to the apostle Paul, and he writes concerning this in 1 Corinthians 15:51:

Behold, I show you a mystery, [that is, 'Behold, I tell you a secret. I am going to tell you something that has been hidden and been kept secret until now'—just as the secret with regard to the Church—the Body of Christ—had been kept—emphasis mine], Behold, I tell you a secret, we shall not all sleep, but we shall all be changed.

The event Paul spoke of had to be different from the "first resurrection" since Job knew of the resurrection (Job 19:26), David (Ps. 16:10), Isaiah (Isa. 26:19), Daniel (Dan. 12:2), Hosea (Hos. 13:14), and Martha (Jn. 11:24). Certainly, this *resurrection* could not be the "mystery" or "secret" Paul spoke of!

Chapter Nine

PARABLES OF CHRISTIAN ADMONITION

THE PARABLE OF THE GOOD SAMARITAN

A certain man went down from Jerusalem to Jericho, and fell among thieves, which stripped him of his raiment, and wounded him, and departed, leaving him half dead. And by chance there came down a certain priest that way: and when he saw him, he passed by on the other side. And likewise a Levite, when he was at the place, came and looked on him, and passed by on the other side. But a certain Samaritan, as he journeyed, came where he was: and when he saw him, he had compassion on him (Lk. 10:30-37).

A large part of the message Jesus brought was to **"love our neighbor as our self."** Perhaps this parable more than any other portrays this vital lesson.

Would someone with God's Holy Spirit have acted like the

pious priest who was dressed in godly attire outwardly—but was unworthy of the name *Christian* inwardly? Would someone with God's Holy Spirit have found excuses like the Levite and not help this needy fellowman? Did the Levite reason, "He's not one of us—why should I help this heathen?" The road leading from Jerusalem to Jericho was known to be a haven for thieves and therefore very treacherous. Perhaps the Levite thought it was too dangerous a location to stay for very long.

Would someone with God's Holy Spirit have failed to lend a *helping* hand to someone in dire straights, such as a stranded motorist or an elderly person crossing the street? Let's face it—there are a million reasons for not doing something if we have a mental block against helping someone!

Undoubtedly, one must exercise *wisdom* and *caution* these days when dealing with every pan-handler and stranded motorist. There are many who would take advantage of a Christian's good nature.

Instead, we should consider what our Lord and Savior would have us do. Jesus was the *kindest* and most COMPASSIONATE person who ever walked this earth! He put a great deal of emphasis on kindness toward our neighbor. In fact, He identifies Himself with the unfortunate—and candidly tells us we cannot be His friend if we are indifferent to the needy (Matt. 25: 40-45).

It is true that no amount of love or kindness toward our neighbor can earn salvation for us. But at the same time, Jesus declares, not one act of kindness, regardless of how trivial, will go unrewarded (Matt. 10:42).

Christians must HUMBLE themselves in times of *service*! They must be willing to help the unfortunate regardless of race or creed. To answer the question: "Who is your neighbor?"—everyone in need! Christ fellowshipped with publicans and harlots—sinners!

James, the brother of our Lord, drives the final nail in the coffin on this subject:

> **If a brother or sister be naked, and destitute of daily food, and one of you say unto them, Depart in peace, be ye warmed and filled; notwithstanding ye give them not these things which are needful to the body; what doth it**

profit? Even so, faith, if it hath not works, is dead, being alone (Jas. 2:15-17).

The question has never been: "Who is my neighbor?—but am I neighborly?"

Jesus personifies the "good Samaritan" as He had compassion on the sinner in his helpless state. We are all indebted to Him! In our Lord's absence, His ministry is to supply the needs to those He has saved.

THE PARABLE OF THE PHARISEE AND THE PUBLICAN

And he spake this parable unto certain which trusted in themselves that they were righteous and despised others: Two men went up into the temple to pray: the one a Pharisee and the other a publican, The Pharisee stood and prayed thus with himself, God, I thank thee, that I am not as other men are, extortioners, unjust, adulterers, or even as this publican.

I fast twice in the week, I give tithes of all that I possess. And the publican, standing afar off, would not lift up so much as his eyes unto heaven, but smote upon his breast, saying, God be merciful to me a sinner. I tell you, this man went down to his house justified rather than the other: for every one that exalteth himself shall be abased; and he that humbleth himself shall be exalted (Lk. 18:9-14).

The Pharisees in Jesus' day were the epitome of self-aggrandizement. They were so HYPOCRITICAL in their religious worship of God that oftentimes Jesus blatantly called them "hypocrites." Jesus loathed their religious pretense and especially despised their failure to recognize their need for a merciful Savior.

These "children of Satan" thought their "tedious works" of fasting, praying, tithing and strict adherence to the letter of observing the Sabbath [which was their interpretation, and in which they abused in thinking they were going beyond their duty]—would earn them favor in the eyes of God.

Jesus did not condone sinners—yet these arrogant "spiritual masochist" were the most despicable of all sinners in His eyes. The Pharisee in this parable had a contemptuous look upon the lowly publican—and an *exalted* opinion of himself. Contrariwise, the publican was *humble* enough to perceive he was a sinner and relied upon God's loving MERCY to deliver him.

Jesus went on to say that we must become like little children if we want to enter the Kingdom of God (vs. 17). This will take a great deal of humility! This parable makes God's outlook on self-righteous individuals quite succinct!

To come to the state of mind where one is "poor or beggarly in spirit", is to be mentally aware that your every breath is contingent upon the omnipotent God. Without God to sustain our physical and spiritual lives, we wouldn't last 10 seconds in Satan's world.

It is God's Holy Spirit that gives us spiritual tenacity—and we must be conscious of our utter dependence upon God for it each day. Without our Great God's help, we cannot produce spiritual growth as Jesus proclaimed in John 15:4-5: **"I am the vine, you are the branches. He who abides in me, and I in him, he it is that bears much fruit, for apart from me you can do nothing."**

Contrary to the "beggarly attitude" is that of a "proud disposition" and trusting in oneself. These contrasting temperaments are brought out by Jesus in this parable.

This parable clearly portrays the vast difference in the "beggar in spirit" and the "haughty in spirit" attitudes toward worshipping God.

The Publican [tax collector] represents individuals who realize they are spiritually destitute and physically naked without God in their lives. Such people depend upon God for forgiveness of sin as well as spiritual development and maturity.

The Pharisee in this story is *symbolic* of every SUPER-SELF-RIGHTEOUS person who thinks he can be saved by his own works. This type of individual believes in his own strengths. He has prominence in himself and does not give God credence for his spiritual knowledge. His spiritual blanket of security is in his own merits—he fails to see God in his life!

PARABLES OF CHRISTIAN ADMONITION

What this Pharisee failed to perceive was that—simply going through the motions of keeping certain aspects of God's laws with the wrong attitude is in vain! This Pharisee's heart was filled with vanity, not humility!

This braggadocio found deep pleasure in "fasting twice a week," "giving tithes" and "praying openly" in public. He thought his Creator was well pleased with his way of life. After all, he was not an "extortioner" or "adulterer" like others. It was a classic case of the kettle calling the pot black. The haughtiness of this insolent Pharisee reached to high heaven and was manifested in his prayer, as he looked upon other sinners with contempt.

One hall-mark that is absolutely essential for all Christians to have is the virtue of HUMILITY. It is the gold standard of Christian mintage. Jesus, the standard of our Christian assay, said this of humility to everyone represented by these two divergent attitudes: **"Every one that exalteth himself shall be abased; and he that humbleth himself shall be exalted."**

The Moral of the Story

What can we glean from this *picturesque* story Jesus told? Simply this. We must all come to the point in our lives where we acknowledge our sins, and realize our desperate need of God's love and mercy to attain salvation. We must comprehend, unlike the egotistical Pharisee, that no amount of good deeds on our part will pay for these sins! There cannot be any delusions about sustaining our spiritual lives of and by ourselves. God must receive credit for everything—and we must be cognizant of our deficiency of spiritual resources without Him.

The apostle Paul was well aware of God in his life and constantly gave Him praise for his accomplishments. Paul wrote of his physical achievements and how he could have gloated over them in Philippians 3:4:

> **Though I might also have confidence in the flesh. If any other man thinketh that he hath whereof he might trust in the flesh, I more: Circumcised the eighth day, of the stock of Israel, of the tribe of Benjamin, an Hebrew of the Hebrews, as touching the law, a Pharisee,**

Concerning zeal, persecuting the church; touching the righteousness which is in the law, blameless.

Paul then relates how all of these physical attributes meant nothing without Christ in his life (verses 7-8).

To be "poor in spirit" means to be constantly aware that we have no spiritual self-sufficiency in ourselves—that we are totally in need of God's help. This kind of "spiritual poverty" is what is needed to attain eternal life! Christians must not let a deficiency of humility become our spiritual waterloo!

THE PARABLE OF THE TWO DEBTORS

There was a certain creditor which had two debtors: the one owed five hundred pence, and the other fifty. And when they had nothing to pay, he frankly forgave them both. Tell me therefore, which of them will love him most? (Lk. 7:41-43).

This parable has overtures of *The Pharisee and the Publican*. The two debtors in this story depict everyone of us as sinners to a greater or lesser extent. Each of us must be FORGIVEN by God Almighty—the greatest creditor of all!

Though there are degrees of sin—ALL must have them *wiped* clean by the precious blood of Jesus Christ! From this parable, it is evident that those who have sinned the most, would be more aware of their need for a Savior! This is not to say that love is the *cause* of forgiveness—but that it precipitates repentance!

Spiritually speaking, we are all in *debt* to Jesus Christ for giving His very life for us: **"For all have sinned"** and therefore all need a Savior to forgive our debt. As debtors to Christ, the greatest repayment we can give Him—is our *willingness to serve Him* now as loyal servants and help carry out His Father's plan for humankind.

This parable also portrays the jealousy of the Jews at the Gentiles receiving favor under the New Testament! Both Jews and Gentiles are *indebted* to Christ for sacrificing His life for them!

Jesus is the pied-piper that we must all pay if we want to

PARABLES OF CHRISTIAN ADMONITION

dance during God's utopia reign on earth. May God help us to escape the octopus-like clutches of the world, before they strangle the love of God in us!

THE PARABLE OF THE UNFORGIVING SERVANT

Therefore is the kingdom of heaven likened unto a certain king, Which would take account of his servants. And when he had begun to reckon, one was brought unto him, which owed him ten thousand talents. But forasmuch as he had not to pay, his lord commanded him to be sold, and his wife, and children, and all that he had, and payment to be made.

The servant therefore fell down, and worshipped, saying, Lord have patience with me, and I will pay thee all. Then the lord of that servant was moved with compassion, and loosed him, and forgave him the debt. But the same servant went out, and found one of his fellowservants, which owed him an hundred pence: and he laid hands on him, and took him by the throat, saying Pay me that thou owest.

And his fellowservant fell down at his feet, and besought him saying, Have patience with me, and I will pay thee all. And he would not: but went and cast him into prison, till he should pay the debt (Matt. 18:23-35).

Peter had just asked our Lord in verse 21, **"...how often shall my brother sin against me, and I forgive him? Till seven times? Jesus saith unto him, I say not unto thee, until seven times; but seventy times seven" (verse 22).** Then Jesus gave the parable of *The Unforgiving Servant.*

The comparison of forgiving *physical debts* in this parable to that of FORGIVING SINS is quite obvious. A talent in the time of Jesus was worth between $1,000 to $30,000 in todays currency. Therefore, a debt of ten thousand talents was a lot of money! Therefore, a debt of about one million dollars was forgiven this man, yet he was unwilling to forgive a measly $17.00 debt. This is tantamount to God forgiving the multitudes of our abominable sins, and we are unmerciful in forgiving those who have transgressed against us.

The point Jesus was trying to get across to Peter, was that there is no limit to the amount of times one should forgive those who are sincere in repentance.

Those who are *heartless* in forgiveness as this fellow and shamefully unreasonable in their conduct—will be treated with the same measure. Jesus cautioned: **"For with what judgment ye judge, ye shall be judged: and with what measure ye mete, it shall be measured to you again"** (Matt. 7:2).

THE PARABLE OF THE LOWEST SEAT AT THE FEAST

As he put forth a parable to those which were bidden, when he marked how they chose out the chief rooms; saying unto them, When thou art bidden of any man to a wedding, sit not down in the highest room; lest a more honourable man than thou be bidden of him: And he that bade thee and him come and say to thee, Give this man place; and thou begin with shame to take the lowest room.

But when thou art bidden, go and sit down in the lowest room; that when he that bade thee cometh, he may say unto thee, Friend, go up higher: then shalt thou have worship in the presence of them that sit at meat with thee. For whosoever exalteth himself shall be abased; and he that humbleth himself shall be exalted (Lk. 14:7-11).

The gist of this parable is that HUMILITY is better than *selfseeking assertiveness* for the spiritual advancement in God's government.

Jesus remarked over and over that the humble shall be *exalted,* but those who *exalt* themselves will be *abased*! The meek publican rather than the supercilious Pharisee was just in

God's eyes. Those who debase themselves even as little children, will be the greatest in the Kingdom of heaven (Matt. 18:4).

It will be the "meek" who will inherit the earth (Matt. 5:5). They will attain positions of exaltation and grandeur being kings and priests in God's copious Kingdom (Rev. 20:6; 5:10).

What a reward of serendipity!

THE PARABLE OF THE GREAT SUPPER

Then said he unto him, A certain man made a great supper, and bade many: And sent his servant at supper time to say to them that were bidden, Come; for all things are now ready. And they all with one consent began to make excuse...And the servant said, Lord, it is done as thou hast commanded, and yet there is room. And the lord said unto the servant, Go out into the highways and hedges, and compel them to come in, that my house may be filled. For I say unto you, That none of those men which were bidden shall taste of my supper (Lk. 14:15-24).

This parable has overtones from the preceding teaching of *humility* and *kindness* to the unfortunate (verses 7-15). Jesus had just admonished His disciples to bid those who were poor, maimed and blind to sup rather than those who could repay them. Then He gave the parable of *The Great Supper*.

This parable sensitizes the Christian's calling. It is the poor, blind, maimed and foolish of this world *spiritually,* that God has called to confound the so-called "wise" (1 Cor. 2:25-27).

Jesus then asserts several reasons why people have neglected their calling to sup with Him in His Kingdom (vs. 15). Our soon ruling King lists three excuses people would give which coincides with the parable of *The Sower*.

The cares of this world (vs. 18), the deceitfulness of riches (vs. 19), and the pleasures of this world (vs. 20), all *choke* God's Word (Matt. 13:22).

Originally, God's calling was to His own nation of Israel. But when they REJECTED Him, Gentiles from the *highways* and byways of this world were allowed to be invited to the marriage supper (verses 21-24).

In a *typical* fulfillment of this parable, ancient Israel represents the first call or invitation given. They of course rejected their invitation, and it was then given to the spiritually maimed of this world *(symbolic* of Gentile sinners).

Jesus concludes this parable by describing the responsibility of a discipleship in (verses 25-35). Here in parabolic, Jesus makes us fully aware of the need to be willing to forsake *all* our worldly affluence to be His disciple (vs. 33).

We must be willing to SACRIFICE family, friends, job, wealth, *anything that could stand in our way* from entering the Kingdom of God! Finally, Jesus says to consider all of this, or "count the cost" (vs. 28), before we embark on this hard and difficult—yet truly rewarding journey!

Can we see the light at the end of the tunnel—or as the saying goes, has the cream in our cup gone sour? For those who are blessed to make it into God's Kingdom, like a caterpillar, they shall be *transformed* into a beautiful butterfly!

THE PARABLE OF UNPROFITABLE SERVANTS

> *But which of you, having a servant plowing or feeding cattle, will say unto him by and by, when he is come from the field, Go and sit down to meat? And will not rather say unto him, Make ready wherewith I may sup, and gird thyself, and serve me, till I have eaten and drunken; and afterward thou shalt eat and drink? Doth he thank that servant because he did the things that were commanded him? I trow [think] not. So likewise ye, when ye shall have done all those things which are commanded you, say, We are unprofitable servants: we have done that which was our duty to do (Lk. 17:7-10).*

The parable of *The Unprofitable Servant* is the result of a conversation Jesus had with His disciples on FAITH. Previously, Jesus had given His ardent students admonition in forgiving their brother seven times seven (vs. 4). Peter had asked this question before: **"How often must we forgive" and Jesus replied,** "seventy times seven" (Matt. 18:21-35).

Realizing their *unwillingness* to forgive was connected to a lack of faith—Jesus further elaborated by giving the example of uprooting a sycamine tree and replanting it in the sea (vs. 6). The apostles wanted to *increase* their faith but just didn't know how (vs. 5).

When Jesus gave the masterful story of *The Unprofitable Servant*, He explains that the first place to start building *faith* is through *humility*. Through this very thought provoking parable, Jesus poignantly shows that most people treat their *servants* like dogs. However, a true *servant* of Christ must wait on others, rather than be waited upon. This example was expressed by the great story teller in Matthew 23:11: **"But he that is greatest among you shall be your servant."**

Through the twin virtues of *humility* and *obedience*, a deep abiding *faith* may be acquired!

Profitable servants should be exercising the virtues of humility, obedience, and faith out of LOVE—not out of obligation. It is true we have been purchased by the precious blood of Jesus Christ and are therefore His slaves. As His bondman we should not expect any reward for performing our *responsibility*. But if we serve out of genuine love and not out of mere *duty* for reward, a great prize awaits us! If we "bite the bullet" of *humility* and step out of the boat in faith—a great serendipitous reward awaits us simply because we have a just and loving Master!

THE PARABLE OF THE POUNDS

A certain nobleman went into a far country to receive for himself a kingdom, and to return. And he called his ten servants, and delivered them ten pounds, and said unto them, occupy till I come. But his citizens hated him, and sent a message after him, saying, We will not have this man reign over us. And it came to pass, that when he was returned, having received the kingdom, then he commanded these servants to be called unto him, to whom he had given the money, that he might know how much every man had gained by trading (Lk.19:13-27).

The parable of *The Talents* in (Matthew 25) teaches us that each of us humanly has a certain amount of *human or physical ability*—that will determine what our reward will be in the Kingdom. The parable of *The Pounds* informs us that some of us have the same amount of talent. However, we are not in SPIRITUAL COMPETITION for higher rewards! Each individual has a specific place in God's Kingdom.

Paul made this crystal clear in 1 Corinthians 3:8-9, when he said: **"And every man shall receive *his own reward* according to his own labor. For we are laborers together with God: Ye are God's husbandry, ye are God's building."** Read that again! Our reward is based upon the individual *labor* we Christians personally perform!

But what labor is God doing in us that we must help? God is building CHARACTER in us personally. The ministry establishes the foundation of this *character* building by getting us in contact with Christ (verses 10-11). We then can build *character* of a certain value on this foundation (vs. 12). These values *symbolically* range from gold, silver, and precious stones, to wood, hay, or stubble.

Spiritually speaking, each of us is given a certain material in the form of "talent" to build this *character* from. But if all we are given to build with is wood; then we must build with wood! We have to start with what God gives us as our talent, or physical abilities!

People who have the same talent or physical abilities and increase their character more than their equals—will be given different levels of reward as the parable of *The Pounds* indicates. Yet, it is evident that if you give a specific city to one man, no other man can be given that particular city.

Since there can be no competition for rewards—God assigns each person a particular labor, using a particular material, in a particular quantity, with a specific amount of talent available to do the job. In other words, each of us has a UNIQUE LABOR to do in order to inherit our reward. We then inherit a specific position in the Kingdom based on our completion of the unique job assigned to us at the start.

A good analogy is that of two men each given individual houses to build for *two different* sums of money, rather than two men racing to see who can build his house the fastest in competition for the most pay.

Christ is in heaven preparing a specific place of residence or responsibility for each Christian (Jn. 14:1-3). Remember, each of us receives his *own* reward. This has the connotation of individual ownership of an individual reward. That's why when some of the wedding guests failed to show up, they had to be directly replaced by going out into the streets and get newcomers to the wedding! (Matt. 22:2-14).

Here's another way of looking at how our reward is determined. Let's imagine a system of rank in the Kingdom from one to one-hundred where each man has been assigned his position in advance. Suppose the 50th man in the ranking system then fails to make it into the Kingdom. You do not merely eliminate the position for the Kingdom. Neither do you promote number 49 up to the 50th position—because you would have to promote everyone below number 49 up a notch.

This principle would cause everyone to hope that people assigned to be above them would somehow fail. That way number 49 could conceivably be promoted to the number one position over the spiritually dead bodies of those originally above him. Instead, when one Christian fails, God merely brings in an outsider or someone with equal talent or ability—and assigns the open position to him. This eliminates competition completely!

Judged according to our Works

The first principle of judgment is that "we shall be judged according to our works." Peter exhorts Christians:

> **And if ye call on the Father, who without respect of persons judgeth** *according to every man's work*, **pass the time of your sojourning here in fear (1 Pet. 1:17).**

And Jesus spoke these piercing words:

> **For the Son of man shall come in the glory of his Father with his angels; and then he shall reward every man according to his works (Matt. 16:27).** This principle is repeated many times in the New Testament. See (Rom. 2:16; 1 Cor. 3:8; Jas. 2:14; Rev. 2:23; 11:18; 20:12).

Our "works" means our "way of life"—our Christian overcoming, growing, serving—or lack of it. Our "works" also includes our part in helping do the Work of God today.

THE PARABLE OF THE TALENTS

The second principle of judgment is explained in the parable of "The Talents" given in (Matthew 25 and Luke 19). Jesus explained:

> *For the kingdom of heaven is as a man traveling into a far country, who called his own servants, and delivered unto them his goods. And unto one he gave five talents, to another two, and to another one; to every man according to his several ability; and straightway took his journey. Then he that had received the five talents went and traded with the same, and made them other five talents. And likewise he that had received two, he also gained other two (Matt. 25: 14-17).*

Notice that the quantities were not equal. The amounts were given according to each servant's ability. The Greek word translated "talent" is *talanton*, which was a measure by which gold or silver was weighed. These units of money *picture* spiritual gifts. God knows some have more hereditary ability, aptitudes, personality or physical strengths than others. Some also have had more education and better opportunities.

The servant who was given "five talents" doubled his spiritual stock-in-trade. Likewise, although the man with two produced less in number than the one with five, he also doubled what he started with. He did as well in proportion to his ability.

Notice how fair God is. Even though each servant was originally given an amount based on his natural abilities, both of the first two servants grew 100 percent. Christ therefore puts both essentially on an equal level in rewarding them. The Bible here reveals the principle that God will judge us according to how well we do with what we have to work with.

This parable reveals that each servant who is faithful "over a few things"—that is, over his or her limited abilities and opportunities of this life—will be rewarded with rulership over "many things" when Christ returns (vss. 21;23).

Christ will not establish world rule until He has first trained His assistants. God will entrust the incomprehensibly great powers of His ruling Family only to those who, in this human life, obeyed Him and learned to properly control the small powers we all have at our disposal. God wants to know that we will use His incredible power in love and self-control and for the good of all those under our authority.

We prepare to responsibly rule for the good of ourselves and others in God's kingdom by learning to better manage the affairs in our control today—no matter how small they may be. There are many chances to grow right on our job, at school or in the home—in whatever our circumstances.

The words "traded with" in the original Greek language imply "working with" or "using." Jesus continued: **"After a long time the lord of those servants cometh, and reckoneth with them" (vs. 19).**

When Christ returns, He will call all of us to Him to find out how much we have grown or increased the "talents" He has given us. To those who have used and increased their God-given abilities, He will say: **"Well done, thou good and faithful servant: thou hast been faithful over a few things, I will make thee ruler over many things: enter thou into the joy of thy lord" (vs. 21).**

The servant who did not use or develop his one "talent" made excuses and said: **"I was afraid, and went and hid your talent in the earth: lo, there thou hast that is thine" (vs, 25).** The servant *knew* Christ expected him to grow and bear fruit (vs. 24), but he was lazy and didn't do it.

In Luke's account of this same parable, Jesus gives this unprofitable servant his dreadful reward:

> **Out of thine own mouth *will I judge thee*, thou wicked servant. Thou knewest that I was an austere man, taking up that I laid not down, and reaping that I did not sow... And he said unto them that stood by, take from him the pound, and give it to him that hath ten pounds....For I say unto you, that unto every one which hath shall be given; and from him that hath not, even**

that he hath shall be taken away from him (Lk. 19:22,24,26).

Simply put, this principle of judgment is: **We shall be judged** *according to what we do with what we have been given.* Christ will consider everything when He judges us—our heredity, environment, upbringing, educational opportunities, etc. Everyone has different abilities and varying amounts of education.

Some have inherited more "talents" than others. Some have had better and more opportunities in life. This is why Christ said: **"For unto whomsoever much is given, of him shall be much required..." (Lk. 12:48).**

Christ will judge each one of us according to what we have accomplished with all we have been given. But if we don't grow at all—we will be rejected and our reward given to someone who did overcome and grew spiritually (Matt. 25: 29-30).

Overcoming Environment

Humankind is a procrastinator of his environment—but God has put a built in mechanism into our brain that makes us act when the need arises. The energy crises is a perfect example!

The human mind has a potential reserve to be taped that is utterly unique. In fact, it has been said that the best minds in the world only use approximately 10% of their brain capacity—because that's all we need now!

In order to grow spiritually, *character* must be exercised through experience, and overcoming ones environment can help provide this vital spiritual nutrient.

Joseph in Egypt during a famine is a perfect example of one overcoming his environment by drawing upon his spiritual resources. Joseph accepted this hostile environment he was placed in by his brothers, and became head over the chief bodyguard. Then when he was arrested, he became chief jailer, and second only to the Pharaoh of Egypt.

Christians can learn from Joseph's example. We don't need a new environment to live in—we need to learn how to survive in the one we have! Should we be thrown in a river and can't swim—we must learn how to swim instead of screaming and drowning!

There is a story of a woman who survived in a concentration camp while most others died. This woman's will to live was coupled with wisdom. Because she wasn't famished when she entered the camp, she sold her food to the guards for razor blades. Then, later when she was hungry, she resold her razor blades for food! She lived!

Does our great God know what He is doing by allowing us to live in ghettos, among poor families, with uneducated parents, alcoholic parents, etc? The answer is a resounding yes!

God is not putting the horse before the cart! He is not giving us the best possible environment to live in yet. We must prove to Him that we are capable to get along in whatever lot in life we are given. Christians must use the ways and laws of our great God to exist in a contented state of mind! Then, one day, our benevolent God will provide a most rewarding environment to live in for all eternity!

Our reward based on Service

Jesus said to His disciples in determining their spiritual reward: **"Whosoever will be great(est) among you [in authority] let him be your minister [servant]" (Matt. 20:26).**

Any position in God's future Kingdom, will be based upon the execution of our natural abilities in the form of SERVICE to others. Future rewards will be given in the form of greater opportunities to serve others. Again, Jesus proclaims this truth: **"...for whether is greater [who is the better servant], he that sitteth at meat, or he that serveth [the meat]? Is not he that sitteth at meat? [that's what most would say], but I am among you as he that** *serveth...***" (Lk. 22:27-30).**

What Jesus is emphasizing here through His example—is that the server will have the *greatest* position in His soon coming government!

Each of us must develop his or her natural god-given talents into serving God's Church and humankind. This may be on a small scale or a grand scale depending upon our talents.

However, in order for us to make sure we are developing our natural abilities—we need to build the character of gold, silver and precious stones that will not be destroyed like wood, hay and stubble in a fire [trials] (1 Cor. 3:12-15). Every man's work or *life* will be made manifest to see what kind of character we are made of!

The surest way to build the character *symbolic* of these non-combustible materials, is to build our house on the foundation of Jesus Christ as Peter reiterated: **"Behold, I lay in Sion a chief corner stone, elect,** *precious***: and he that believeth on him [Christ] shall not be confounded" (1 Pet. 2:6).**

Belief in Christ is fundamental to building strong character, but so is FAITH, notice: **"That the trial of your** *faith***, being much** *more precious than gold* **that perisheth, though it be tried with fire..." (1 Pet. 1:7).**

These two ingredients are absolutely necessary in building the kind of character that will enhance our service toward others—and ultimately determine our reward in God's Kingdom.

But there is one more vital constituent that growing Christians must have to become great servants of Christ: **"And now abideth faith, hope, love, these three: but the** *greatest* **of these is** *love***" (1 Cor. 13:13).**

Love is the all-encompassing spiritual adhesive that must hold our spiritual house together. We must LIVE to serve others! That's why Christ said, **"...the greatest commandments are to** *love* **God with all our heart and** *love* **our neighbor as ourself" (Matt. 22:37-39).**

The apostle John placed love above all else in character development as he exhorted: **"Herein is our love made** *perfect***, that we may have boldness in the day of judgment because...***there is no fear in love***, but perfect love casteth out fear" (1 Jn. 4:17,18).**

Without belief or *faith* in Christ—we might not desire to serve others. Void of *love* we might be fearful of serving others. With *faith* and *love* as our superstructure atop the foundation of Christ—these lasting and solid character traits depicted by the building materials of gold, silver and precious stones—will endure the flames of the most intense heat!

This is the kind of character that is needed to be a great servant of Christ, and to receive a tremendous reward under His government!

The expression "first come, first serve" will certainly apply to those God has first called and chosen to be "firstfruits" in His Kingdom. Jesus admonishes us to start serving now and enjoy it—because we will be His servants for all eternity!

Judged as we judge others

In His renowned sermon on the Mount, Jesus made a seemingly paradoxical statement. He said: **"Judge not, that you be not judged" (Matt. 7:1).** Then a few verses later He continued, **"You shall know them by their fruits."**

Certainly, the latter statement would take some form of judgment and therefore contradict the first statement. If this were valid, these scriptures would contradict one another. Obviously, there is an answer—and it is complimentary, not contradictory!

When Jesus said, **"Judge not, that you be not judged",** He was referring to judgment in the sense of *condemnation* or pronouncement of guilt. The original Greek word translated "judge" means "condemnation." Matthew 7:1 should therefore read: **"Condemn not that you be not condemned."**

THE PARABLE OF THE VINEYARD

For the kingdom of heaven is like unto a man that is an householder, which went out early in the morning to hire labourers into his vineyard. And when he had agreed with the labourers for a penny a day, he sent them into his vineyard (Matt. 20:1-16).

This parable has *double meaning* and applies to both Church dispensations. The Jews are represented in this parable as those hired very early in the day [Old Testament dispensation] and began to murmur when the Gentiles were called later in God's plan.

The Time Factor

The parable of *The Laborers in the Vineyard* shows that God will use the factor of time as yet another parameter in determining our reward (Matt 20:1-6).

In this painting of words, all Christians are likened unto LABORERS in a vineyard. The householder hired some laborers "early in the morning." He agreed with them to pay each a penny a day. Later, others were hired "at the third hour" (9:00 a.m.), and still others were hired at the "sixth" (12:00 noon) and "ninth" (3:00 p.m.) hour of the day. Then the householder promised to reward [whatsoever is right] to each of the hired hands.

But there were some that weren't hired till late in the afternoon "at the eleventh hour."

When the householder payed those that had worked all day the same wage as those that worked only the last hour, they thought they deserved more because they worked a full day. Those that had been hired earlier in the day murmured and complained "against the goodman of the house" because they thought they got a raw deal (vs. 11).

They said,

> **These last have wrought but one hour, and thou hast made them equal unto us, which have borne the burden heat of the day. But he answered one of them, and said, Friend, I do no wrong: didst not thou agree with me for a penny? Take that thine is, and go thy way: I will give unto this last, even as unto thee. Is it not lawful for me to do what I will with mine own? Is thine eye evil, because I am good? (verses 12-15).**

How does this parable apply to modern-day Christians? The "day" mentioned in this parable represents the "life span" of each Christian. Some are called into God's Church [His vineyard] early in life, or "early in the morning." Others are called at mid-life (noon) while yet others are called at the end of their life (sunset).

This parable teaches us that God expects more out of those called *earlier* in life than those called at the *end* of their life. There are good reasons for this and shows God's JUSTICE and mercy. A person called to understand God's truths early in life—has the advantage of developing their minds and bodies more properly, and therefore more is expected of them.

One called later in life—who through bad living habits due to spiritual blindness—and has destroyed his health and mind—will have a harder time overcoming. May God help us to use every golden drop of time wisely and to His advantage!

Equality

As shown by the previous parables, we are not equal in this physical life in talent or natural abilities. We are not equal in music, sports or intelligence. But does this mean that God is unfair with us? Why were we born in America instead of India or Africa? Has God been unfair with them?

Throughout the Bible there are many examples of where one might reason that God has been unjust to certain nations and individuals.

Inspired with the mind of God, the apostle Paul points out very plainly in (Romans 9), why God has done things that most people would consider unfair and has not treated everyone equally.

Paul shows that God chose Isaac to be the recipient of the promise made to Abraham, and didn't even consider Abraham's other son Ishmael (vs.7). Paul explains further that when Isaac's wife Rebecca conceived, God knew that her elder son would serve the younger son before they were born (verses 10-11).

We read of the blessings given to each of the tribes of Israel in (Genesis 49) and must conclude they were not equal.

God will give rewards to individuals in the Kingdom that are not equal as already shown through the parables.

The apostle Paul writes concerning God's equality system in Romans 9:14:

> **What shall we say then? Is there unrighteousness with God? God forbid! (vs.15): For He saith unto Moses, I will have mercy on whom I will have mercy, and I will have compassion on whom I will have compassion.**

God has shown us in His Word that we cannot judge His equality system based on man's way of thinking for, Neither are His ways our ways, or—**"His thoughts are not man's thoughts" (Isa. 55:8).** We must also heed the Words of our Savior that "...to whom much is given, much will be demanded" (Lk. 12:48).

The parable of *The Talents* in (Matthew 25) and *Pounds* in (Luke 19) shows us that God has given each of us different physical and mental talents to be developed in this life. Most of us think this is unfair in itself. But besides this, if those who have been given little talent and don't even develop this—it will be taken from them and given to the one who has more talent and is developing it.

The parable of the man working out in the field all day to earn the same amount of money as the man who worked only the last hour—shows again that God's equality system is altogether different from ours.

It has been said by man's standards that the only place we are really equal is the grave. However, even this is not true since those that have been unfaithful in developing their talents—may not be resurrected out of their graves for the first resurrection!

The feeling of wanting to be equal does not stem from God, but rather from Satan who wanted to equal with God (Isa. 14:12).

Summary

There are *four factors* to be considered in this overall equation that determines our spiritual reward: 1) works or attitude; 2) ability or human character; 3) judgment of others based on acquired knowledge, and 4) time.

Human character is the natural physical talent that we have inherited from birth. Knowledge is something we are not born with but can be acquired bit by bit over a period of time. Spiritual knowledge is yet another thing. It can only be imparted by *God's Holy Spirit*. Our attitude is how we accept or reject God's truths.

The parables of the *Laborers in the Vineyard, Pounds and Talents* provides the factors God will use in judging us and determining our reward.

The parable of the *Talents* shows that we are not all born equal. At birth each person receives different talents and abilities from those of every other individual. Then, at conversion, God adds spiritual talents and gifts according to each man's natural abilities. There are many biblical examples in God's Word such as Moses, Solomon, Peter, Paul and the disciples, that show how God enhanced these men's natural ability.

The parable of the *Pounds* reveals that, of those who are of equal talents and abilities, some will use their God given talents more diligently than others. As a result, they will receive greater responsibility in God's Kingdom. The one who multiplies his pound over five times will be given authority over five cities.

The parable of *The Laborers* discloses that God will also take into account the factor of time—the time given after our conversion to apply His truths. Those who are given more time will be held accountable for having overcome and grown more— and for having produced more in God's service.

Remember, many battles are lost in a war that's won! God doesn't judge us by where we *are*, but by where we're going!

Whether our reward in God's Kingdom is great or small depends on us! It depends on our works. It depends on how much effort we go through in OVERCOMING and growing spiritually. It depends on whether we always willingly let Christ *mold* us into His character image or whether we tend to resist change. Notice Paul's advice in Romans 12:2:

> **Don't let the world around you squeeze you into its own mold, but let God remake you so that your whole attitude of mind is changed. Thus, you will prove in practice that the will of God is good, acceptable to him and perfect** *(Phillips Modern English* **translation, paraphrased).**

Each servant's reward will be *directly proportional* to the degree of his growth—his spiritual overcoming and development! But let us also remember that salvation is given at any hour of the day equally.

THE PARABLE OF THE FRIEND AT MIDNIGHT

And He said unto them, Which of you shall have a friend, and shall go unto him at midnight, and say unto him, Friend, lend me three loaves; For a friend of mine in his journey is come to me, and I have nothing to set before him? And he from within shall answer and say, Trouble me not: the door is now shut, and my children are with me in bed; I cannot rise and give thee. I say unto you, Though he will not rise and give him, because he is his friend, yet because of his importunity he will rise and give him as many as he needeth (Lk. 11: 5-8).

After Jesus delivered the outline for prayer, He uttered the parable of *The Friend at Midnight*. The purpose of this parable was for the sole purpose of teaching that God is always there to hear our prayers—even at midnight! God will especially honor *patient* and *persistent* prayer. Jesus commended *importunity* [shamelessness; persisting in the face of all that seemed reasonable, and refusing to take a denial, J.F.B.] in prayer.

Learning to pray without ceasing (1 Thess. 5:17), especially in times of despair or when there is delay in answer, is indeed a lifetime study.

Jesus continued to exhort Christians to: **"...*Ask*, and it shall be given you: *seek* and ye shall find; *knock*, and it shall be opened unto you. For everyone that asketh receiveth; and he that seeketh findeth; and to him that knocketh it shall be opened" (verses 9-10).** This takes PERSISTENCE!

THE PARABLE OF THE UNJUST JUDGE

And He spake a parable unto them to this end, that men ought always to pray, and not to faint; Saying, There was in a city a judge, which feared not God, neither regarded man: And there was a widow in that city; and she came unto him, saying, Avenge me of mine adversary. And he would not for a while: but afterward he said within himself,

Though I fear not God, nor regard man; Yet because this widow troubleth me, I will avenge her, lest by her continual coming she weary me. And the Lord said, Hear what the unjust judge saith. And shall not God avenge his own elect, which cry day and night unto him, though he bear long with them? I tell you that he will avenge them speedily. Nevertheless when the son of man cometh, shall he find faith on the earth? (Lk. 18:1-8).

The parable of *The Unjust Judge* is akin to that of *The Friend at Midnight* and teaches that God does hear the prayers of His people—especially when they are "persistent." Notice how this widow came continuously [persistence] before this judge who finally gave her *satisfaction* (vs. 5).

Jesus tells us through this colorful word painting that our heavenly Father [the most just Judge of all], will hear and answer the PERSISTENT prayers of the faithful. God indeed cares for us—but we must *never* lose faith in Him! This parable also has a *dual* meaning. The widow is *symbolic* of the Old Testament Church who is temporarily *widowed* from her husband, Christ. Jesus asked this question upon His return—**"Will I find faith on the earth?"** Persevering, consistent, persistent prayer is the exercise of the *faithful* that will enhance our faith!

Meanwhile, we must *trust* in God to bring vindication or justice upon predicaments that befall us. If we are persecuted for righteousness sake—our merciful God will deliver us! How much better for us to have a God of love and justice on our side—than a vengeful judge!

The widow in this parable is also a *portrait* of Israel suffering at the hand of her enemies, only to be forgiven by a merciful God! Old and New Testament prophecies declare vengeance upon the enemies of Israel!

Enemies of Zionism will say with a chorus of hate-ridden voices, **"Come, and let us cut them off from being a nation"** (Ps. 83:4; Zech 1:5, 14:2; Joel 3:2).

This widow's vengeance was repaid as will Israel's by the God of love and vengeance! (Isa. 35:4; 61:2; Lk. 4:18-19; Rom. 12:19).

Chapter Ten

THE FUTILITY OF RICHES

THE PARABLE OF MOTHS AND THIEVES

Lay not up for yourselves treasures upon earth, where moth and rust doth corrupt, and where thieves break through and steal: But lay up for yourselves treasures in heaven, where neither moth nor rust doth corrupt, and where thieves do not break through nor steal: For where your treasure is there will your heart be also (Matt. 6:19-21).

Through the analogy of a *moth*, *rust* and *thieves*, the Master Story Teller graphically paints a bleak picture of the utter FUTILITY to acquire earthly possessions.

Earthly possessions are only TEMPORARY and Jesus suggests how perishable they are by moths and rust. Moths and rust both attack perishable items; rendering them useless. Moths eat away at physical things while rust corrodes them—decay and worthlessness is the end result!

Thieves, while not corrupters of perishable possessions, accomplish the same purpose. All three are silent robbers of material wealth!

Jesus exhorts Christians to seek the ETERNAL RICHES of His Kingdom, **"rich in good works" (1 Tim. 6:18),** and **"rich in faith" (James 2:5);** and be partakers of **"unsearchable riches" (Eph. 3:8,16).** These are not perishable riches but *heavenly treasures!*

The parable of *Lazarus and the Rich Man* (Lk. 16); *The Rich Young Man* (Matt. 19:16); *The Talents* (Matt. 25:14); *The Pounds* (Lk. 19:13-27); *and Laborers in the Vineyard* (Matt. 20:1-16)—all show spiritual lessons through the proper use of money.

Jesus said it would be easier for a camel to go through the eye hole of a needle—than it would be for a rich man to enter the Kingdom of God (Matt. 19:24).

Was Jesus against having wealth or treasures in this life? Absolutely not! Having possessions or money are not sinful in themselves—it is the *improper* use of them that make them a curse. Merely hoarding up treasures or money for one's own profit or pleasure, instead of sharing them with the needy is an abomination to God!

In fact, there are countless proverbs which exhort Christians to share their wealth with those less fortunate as we have read under, "God, the Financial Advisor."

God's Word exhorts Christians to be *content* in this life regardless of the financial state they are in (Phil. 4:11). They should not TRUST in riches (1 Tim. 6:17-19), realizing, **"A man's life consisteth not in the abundance of things. For what does it profit a man if he gain the whole world and lose his soul?" (Lk. 12:15).**

Instead, Christians are encouraged to, **"Seek *first* the kingdom of God and all these things will be added unto you" (Matt.6:33).** Seek *faith*, *love*, *patience* and *meekness* instead of wealth (1 Tim. 6:3-11). Seek *wisdom* rather than gold and silver or rubies (Prov. 8:10,11,19). With wisdom, King David a man after God's own heart wrote, "A little that a righteous man hath is better than the riches of many wicked" (Psalm 37:16).

Positively, it is definitely not wrong or evil to have wealth or riches. But one should be content with what he has—and should use what wealth God has blessed him with wisely—by giving to the poor and for God's work!

One should not set his heart on wealth in this life—but

THE FUTILITY OF RICHES

rather on wisdom, understanding, faith, love, patience, meekness, virtuousness, and purity! These are the incorruptible treasures of heaven! We Christians must remember the words of our Savior that, we cannot serve both God and mammon (Matt. 6:24). There is a cliché that says, though the toilet may be covered with silverplate—it's still a toilet! And if people only appear to be Christian on the surface—they are only as tinkling brass if they have not charity! (1 Cor. 13:1).

THE PARABLE OF LAZARUS AND THE RICH MAN

There was a certain rich man [Jesus meant there really was] who was clothed in purple and fine linen, and fared sumptuously every day...there was a certain beggar named Lazarus, which was laid at his gate full of sores, and desiring to be fed with the crumbs which fell from the rich man's table: moreover the dogs came and licked his sores...and it came to pass, that the beggar died, and was carried by the angels into Abraham's bosom: the rich man also died and was buried; and in hell he lift up his eyes, being in torments, and seeth Abraham afar off, and Lazarus in his bosom. And he cried and said, Father Abraham, have mercy on me, and send Lazarus, that he may dip the tip of his finger in water, and cool my tongue; for I am tormented in this flame...(Lk. 16:19-31).

Observe, this beggar was carried into Abraham's bosom! What exactly is a bosom? If we can find out what a "bosom" is—in this case Abraham's—we will know where the beggar was taken.

Any dictionary will tell you that a bosom is an embrace or loving or affectionate enclosure; a loving embrace by the arms of one person about another; an intimate relationship.

Lazarus then, was carried into an intimate relationship with Abraham. Lazarus is pictured here as a Gentile who received salvation, by becoming Christ's follower or disciple. Notice, **"And if ye be Christ's then are ye Abraham's seed [children],** and heirs according to the promise" (Gal. 3:29).

Through Christ, Gentiles may become Abraham's children. Through faith we all become "the children of Abraham" (Gal. 3:7).

God actually made *two* separate promises to Abraham, notice: **"Now from thy kindred and from thy father's house, unto a land that I will show thee: and I will make thee a great nation...And in thee shall all the families of the earth be blessed" (Gen. 12:1-3).**

There are *two* separate and distinct promises God made to Abraham: **1) the birthright promise, of national wealth and prosperity and 2) the sceptre promise of salvation by grace: "...And in thee shall all the families of the earth be blessed."**

God promised Abraham that all of the families of the earth would be blessed because of his seed which culminated in the one seed Jesus Christ (Gen. 22:18; Gal. 3:8,16).

The promise God gave to Abraham was the land of Palestine, on this earth. The beggar, like all Christians are *heirs* to the promise to Abraham. A *heir* is not yet an inheritor or possessor of the promise.

In (Acts 7), Stephen, the first Christian martyr, speaks of Abraham:

> **And he said, Men, brethren, and fathers, hearken; The God of glory appeared, unto our Father Abraham...and said unto him, Get thee out of thy country, and from thy kindred, and come into THE LAND which I will show thee. Then came he out of the land of the Chaldeans...into this land, wherein ye now dwell (Palestine). And He gave him none inheritance in it...yet He promised that he would give it to him for a possession, and to his seed after him...(vss. 3-5).**

This truth is also stated in Hebrew 11:8-13:

> **By faith Abraham, when he was called to go out into a place which he should after receive for an inheritance, obeyed...By faith he sojourned in the land of promise, as in a strange country,**

> dwelling in tabernacles with Isaac and Jacob, the heirs with him of the same promise...These all died in faith, **NOT HAVING RECEIVED THE PROMISES,** but having seen them afar off...

In (John 8:52) we read, **"Abraham is dead."** Notice it! Abraham was not up in heaven—but dead in the days of Christ!

Jesus said Abraham would receive the promises, including eternal life, through the RESURRECTION:

> **But as touching the resurrection of the dead, have ye not read that which was spoken unto you by God, saying, I am the God of Abraham, and the God of Isaac and the God of Jacob? God is not the God of the dead, but of the living (Matt. 22:31-32).**

Jesus told the Pharisees they would see Abraham in the Kingdom because Abraham, now dead, will be RESURRECTED from the dead (Lk. 13:28).

Conclusively, Abraham is dead and so is the beggar! Both will receive the promises at the resurrection when Christ returns to set up His glorious Kingdom, notice:

> **When the Son of man shall come in His glory, and all the holy angels with Him, then shall he sit upon the throne of his glory: And before him shall be gathered all nations: and he shall separate them one from another, as a shepherd divideth his sheep from the goats: And he shall set the sheep on his right hand, but the goats on the left. Then shall the King say unto them on his right hand, Come, ye blessed of my Father, inherit the kingdom prepared for you from the foundation of the world (Matt. 25:31-34).**

Carried by Angels

Luke's account makes it crystal clear that Lazarus was to be carried by angels into Abraham's bosom. We know that Lazarus was not carried up to heaven as many suppose—but is awaiting the promises—at the return of Christ when the resurrection will occur! Many believe he is in a state of sleep.

This state of sleep has been termed "sole sleep" and there are many scriptures which support it such as (Ecc. 9:5, 12:7).

We have just read where angels will be coming with Christ upon His return to the earth. In (Matthew 24:31) we read more of what these angels will do. Christ shall **"...send his angels with a great sound of a trumpet, and they shall gather together His elect from the four winds"**—out of their graves in a RESURRECTION! Lazarus and Abraham are to be carried by the angels through the air to meet Christ, at His return, and to be with Abraham, in the intimate relationship of father and son.

There is no doubt as to how the Bible uses the word "bosom." In (Isaiah 40:11) God shows he will care for His people as a shepherd cares for his sheep, which He will carry "in his bosom."

Jesus says He was in the bosom of the Father (John 1:18), enjoying the Father's blessings and close relationship.

To be in one's bosom is to have that one's love and protection, and share his blessings and inheritance. So it will be at the RESURRECTION that Lazarus will be in Abraham's bosom.

The Rich Man in "Hell"

What did Jesus mean when He said **"...the rich man also died, and was buried; and in hell he lift up his eyes, being in torments, and seeth Abraham afar off, and Lazarus in his bosom"? (Lk. 16:22-23).**

The first thing we need to realize is that the Greek word used for "hell" in this verse is *hades* which means "grave" or "tomb."

Jesus said, **"When the rich man lifts up his eyes he will see Lazarus and Abraham."** We have already shown that Lazarus and Abraham will not be together untill the resurrection—this is when the rich man will open up his eyes and see them.

Daniel speaks of the resurrection of the just, and of the unjust, notice:

> **And many of them that sleep [their eyes are closed while sleeping] in the dust of the earth**

> **[their graves, buried—in 'hades'], shall awake [lift up their eyes] some to everlasting life [Lazarus and Abraham] and some to shame and everlasting contempt (Dan. 12:2).**

Concerning this time, Jesus said:

> **...the hour is coming, in which all that are in the graves shall hear His voice, and shall come forth: they that have done good, unto THE RESURRECTION OF LIFE: and they that have done evil [including the rich man], unto the RESURRECTION OF JUDGMENT (Jn. 5:28-29).**

Here, Jesus speaks of TWO DIFFERENT, SEPARATE RESURRECTIONS. The first resurrection will be for the righteous at Christ's coming. All through the Millennium, there will be a separation of "sheep and goats" or those who will accept Jesus and those who will not. Then will come the final resurrection of judgment to occur one thousand years later after the Millennium!

So, while Jesus in speaking about the rich man and Lazarus, did not say WHEN the rich man will open his eyes and be resurrected out of his grave. From other scriptures it appears that it will be after the Millennium.

What is this Flame?

But when the rich man is resurrected after the Millennium, he will open up his eyes—and see Lazarus and Abraham and also a "flame" which torments him. What is this flame?

Jesus spoke of the third Greek word for Hell, "ghenna" fire or "a lake of fire" that will be used to destroy the wicked. This is the second death, which will be by fire. This death is for all eternity! ETERNAL PUNISHMENT—but not ETERNAL PUNISHING!

When the rich man opens his eyes, he will see Lazarus in Abraham's bosom—his embrace. He will also see this awful flame of fire—this lake of fire which is about to destroy him forever! He becomes terrified. His mouth suddenly becomes very dry, and his tongue sticks to his mouth, The rich man cries out in mental anguish, **"Father Abraham have mercy on me, and send Lazarus, that he may dip the tip of his finger in water, and cool my tongue; for I am tormented in this flame."**

The rich man will be in a condition of WEEPING AND GNASHING OF TEETH at this time—for he knows he is about to be burned up and destroyed! Jesus said this same thing to the Pharisees in Luke 13:27-28:

> **Depart from me, ye workers of iniquity. There shall be weeping and gnashing of teeth, when ye shall see Abraham, Isaac, and Jacob, and all the prophets in the Kingdom of God, and you yourselves thrust out.**

What is the Great Gulf?

Jesus continues the story of the rich man in (verse 25) describing what Abraham would say to the rich man. That he had his reward in material things he sought and craved, instead of God's Kingdom—and because of this he is now doomed!

The "great gulf" mentioned in (verse 26) by Abraham represents IMMORTALITY and prevents the wicked from escaping death by hell fire—and also keeps the righteous from being burned!

The rich man realizes he is doomed in (verse 27) and now asks if Abraham would send Lazarus to his father's house to plead with his brothers—lest they come to his terrible fate. Abraham replied they had the writings of Moses and the prophets. But the rich man realized they would not hear these scriptures. **"Nay, Father Abraham"** he screamed, **"but if one went unto them from the dead they will repent" (vs. 30).**

The rich man knew Lazarus was RAISED FROM THE DEAD! This one statement proves that the whole experience of Lazarus and the rich man—was given by Jesus to show THE TRUTH OF THE RESURRECTION—not to teach any immediate going to "heaven" or "hell" at the instant of death!

It shows MORTALITY which dies and is DEAD—not *immortality* which never loses consciousness, and lives forever in an eternal punishing of an imaginary "hell" of Dante. We will cover "the origin of the immortal soul" in Vol. 4.

The Worm that Dieth not

In Mathew 9:44, the phrase where **their worm dieth not, and the fire is not quenched** is an allegorical expression of the fate of the wicked in which many take literally. The valley of Hinnom or Gehenna was a garbage dump outside of the city of Jerusalem, where dead bodies of animals, trash and filth were thrown into a continuous burning fire. In Old Testament times, children had been sacrificed to idols there (2 Kings 23:10). If a dead body of an animal landed on a ledge outside of the burning fires, it would be devoured by many worms or maggots which were kept alive by the constant rubbish of the dead animals and vegetable substances thrown there constantly.

But did Jesus mean these worms would live forever? Actually, these worms were maggots or larvae which develop from eggs deposited by flies. They continue for only a few days in the larvae state and then become flies which eventually die! The Greek word translated as "worm" simply means "grub or maggot." The flies like all animals will eventually die and return to dust again, not live forever as the inspired Word of God says (Eccl. 3:19-20). The same reference to worms is found in Isa. 66:24 where the worms or maggots die not, but continue to develop into flies. In Mark 9:48, when Jesus says, "Where their worm does not die and the fire is not quenched", He is quoting from Isaiah 66:24.

The nation of Israel may be seen in this parable as those, like Lazarus who refused to share their God-given blessings with the poor (Gentiles). Christ said of this ungrateful people: **"If they hear not Moses and the prophets, neither will they be persuaded though one rose from the dead. Had ye believed Moses, ye would have believed Me, for he [Moses] wrote of me" (Jn. 5:46).**

The reader is encouraged to study the scriptures in (Isa. 66:22-24; Dan. 12:1-2; Matt. 18:6-90; 25:31-41; Mk. 9:42-49; 2Thess. 1:5-10; Jude 7,13; Rev. 14:9-11; 20:10,14-15) which are the main scriptures that Christians have different opinions on Eternal life.

Soul Sleep

Although God's Word does not use the words "Soul sleep," this teaching associated with several denominations, is the belief that when a person dies, their soul "sleeps" until the time of a future resurrection. In this condition, the person is not aware or conscious.

The Bible uses different language in different places to describe what happens to us when we die. Often it refers to death as "sleep" (e.g. Ps. 1:1-3, 9:5, 12:7, 13:3; Dan. 12:2, 13; John 11:11-14; Acts 13:36; 1 Cor. 11:30; 15:6,18,20,51; 2Cor. 5:8; Matt. 17:1-8; Lk. 23:42-43; Eph. 5:14; 1 Thess. 4:13-17; Rev.6:10).

It is not our intention to prove or disprove what happens to people when they die, but to objectively allow each person decide for themselves based upon the foregoing scriptures.

THE PARABLE OF THE RICH FOOL

> *And he spake a parable unto them, saying, The ground of a certain rich man brought forth plentifully: And he thought within himself, saying, What shall I do, because I have no room where to bestow my fruits? And he said, This will I do: I will pull down my barns, and build greater; and there will I bestow all my fruits and my goods. And I will say to my soul, Soul, thou hast much goods laid up for many years; take thine ease, eat, drink, and be merry. But God said unto him, Thou fool, this night thy soul shall be required of thee: then whose shall those things be, which thou hast provided? So is he that layeth up treasure for himself, and is not rich toward God (Lk. 12:16-21).*

The Greek derivation of the word "Fool" in this parable, means "without spiritual perception" or "without mental reasoning toward carnal and spiritual things."

Despite the fact that the "rich fool" acquired his money through legitimate means [productivity of his land]—in God's eyes he was considered a foolish person (vs. 20). Why? Because his heart was on the material possessions of this *temporary* life!

Instead, he should have spent his energies on seeking God's Kingdom—which is ETERNAL!

This man's folly was that he TRUSTED in his own wealth to provide for him—rather than God! He had not thought of his eternal future, but only of the temporary enjoyment and pleasures of this existence!

Jesus counsels us not to be anxious with how we will be provided with food, clothing or shelter in this life (verses 22-23). Rather, God will take care of our physical sustenance even as the birds of the air and lilies of the field (verses 23-28). Our heavenly Father is aware of our physical needs and will provide them accordingly (vs. 30). Jesus then gave the ultimate reason for our physical life: **"...seek ye [first, emphasis mine] the kingdom of God; and all these things shall be added unto you" (vs. 31)**

The statement Jesus gave leading into this parable was: **"...take heed, and beware of *covetousness:* for a man's life consisteth not in the abundance of things which he possesseth" (vs. 15)**. Instead of seeking to "get" more sensual items for ourselves, or build "bigger barns" as the "rich fool," we should concentrate on "giving" more to others!

This is the greatest stupor of the rich and why **"the love of money is the [a] root of all evil" (1 Tim. 6:10)**. As in the parable of *Lazarus and the Rich Man,* both rich men allowed "the deceitfulness of riches" to *choke* God's way of life. The "rich fool" garnered his opulence to merely hoard things for himself, while the "rich man" lavished in his wealth. Both were wrong attitudes toward the proper use of money.

Perhaps the most glaring mistake made by both of these rich men was their ignorance and neglect of acknowledging the *source* of their prosperity. Neither one gave God thanks or credit for their accrued prosperity. Truly, **"There is a way that seemeth right unto a man, but the end thereof are the ways of death" (Prov. 14:12)**.

Many times Jesus gave pungent warnings to "rich men" who would make improper use of their inherent blessings. May God help those who are blessed with riches to take heed of the "pearls of great wisdom" in this parable! Christians who have been blessed with great wealth must take heed and not allow riches to be their Achilles' heel!

THE PARABLE OF THE UNJUST STEWARD

And he said also unto his disciples, There was a certain rich man, which had a steward; and the same was accused unto him that he had wasted his goods. And he called him, and said unto him, How is it that I hear this of thee? give an account of thy stewardship; for thou mayest be no longer steward. Then the steward said within himself,

What shall I do? for my lord taketh away from me the stewardship: I cannot dig; to beg I am ashamed. I am resolved what to do, that when I am put out of the stewardship, they may receive me into their houses. So he called every one of his lord's debtors unto him, and said unto the first, How much owest thou unto my lord? And he said, An hundred measures of oil. And he said unto him, take thy bill, and sit down quickly, and write fifty...And the lord commended the unjust steward, because he had done wisely: for the children of this world are in their generation wiser than the children of light (Lk. 16:1-8).

This parable is addressed to Jesus' disciples and contains many important lessons about God's purpose being worked out here below.

A steward [or overseer] of a wealthy man's estate was accused by the owner of "wasting his goods." Evidently this rich man's friends had informed him that his steward was involved in some improprieties. This shady character was then called on to give an account of his activities to his master. If the steward failed to satisfy this rich man in his defense—he would be fired! What was he to do?

"And the steward said within himself" [he admits his impropriety to himself only]—**"What shall I do, seeing that my lord taketh away the stewardship from me? To dig I have no strength"** (he knew he couldn't make a living at being a ditch digger), **"to beg I am ashamed"** (begging was not his cup of tea). He pondered, "how am I going to make a living to survive?" Then it came to him—**"I am resolved *what to do*, that, when I am put out of the stewardship, *they* may receive me into their own houses."**

This steward was a sharp cookie—he was now going to solve his problem with a clever idea. He was going to continue his *double dealing* with his employer's estate by writing off the rich man's debtors for a bargain. This way he would make friends with his bosses's debtors—and when he was fired, perhaps he could get a job from one of them?

This guy was a real shrewdee! These debtors couldn't refuse him, for after all, they were accomplices in this deceitful scheme of fixing the books.

When the steward was called upon by his master to give a rendering of the accounts—the rich man was impressed with the stewards "worldly ingenuity." He could find nothing wrong with the altered accounts, **"And the lord commended the steward of unrighteousness for doing wisely."** It must be noted, the "lord" here is the rich man of the estate and not Jesus Christ. The steward was not commended for wasting the estate, but rather for his shrewd, *worldly* business practice. He had solved his problem by buying friends!

The Foolish Things of this World

What did Jesus mean when he said, **"...for the children of this world [margin, 'age'] are in their generation wiser than the children of light" (vs. 8)?**

From the parable of *The Unjust Steward* just given to His pupils—Jesus is telling us that there is a kind of *worldly wisdom* that nonbelievers have [the children of this world] that the children of light [believers] do not possess. These people are by nature wiser in certain respects than the ones God is calling in this age. The apostle Paul put it thusly: **"For ye see your calling brethren, how that not many wise men after the flesh, not many mighty, not many noble are called" (1 Cor. 1:26).**

God is not calling the "wise" of this world whose "wisdom is foolishness with God" (1 Cor. 3:19). Such are "wise" in themselves and become insolent. Instead,

...God has chosen the *foolish* things of the world

> to confound the wise; and God hath chosen the *weak* things of the world to confound the things which are mighty. And *base* things of the world, and the things which are *despised*, hath God chosen, yea, and things *which are not* [nothings] to bring to nought things that are: That no flesh should glory in His presence (1 Cor. 1:27-29).

God speaks through Paul that He [God] has chosen the *nothings* of this world to confound the wise (what the world considers intelligent). Why? Simply because these arrogant people would think they earned salvation through their own intelligence! These "rich in worldly ways" have the smarts to make a lot of money—and would probably use their large bank rolls to influence church authorities. They would gloat over their financial and spiritual success as though God had no intervention in their lives.

Realizing this, God has called those lacking wisdom and given them a way to accrue it. James informs us,

> But if any of you lacketh wisdom, let him ask of God, who giveth to all men liberally and upbraideth not; and it shall be given him. But let him ask in *faith*, nothing doubtful (Jas. 1:5,6).

Paul wrote of God's wisdom,

> Howbeit we speak wisdom among them that are perfect: yet not the wisdom of this world, nor of the princes of this world [age] that come to nought: But we speak the wisdom of God...even the hidden wisdom, which God ordained before the world unto our glory (1 Cor. 2:6-7).

The Mammon of Unrighteousness

Because we, [the spiritual nobody's of this world] lack wisdom—Jesus provides a means for us to accumulate some. He says after this parable: **"And I say unto you, make for yourselves friends out of the mammon of unrighteousness..."**

THE FUTILITY OF RICHES

(verse 9). Was this "spiritual double talk" on the part of Jesus? Did He really expect us to gain mammon [money] through unrighteous means like the unjust steward?

This is not what Jesus meant! But through the colorful illustration of this parable, we can become as **"...wise as serpents, and harmless as doves" (Matt. 10:16).** This story is an example in RESOURCEFULNESS or spiritual prudence, not an example of corruption!

Mammon and money are *synonymous* in this parable. What Jesus was implying is that, while nonbelievers use money for evil purposes, believers should use it for preaching the gospel! This is how we make eternal friends after we *fail* (vs. 9 or die).

Jesus admonished us to use money properly by saying: **"No servant can serve two masters: for either he will hate the one, and love the other; or else he will hold to the one, and despise the other. Ye cannot serve God and mammon [money]" (Lk.16:13).** Like anything else God has created—money can be used for good or evil purposes. Christians can put their money to good use by helping those who are preaching the gospel. This is real *wisdom!* We can then make spiritual friends rather than carnal minded temporary friends! Heaping treasures to ourselves, building bigger barns; etc. is not what God desires in His children. The advice from our Savior is to, **"Lay up for yourselves treasures in heaven...for where thy treasure is, there will thy heart be also..." (Matt. 6:19-21).**

Faithful Stewards

At the end of this parable, Jesus cautioned:

> **Who is faithful in very little is faithful also in much: and who is unrighteous in very little is unrighteous also in much. If therefore ye have not been faithful in the unrighteous mammon, who will commit to your trust the true riches? And if ye have not been faithful in that which is another man's who shall give you that which is your own? (verses 10-12).**

As God's stewards over all His goods—we are expected to be *faithful* stewards and not waste our Master's goods! God has entrusted us with His *pearls of truth* that are not to be given to swine [those who would mock and trample upon God's truth] (Matt. 7:6).

God has also given us children to train up His way. They are to be taught God's laws and the penalties for breaking them. God desires that we should maintain our homes, cars, bodies; etc. (everything He has allowed us to have while in this temporary life). We are to **"dress and keep"** them (Gen. 2:15).

Oftentimes the parables relate characters to that of God the Father and God the Son. However, sometimes this *analogy* does not *parallel* the God-head and can be misleading. For example, God the Father is *not* represented by the parable of *The Unjust Judge*. In this parable, Jesus desires Christians to be wise in spiritual ways as the steward was wise in worldly wisdom.

On the other hand, we are not to be unrighteous or unfaithful in handling the material blessings given by our benevolent Father. If we, as God's stewards waste them—God will not commit to us the eternal treasures which He has "cast upon the waters."

As heirs of all of God's treasures, along with Jesus, our elder spiritual brother—we shall inherit all of God's hidden riches [the universe] if we are faithful now! Let us be *faithful* and *wise* stewards so we can claim these wonderful promises! The "unjust steward" lacked integrity and fidelity, but may we learn from his foresight and acting quickly and without delay!

Parable Summary

Oftentimes there is a three-fold meaning in many of the parables! There was a past fulfillment of Israel; there is a present fulfillment and yet a future fulfillment! This is also consistent with the feast days God gave the nation of Israel.

Without the understanding of the parables, it would be virtually impossible to comprehend the *deeper* meaning of the prophecies! Many of the parables relate to Israel's past history, some to the Gentiles, and yet others to the Church.

Each one is intended to teach an object overall spiritual principle to God's people throughout all dispensations!

Clearly, from the parables, God's plan is far greater than any thought of a "Jewish" or "Church" dispensation—His principles apply to all! To try and lump the present Church dispensation

THE FUTILITY OF RICHES

into the whole of God's plan without including Israel, would indeed be a gross error!

This present dispensation is but a small part of God's great Kingdom over which He will very soon rule! To spiritualize all of the Old Testament prophecies in regards to their fulfillment—is indeed unwise and a big mistake!

The parables *graphically* show in beautiful word technicolor, the consistency of many unfulfilled blessings to Israel. To claim Israel's blessings for the Church is not only misleading, but disrespective of the masterful mind who promised them!

Through the colorful imagery of *parabolic* we find the history of Israel—past, present and future! The parables portray in prophetic puzzle, the pieces of God's messengers sent to Israel of old and in the future! Finally, the nation of Israel will once again bloom as God's fruitful bow!

Needless to say, although the parables are directed towards the nation of Israel prophetically—they contain jewels of wisdom for today's Christian!

Just as we will observe God's plan of salvation through the atoning work of Christ in the offerings and Feast Days—the parables likewise hold the future of God's chosen people [Israel] and the world!

In our Lord's absence, the parables are to teach and edify us in how to complete His work upon planet earth! The Sower is to *sow* the gospel message, while the Holy Spirit invites potential family members to the wedding feast!

The Steward *protects* his Master's goods by not giving His truths to those who trully are not interested, as the Porter *watches* faithfully for his Master's return!

The Husbandman *dresses* the Vineyard [God's Church] of his Master to keep it fertile while the Trader *invests* his Master's money to preach the gospel wisely!

The Reaper [God's angels] *gathers* the Master's harvest in due season, while the Laborers [God's ministry] *plough* the Master's field and feed His flock!

Two or more classes of individuals are represented in many of the parables. There are the good and bad, fruitful and unfruitful, wise and foolish, profitable and unprofitable.

Sometimes our Lord introduces Old Testament *symbolism* into the parables such as oil, leaven, salt, wine, meal, candlestick, etc. Each *symbol* teaches a similar object lesson regardless if it is found in the Old or New Testament!

We have already experienced the fine thread of *duality* running consistently throughout the Word of God—and the parables are no exception to this rule of thumb!

The "Woman and the Meal"; the "Mustard seed"; the "Birds of the Air"; the "Leavened Meal"; are parables with a double meaning. Through "double symbolism", different aspects of the Church and Israel are illuminated!

What a beautiful word painting we have in the parables, drawn by a Masterful hand!

Chapter Eleven

NUMBERS AND THEIR SPIRITUAL SIGNIFICANCE

Numbers as they appear in scripture, oftentimes have a deep *spiritual significance*. They portray God's supernatural algebraic design and can be summarized as follows:

ONE—UNITY, COMMENCEMENT, BEGINNING.

One denotes *unity* as the evening and morning became the *first* day (Gen. 1:5). **"In the beginning God"**—Genesis, the *first* book of the Bible contains the *beginning* of life and prophecy of the "one seed" through the woman. Here we also have the *beginning* of the woman's [Church] adversary—the seed of Satan (the serpent).

1 Cor. 8:6; 12:13	"...*one* God, *one* Lord, *one* Spirit, *one* baptism, *one* body..."
Mk. 9:35	"...desires to be *first* he shall be last."
1 Cor. 12:28	"...*first* apostles, secondarily..."
1 Cor. 15:45	"...the *first* man Adam a living soul..."

Eph. 6:12	"...which is the *first* commandment..."
1 Thess. 4:16	"...in Christ shall rise *first*."
Heb. 8:7	"...the *first* covenant."
Heb. 9:12	"...*first* tabernacle, wherein."
Rev. 20:5	"...this is the *first* resurrection."
Rev. 21:1	"...*first* heaven and *first* earth were..."
Ex. 12:2	"...the *first* month of year to..."
Ex. 12:18	"...*first* month eat unleavened bread..."
Lev. 12:6	"...bring a lamb of the *first* year..."
Rev. 1:5	"Jesus; who is *first*born from the dead."
Rev. 14:4	"...being the *first*fruits unto God."

TWO—DIVISION, DIFFERENCE, OPPOSITION.

Two mainly denotes *difference* as indicated by the work of the second day. Of course this is not always true as indicated by "two angels at the tomb, two Witness"; etc. All words relating to *two* such as "double" imply difference, e.g. "double-tongued." *Two* is prevalent in male and female, two eyes, ears, legs, and arms.

Gen. 1:4	The very purpose of the light on the *2nd* day was to DIVIDE the light from darkness.
Gen. 25:23	"...*two* nations are in thy womb, and *two* manner of people shall be..."
Gen. 7:2; 9:15	"...of beasts that are not clean by

SPIRITUAL NUMBERS

	two..."
Lev. 16:7-8	"Aaron shall take *two* goats and cast lots upon *two*..."
Duet. 21:15	"...if a man have *two* wives."
Amos 3:3	"...can two walk together except they be agreed?"
Matt. 6:24	"...no man can serve *two* masters."
1 Cor. 6:16	"...for *two* shall be one flesh."
Gal. 4:24	"...these are the *two* covenants."
Rev. 11:3-4	"I will give power to My *two* witnesses..."
Rev. 13:11	"...he had *two* horns like a lamb..."
Gen. 1:6	The firmament DIVIDED the waters which were above the firmament from those below the firmament on the *2nd* day.
LK. 7:41	The parable of *two* debtors.
Gen. 4	Cain and Abel picture *two* divergent ways of life. Righteous Abel depicted the way of God (Acts 18:26) and Cain—the way of Satan (Jude 11).
Gen. 12:4	Abraham and his Nephew Lot portray *difference* in attitude towards serving God. After entering the land of Haran to go into the land of Canaan—"strife" began to manifest itself between them. Abraham's dwelling place was chosen by the Eternal (Gen. 13:14), while Lot chose to dwell in the plain of Jordan

where the cities of Sodom and Gomorrah were located (Gen. 13:11). Lot was a very wealthy and righteous person in Sodom (Gen. 14:12; 19:1), despite their ungodly abominations (Gen. 13:13; 2 Pet. 2:6-9).

Lot's uncle came to his rescue after hearing of his captivity by these barbarious cutthroats (Gen. 14:11-14). Now Abraham walked by *faith* in serving God and was rewarded accordingly.

Gal. 4:21-31

There was a vast *difference* in attitude in how Abraham and Lot worshipped the Eternal. But this *difference* was even greater between their wives. Abraham's wife Sarah was a *type* of Jerusalem above while Lot's wife "became a pillar of salt." Jesus said, "..remember Lot's wife" and to continue in deep abiding faith!

Rom. 9:7

Abraham's *two* sons, Isaac and Ishmael also show a *difference* in two ways of worshipping God. Isaac was born through "promise" of God by Abraham's wife Sarah when he was 100 years old. But Ishmael was born after "fleshly" desire by Hagar— Abraham's handmaid. Isaac was born after the "spirit" while Ishmael after the "flesh." Here then is the *difference* between the two covenants and two ways of life!

Gen. 25:22

Once again God shows us *differences* of two ways of worshipping Him through the lives of Jacob and Esau. These twin brothers had the same father in Isaac and the same mother in

Rebekah—but that is where the oneness ended!

Contention between these two developed when they were yet in the womb. Esau became a fornicator and a "profane person" selling his birthright for a bowl of pottage (Heb. 12:16-17). Jacob coveted the birthright so much that he committed deception to acquire it. However, God saw Jacob's zeal and turned it around for good, once Jacob repented. After several years of testing Jacob; God changed his name from Jacob, meaning "supplanter", to Israel or "overcomer with God." Jacob became to be deeply loved by the Eternal (Mal. 1:2-3; Rom. 9:13).

Matt. 13:24-30	*TWO* kinds of seed in the Wheat and Tares.
Matt 25	*TWO* groups of watchers in the 10 Virgins.
Matt. 13:47-50	*TWO* sorts of fish gathered in the Net.
Lk. 17:7-10 Matt. 18:23-35	*TWO* classes of servants.
Matt. 7:26	*TWO* builders of houses.
Lk. 18:9-14	*TWO* forms of righteousness in the Pharisee and Publican.
Lk. 16:19-31	*TWO* contrasting ways of life in the history of Lazarus and the rich man.

Dualities of Israel and the Church

It is indeed most fascinating, but the entire *plan* of God is *dual* to Old Testament Israel and the New Testament Church.

The following are some of the dualities we shall observe as we journey through the *types*.

Two Israel's	Two Royal Priesthoods
Two Church's	Two Holy People
Two Harvests	Two Brides
Two Marriages	Two Suppers
Two Wives	
Two Resurrections	
Two Comings	
Two "Firstfruits"	

In summation, there are *two ways of life*—God's and Satan's! There are therefore *two kinds of individuals*—God's and Satan's!

Consequently, there are *two Church's* in existence—God's and Satan's! Finally, there will be *two harvests*—one to remove Satan's people, and one to bring God's people into everlasting happiness, and to be rulers over His Kingdom!

THREE—FINALITY, COMPLETENESS, DIVINE PERFECTION OF TESTIMONY, RESURRECTION.

Three denotes *completeness* as the fundamentals of the creation work were completed by the *third* day. It represents *resurrection* to life in that on the *third* day the earth *rose* up out of the deep and fruit rose up out of the earth.

Our Lord was resurrected on the *third* day even as Jonah was in the belly of the great fish for *three* days and *three* nights. Hence, the *third* day is *symbolical* of a Christian's "resurrected life" in Jesus!

Dan. 7:5	"...it had *three* ribs in the mouth."
Dan. 8:20-24	"...were *three* of the first horns..."
Dan. 11:2	"...there shall stand up *three* kings."
Matt. 13:33	"...let us make here *three* tabernacles."
Matt. 4:3	Christ was tempted *three* times by Satan.

Lk. 13:32	Jesus was *perfected* on the *third* day. It was the *third* hour He was crucified.
Matt. 27:46	Jesus gave up the Spirit at about the ninth hour (3x3).
Acts 5:7	"...*three* hours after, when his..."
Acts 10:16	*Three* times the sheet was let down to Peter as *testimony* to the sanction of Gentiles into the Church.
1 Cor. 13:13	"...faith, hope, charity..of the *three*..."
1 Jn. 5:7	"...there are *three* that bear record in heaven: these *three* are one."
1 Jn. 5:8	"...*three* bear witness in earth [water, blood, spirit] and these *three*..."
11 Cor. 12:8	The apostle Paul asked God to heal his thorn in the flesh *three* times—then he realized this was God's *final* answer.

Lineages of Completeness

1. Shem Ham and Jephthah.
2. Abraham, Isaac and Jacob.
3. Saul, David and Solomon.
4. Shadrach, Mechach and Abednego.
5. Peter, James and John.

Three Called before the Flood

Only three individuals are recognized as being called prior to the flood as evident from (Hebrews 11). Each of these people typify a *type* of calling God expected of those in the future:

1. Abel   *symbolic* of love toward neighbor.
2. Enoch   *symbolic* of love toward society.

3. Noah   *symbolic* of love toward races.

FOUR—CREATIVE WORKS, UNIVERSAL, AND WORLD RULERSHIP, MATERIAL COMPLETENESS

Four denotes *nature* or *creation* and pertains to the rulership of the *heavens* and the *earth*. It denotes spiritual as well as *material creation* (3+1).

God's *material* creation was actually completed on the *fourth* day. Man and the animals were merely added on the *fifth* and *sixth* day.

The sun, moon and stars were created to tell the seasons and times—and were made visible on the *fourth* day.

There are *four* renowned elements of the earth (air, fire, water and land). There are *four* directions of a compass (north, south, east and west). There are *four* seasons of the year (summer, fall, winter and spring).

Because *four* is the world number, we should expect to find *four* visions about world-empires.

Dan. 2	Nebuchadnezzar's dream contained *four* different metals picturing *four* world ruling powers.
Dan. 7:2,3	Nebuchadnezzar also saw *four* wild beasts (leopard, lion, bear and the *fourth* was more dreadful than the other three). Here again, these four beasts envision *four world ruling* empires to dominate the *world* prophetically.
Ex. 20:8	The *fourth* commandment is the only one that refers back to the creation of the heavens and the earth.
Ex. 27:2	"...the horns of it upon the *four* corners..." (corners of the earth).
Ex. 29:12	"...put of the blood on the [four] horns..." (corners of the earth).

Matt. 24:31 "...and they shall gather the elect from *four* winds" (corners of the earth).

Rev. 7:1 "...*four* angels, on *four* corners, holding *four*..."

Rev. 9:13 "...a voice from the *four horns of*..."

FIVE—GRACE.

Five is a leading number in the Tabernacle measurements. It is God adding His gifts and blessings to the works He has made. It is the number of man dependent upon God (4+1).

Dan. 2:44 The *fifth* kingdom of the earth succeeding the previous four world-powers will be the kingdom of God. It will smash the demonic controlled governments of this evil age—and rule them with POWER and GRACE!

1 Sam. 17:40 David, the shepherd boy chose *five* smooth stones to slay Goliath with. Although he only needed one—these were *symbolic* of God's extended *grace* to supplement for his human frailty. Bathsheba was one of five women in David's (or Christ's genealogy). She was David's wife and Solomon's mother through grace.

The number *five* is predominant in the design of the Tabernacle—which itself is a picture of *grace*.

Ex. 25-31 The Tabernacle was 10 cubits high (5x2), 10 cubits wide and 30 cubits long (5x6). The holy place was 20 cubits long (5x4), and the Holy of Holies was 10 cubits (5x2).

Multiples of *five* are seen in the outer court (100 cubits long and 50 cubits wide). Twenty (5x4) pillars were located on each side of the Tabernacle, while 10 pillars (5x2) were placed at each end. A *pillar* in the Bible is a support structure because of its *strength* and endurance.

Here we have a total of 60 pillars (5x12) displaying visibly God's *government of grace*. *Five*, the number of *grace* and *twelve* the number of *government*.

Ex. 35-40

The curtains, 10 in number, that were held up by the pillars were 5 cubits apart and 5 cubits high. The whole of the outer curtain was divided in squares of 25 cubits (5x5). The dimension of the brazen altar was 5x5).

Ex. 30:23-25

The Eternal commanded the priests to make *holy oil* for anointing as follows:

1) Myrrh, 500 shekels (5x100).
2) Sweet Cinnamon, 250 shekels (5x50).
3) Sweet Calamus, 250 shekels (5x50).
4) Cassia, 500 shekels (5x100).
5) Olive, 1 hin.

Hence, grace was implied by the *five* component mixture to those who were anointed with it. The qualities of the individual ingredients were also multiples of *five*—indicative of *grace*. There were eight holy things that received anointing with this

SPIRITUAL NUMBERS

consecrated oil by Moses:

1) The Tabernacle.
2) The Ark of the testimony.
3) The Table and its vessels.
4) The Candlestick and its vessels.
5) The Altar of Incense.
6). The Altar of Burnt-offering.
7) The Laver and its foot.
8) Aaron and his sons.

Ex. 7:12   The first four plagues in Egypt were poured out on Israelites and Egyptians alike. But starting with the 5th plague—God spared His people the remaining six terrible judgments through His GRACE!

SIX—HUMANKIND, IMPERFECTION.

Six denotes *humankind* as man was created on the *sixth* day. *Six* is hall-mark for man and everything connected with man. Man was to work *six* days and rest the seventh. The hours in the day (24), minutes in an hour (60), seconds in a minute (60) and months in a year (12) are all a multiple of *six*. The number of antichrist (666) epitomizes what man stands for as the nadir of degeneracy.

Gen. 7:11   Noah was 600 years old when God destroyed the world of humankind by a flood. This unprecedented event in the recorded history of humankind was *symbolic* of humankind's 6000 year allotted time span of self-imposed rule. Soon this satanic inspired world, like the world of Noah will be destroyed by the returning Jesus Christ!

Ezek. 46:4   "And the burnt offering...shall be *six* lambs.."

249

1 Sam. 17:4-7	Goliaths height was *six* cubits." He had *six* pieces of amour, and his spear's head weighed *six hundred* shekels of iron."
Dan. 3:1	"...of the image of gold *six* cubits."
Ex. 28:10	"...*six* of their names on one stone, and the other *six* names of ..."
Rev. 4:8	"...beasts had each *six* wings..."
Rev. 13:18	"...for it is the number of a man; and his number is *Six* hundred threescore and *six* (666)."

SEVEN—TOTALITY, SPIRITUAL PERFECTION, COMPLETION, FULLNESS

The number *seven* denotes totality in *spiritual perfection* even as God rested from His completed perfect work on the *seventh* day of creation. *Seven* days complete a week; there are *seven* notes in music and *seven* colors in the rainbow.

Six is the number of MAN and materialism. *Seven* is God's number of perfection and completion. God made the material creation in six days. MAN was created the *sixth* day. But God *completed* the first week, and *perfected* it by creation of His Sabbath, on the *seventh* day. That *seventh* day typified the completed and perfect SPIRITUAL creation.

Thus, God set apart *six* millennia for MAN to be allowed rejection of God's government, and to write the lesson of human rebellion, to be followed by the *seventh* millennium in which God will *perfect* and *complete* His SPIRITUAL creation!

Ex. 20:11	"...and rested the *seventh* day; wherefore the Lord blessed the *seventh* day and hallowed it."
Lev. 23:15	"...*seven* sabbaths shall be..."

SPIRITUAL NUMBERS

Dan. 9:25   "...Messiah shall be *seven* weeks."

Rev. 1:12   "...I saw *seven* golden candlesticks."

Rev 1:4   "...*seven* churches in Asia..."

Rev. 5:6   "...Lamb as slain, having *seven* horns, and *seven* eyes, which are the *seven*..."

Rev. 8:2   "...I saw the *seven* angels which..."

Rev. 12:3   "...having *seven* heads, and *seven* crowns..."

Rev. 17:9   "...the *seven* heads are *seven* mountains..."

Gen. 5:24   "The *seventh* man from Adam" was not, for God took him."

Gen. 7:12   Clean animals were taken into the ark by *sevens*.

Gen. 29:27   Jacob and Leah's wedding feast lasted *seven* days—*symbolic* of the 7th day millennial feast of Christ and His Bride.

Levitical system and Seven

Lev. 25:2,4,6   Every *seventh year* a Sabbatic year of land rest.

Lev. 25:9-13   Every *seventh Sabbatic year* a Jubilee year.

Lev. 23 feasty   Every *seventh month* has 3 annual days (Atonement, Trumpets, and Tabernacles).

Lev. 23:15   Pentecost is counted *seven weeks* from

THE FOOLISHNESS OF GOD

	the Sabbath during the days of Unleavened Bread.
Lev. 23:6	The days of Unleavened Bread are for *seven days*.
Lev. 23:34	The Feast of Tabernacles is the *seventh* Feast in the *seventh* month lasting *seven* days.
Num. 28:19	*Seven lambs* were offered daily during the days of Unleavened Bread.
Lev. 23:18	*Seven lambs* were offered at Pentecost.
Num. 29:2	*Seven lambs* were offered at Trumpets.
Num. 29:8	*Seven lambs* were offered at Atonement.
Num. 29:13	Fourteen lambs (7x2) were offered each day during the Feast of Tabernacles.
Num. 29:36	*Seven lambs* were offered on The Last Great Day.

**There are 77 names from God through His son Adam, to Christ, the second Adam.

EIGHT—NEW ORDER, NEW BEGINNING, REGENERATION

The number *eight* succeeds the number seven which is representative of *perfection*. After perfection can only come a "new beginning" or "new order"—and that is precisely what the number *eight* represents. The following examples of the number eight illustrate its relationship to a "new beginning."

- The Israelites were told by God to circumcise their children upon the *eighth* day after birth (Gen. 17:12; 21:4; Lk. 2:21).

SPIRITUAL NUMBERS

This event is what made them an Israelite and is *symbolic* of the Christian's initiation of baptism. Throwing away of the foreskin was *symbolic* of discarding the "old man." This event or initiation started a "new life" or "new beginning" for both Israelite and Christian.

- Noah and his family [a total of *eight* souls] were saved from the flood in the safety of the ark (1 Pet. 3:20). The ark is a *type* of Christ and the water a *type* of baptism. Just as Christians are saved in the haven or ark of Christ through baptism, so were these *eight* souls saved from the flood. These *eight* souls began a "new order" of life after the flood.

- The final resurrection of the Roman Empire will be *eighth* and of the seven (Rev. 17:11). The Babylonian Empire, Persian, the four divisions of Greece and the original Roman Empire constitute 7 HEADS as *symbolized* by the heads of (Daniel 7). These 7 heads were not dominated by religion. Pagan Rome was the 7th head and was wounded to death.

Yet later, Rome continued as a "revived" or "healed" Beast as described in (Revelation 17). It's system is called the "eighth" because it is different than the previous seven; that is, it has always been ridden by a "fallen woman."

Therefore, it is a part of the original 7th head and hence of the seven, but it is called "eighth" because it is a different system, being dominated by religion.

- The seventh sanctuary of God will be the Church—God's spiritual building. We will read more of this in the chapter on the sanctuaries of God in volume 3. The Church is now being fashioned into the spotless Bride of Christ as each member is qualifying to be a "spiritual stone" of this spiritual House. This will be followed by the *eighth* and final sanctuary "New Jerusalem" which comes down out of heaven to start the "new order" of things as the "new heavens" and "new earth" begins.

It is also highly significant that the Holy of Holies in both the Tabernacle and the Temple were cubes. *Eight* is the first *cubic* number (2 x 2 x 2). Here is the first geometric figure of perfection in which the length, breadth, and height are equal. The Holy of Holies in the Tabernacle was a cube of 10 cubits, The Holy of Holies in the Temple was a cube of 20 cubits. Most likely "New Jerusalem" which is the culmination of God's Most Holy Place will be a cube of 12,000 furlongs (Rev. 21:16).

There is some speculation that the window of the ark of Noah was shaped in a cube of one. This was a kind of sacred "Shechinah." If this were true, we would then have a series of the following cubes:

1 = The Ark of Noah
$10^3 = 1,000$ = The Tabernacle.
$20^3 = 8,000$ = The Temple.
$12,000^3 = 1,728,000$ = New Jerusalem.

- The "Last Great Day" of the annual fall Feast days God gave to the nation of Israel occurred on the *eighth* day of the Feast (Lev. 23:36). Some believe this Feast day represents the final judgment and *resurrection* of those who have never known of God's truths. This will be the *final* opportunity for these individuals to make it into God's Kingdom.

- As already demonstrated, the spiritual significance of the number *eight* appears to emphasize "a new beginning" and therefore the eighth day of the Feast of Tabernacles is believed to *picture* the first day of the new week of ETERNITY!

The speculation is thus. If the Feast of Tabernacles pictures the Millennium, then the day after would picture the beginning of Eternity! After the Millennium, when the "New Heavens" and "New Earth" with a "New Jerusalem" are created—the eighth day of the Feast of Tabernacles will find its fulfillment in the eternal week which has no end!

The first seven days of the Feast of Tabernacles *pictures* the first seven days of the creation week, after which God will finally REST with His people. Thus, redemption will have been completed in man as God now DWELLS with him as we enter into His ETERNAL REST! Then the "first day" of eternity will begin as *symbolized* by the eighth day of the Feast of

SPIRITUAL NUMBERS

Tabernacles. We will study this in more detail in volume 3.

Eight Preachers of Righteousness

1) Abel (not Adam).
2) Seth (Gen. 5:6).
3) Enos (Gen. 5:9).
4) Cainan (Gen. 5:12).
5) Mahalaleel (Gen. 5:13).
6) Jared (Gen. 5:18).
7) Enoch (Gen. 5:22).
8) Noah (Gen. 5:32; ll Pet. 2:5).

Eight New Beginnings

1. *Adam*—Gen. 2:7
   Expulsion from the Garden of Eden—(Gen. 3:22-24).

2. *Seth*—Gen. 4:25
   The Flood—(Gen. 6-8).

3. *Noah*—Gen. 9:2
   Confusion of Tongues—(Gen. 11).

4. *Abraham*—Gen. 12:1-3
   Egyptian Bondage—(Ex. 1:7-14).

5. *Moses*—Ex. 3:1-12
   The Children of Israel

6. *The Church Age*
   The Holy Spirit—(Acts 2)

7. *Christ's Millennial Rule*
   God's Kingdom—(Rev. 20).

8. *The New Heaven and New Earth*
   The Holy City—(Rev. 21).

NINE—FINALITY OF JUDGMENT, DIVINE COMPLETENESS

Nine denotes *Divine completeness* in that it is the product of 3x3. Multiples and factors of nine denote judgment.

Gen. 17:1	"...Abram was *ninety* years old, and *nine*..."
Matt. 18:12,13	"...doth he not leave the *ninety* and *nine*..."
Matt. 27:45	"...was darkness over all the land unto the *nineth* hour."
Matt. 27:46	"...*nineth* hour Jesus gave up the ghost..."
Gal. 5:22-23	There are nine fruits of the spirit.
Acts 10:3	It was about the ninth hour that the gentile Cornelius had a vision to contact Peter.

TEN—ORDINAL PERFECTION, POWER, JUDGMENT

Ten denotes *ordinal perfection* and *worldly power* as it comes after the nineth digit, when numeration commences anew. Completeness of order, wholeness of cycle.

Duet. 14:22	God's tithing system (l0th) represented what man owes God.
Ex. 18:13,25	Moses had captains of 1,000 (l0x100); 100 (l0x10); 50 (5x10), 10.
Ex. 34:28	"...wrote *ten* commandments."
Matt. 25:1	"...be likened to *ten* virgins."

Matt. 25:28	"...to him that hath *ten* talents."
Lk. 19:13	"...delivered them *ten* pounds."
Lk. 19:17	"...have thou authority over *ten* cities."
Rev. 2:3,13:1, 17:3,7,12,16	"... a dragon having *ten* horns."
Dan. 7:7,20,24,	Ten kingdoms of *worldly power* are represented symbolically by *ten* toes, and *ten* horns. See also (Dan. 2:41).

Ten plagues were brought on the land of Egypt—completing God's judgment on that nation. Noah was the tenth from Adam—his generation ending the antediluvian age. Ten nations or groups of nations will mark the final rising of the Roman Empire in the end-time generation. *Ten* virgins represent the whole of the New Testament Church throughout the ages.

TWELVE—GOD'S GOVERNMENT, GOVERNMENTAL PERFECTION, BEGINNINGS.

Twelve denotes *perfection in God's government.* The number 144 is (12 x 12) and 12 is the number of God's governmental design. It is the number or factor of all numbers that designate government. It is found in all that has bearing on ruling as a multiple, e.g. the sun which rules the day.

Twelve is God's number of spiritual *organizational* BEGINNINGS. God's promises pertain to Abraham's children. His Children *began* with the twelve sons of Jacob. God *began* His organized nation on earth with TWELVE tribes. Christ BEGAN His Church with TWELVE apostles.

"New Jerusalem" has 12 gates with 12 angels standing at them with the 12 tribes of Israel inscribed upon them. The city has 12 foundations on which are written the names of the 12 apostles and the wall of the city is 144 cubits.

Twelve is the number of *organizational* beginnings, not first beginnings. God started off the human race with ONE man, Adam. The first human "father of the multitude" that shall be converted and inherit salvation was the ONE man, Abraham

THE FOOLISHNESS OF GOD

(Gen. 17:5); and this same *one* man is the human "father of the faithful" (Rom. 4:16).

The actual *first* beginning of the Church was the ONE man, Jesus Christ. But the *organizational* beginning was through the *collective* Body of Christ, empowered by the same Spirit, starting with the TWELVE.

Gen. 23:22	"...now the sons of Jacob were *twelve*."
Gen. 49:28	"...all these are the *twelve* tribes..."
Matt. 10:2	"...the names of the *twelve* apostles."
Matt. 19:28	"...sit upon *twelve* thrones judging the *twelve* tribes..."
Jn. 11:9	"...not *twelve* hours in a day?"
Rev. 21:12	"...*twelve* gates, at the gates *twelve* angels."
Rev. 21:14	"...city had *twelve* foundations, and in them the names of the *twelve* apostles."
Rev. 22:2	"...tree of life bare *twelve* manner of fruit..."

FORTY—TRIAL, TESTING, PROBATION, CHASTISEMENT.

The number *forty* denotes *trial* and *testing* before God's judgment was made, or because God's judgment was made.

Gen. 25:20	"...Isaac was *forty* years..."
Gen. 36:34	"...Esau was *forty* years when he took.."
Ex 16:35	"...Israel did eat manna *forty* years..."
Num. 14:33	"...wander in wilderness *forty* years..."

SPIRITUAL NUMBERS

Num. 32:34	"...your iniquities *forty* years..."
1 Kings 2:11	"...David reigned *forty* years..."
1 Kings 11:42	Solomon reigned *forty* years..."
Acts 13:21	Saul reigned *forty* years.
Amos 5:25	"...ye offered sacrifice *forty* years..."
Acts 7:23	"...Moses was *forty* years old, he..."
Acts 13:18	"...the time of *forty* years suffered..."
Heb. 3:9	"...saw my works *forty* years..."
Gen. 7:4	"...to rain on earth *forty* days."
Ex. 24:18	"...in mount *forty* days and *forty* nights."
1 Kings 19:8	"...strength of meat *forty* days" (Elijah fasted *forty* days).
Ezek. 4:6	"...iniquity of Judah *forty* days."
Jonah 3:4	"...*forty* days Nineveh be..."
Matt. 4:2	"...fasted *forty* days and *forty* nights."
Mk. 1:13	"Jesus was *forty* days in the wilderness."
Acts 1:3	"...seen of them *forty* days."
Ex. 34:28	Moses fasted *forty* days.

* There were 480 years (12 x 40) from the Exodus to the building of Solomon's Temple.

Chapter Twelve

PROPHETIC NUMBERS

THE HEBREW CALENDAR

In order to understand any aspect of prophecy relating to prophetic days or years, it is vital to understand the Hebrew Calendar. According to Josephus, the initial formulation of the Hebrew calendar was given in the days of Seth. God intended that the heavenly bodies would intrigue man to study their movements carefully, notice Genesis 1:14: **"Let there be lights in the firmament of the heaven to divide the day from the night; and let them be for signs, and for seasons, and for days, and for years."**

For over two centuries the Israelites had been in severe bondage in Egypt—forced to work with cruel taskmasters over them. There was no Bible—no written Word of God. They were not permitted to worship God as He had ordained. They were forced to work seven days a week. They had lost sight of the true Sabbath—that is why God revealed to them the Sabbath in the wilderness of Sin (Ex. 16).

At that time in Egypt they had also changed the proper time for commencing the year. And so, on delivering His people from Egypt, God straightened His people out as to time. And, as the beginning of our salvation was wrought by Christ's death on the cross, so God said, **"This month shall be unto you the**

beginning of months" **(Ex. 12:2).**

It appears that God first revealed His religious calendar to the nation of Israel prior to their first Passover observance in Egypt. At this time, God set His civil calendar approximately six months backwards, as the first month of the religious calendar became the seventh month of the civil calendar.

The Sabbath day had established the days of the week, the new moons had established the months in proper sequence. Once Israel set foot in their new land, the Sabbatical cycles and Jubilee Year were established (Lev. 25:2-12). With the advent of the computer age, there have been many researchers who have disputed the 360 day cycle for a 364 day cycle. We will cover both calendars and will start with the 360 day cycle calendar.

The 360 Day Cycle

Our modern world calendar is based on the solar cycle, and consists of 365.25 days. The calendar that God gave the Israelites was calculated according to both lunar and solar cycles.

Their twelve months are calculated as containing 354 days, which leaves their year eleven-and-one-fourth days short of the true solar year. This is corrected by adding a "leap month" of 30 days, known as Adhar, seven times during a nineteen-year cycle.

Thus, in the 3rd, 6th, 9th, 11th, 14th, 17th, and 19th years, a "leap month" was added. If on the 16th of the month Nisan, the sun had not reached the vernal equinox, the month was declared to be the second Adhar and the following Nisan.

However, the prophetic year, consisted of 12 months of 30 days or 360 days (Rev. 11:2-3; 12:6). This 30 day month was known in the days of Noah, as the 150 day interval till the waters abated from the earth, began on the seventeenth day of the second month, and ended on the seventeenth day of the seventh month (Gen. 7:11,24; 8:3-4). Thus, in this 5 month period, each month was 30 days.

The book of Esther also gives indication that this 360 day year was in existence, by recording the six-months-long feast of Xerxes as lasting 180 days. Thus, in a 6 month period, each month was 30 days.

Sir Isaac Newton explains: "All nations, before the just length of the solar year was known, reckoned months by the course of the moon, and years by the return of winter and summer, spring and autumn; and in making calendars for their festivals, they reckoned thirty days to a lunar month, and twelve lunar months to a year, taking the nearest round numbers, whence came the division of the ecliptic into 360 degrees" (*Astronomy of the Ancients,* chap. i.; 7).

God's Time Elements

Here is a brief explanation of the time elements God uses to make up His months:

DAY: Genesis 1:5 shows that the day begins in the evening: "And the evening and the morning were the first day." Jesus put His divine approval upon dividing the day into twenty four hours when He said: "Are there not twelve hours in a day" (Jn. 11:9).

HOUR: Instead of being divided into minutes and seconds, the hour is divided into parts, or chalakim. One hour consists of 1080 parts of 3600 seconds.

MONTH: A lunar month is the time needed for the moon to revolve around the earth. Even though this period varies from month to month, 29 days 12 hours 793 parts is the traditional average used for calculation. Actual calendars cannot be based upon 29 1/2 days, so the Hebrew calendar incorporates months of 29 and 30 days.

YEAR: The Hebrew calendar has two basic types of years, common and intercalary. (The latter is also called "embolismic.") An intercalary Hebrew year will have 30 additional days, so it can also be called a leap year. By contrast, recall that the Roman leap year has 366 days instead of 365. Common years will have 353, 354, or 355 days. Leap years may have 383, 384, or 385 days. Since 142 AD, the years in a cycle that are leap years are 3 6 8 11 14 17 19. Before 142 AD, the leap years were 2 5 7 10 13 16 18.

19 YEAR CYCLE: The Western world is accustomed to a solar year of 365.25 days, since the Roman calendar in common use is solar. This means that a given month of the year will always occur during the same season.

On the other hand, the Hebrew year by itself does not closely match the length of a solar year. Twelve months which are each approximately 29 1/2 days result in a year which has only 354 days—about eleven days less than a solar year of 365.25 days. A common Hebrew year is thus *shorter* than a Roman year.

God ordained that His Holy days were to be kept "in their seasons" (Lev. 23:4). He also appointed *both* the sun and the moon "for signs, and for seasons, and for days, and years" (Gen. 1:14). This means that the calendar which God designed to house His sacred festivals for the nation of Israel would be luni-solar. The months were to occur at the proper times for the holy days to fall within the proper season of the year.

How then, are the Hebrew lunar months related to the solar year? Every 19 solar years (of 365.25 days), the moon revolves around the earth 235 times, each "lunation" being on the average 29 days, 12 hours, 793 parts. This remarkable astronomical relationship makes it possible to combine common years and leap years together within a fundamental pattern that repeats itself every nineteen years! The nineteen year cycle is also known as the cycle of Meton, or the Metonic cycle.

THE JULIAN CALENDAR

The Julian calendar was named after Julius Caesar; the Gregorian calendar after Pope Gregory XIII. Both calendars are "Roman." The Gregorian calendar is what we use every day.

When did the Roman calendar, based upon an average yearly length of 365.25 days, come into use? The answer is 45 B.C. With the aid of the Egyptian astronomer Sosigenes, Julius Caesar completely revised the seasons. To effect the reform, "46 BC" had 445 days assigned to it, appropriately called the "year of confusion!" In 45 BC the vernal (spring) equinox occurred on March 25.

The Julian calendar wasn't without faults, however. The average Julian year was eleven minutes and fourteen seconds *longer* than a "tropical year." (A tropical year is measured from one vernal equinox to the next.) After 128 years the Julian calendar had an extra day, compared to an equal number of tropical years.

By the time of the famous Council of Nicea in 325 AD, the Julian calendar was about three days behind the tropical year.

This meant that the vernal equinox was several days "early" on the Julian calendar. Accordingly, the churchmen based their rules for the date of Easter on the spring equinox falling on March 21 of the Julian calendar. It had been March 25 in 45 BC.

Towards the end of the Counter-Reformation in the sixteenth century, the spring equinox had "crept back" to about March 11. To alleviate the problem, Pope Gregory reformed the Julian calendar by deleting ten days from the month of October 15. So, after 1582 the spring equinox shifted back to March 21—where it had been during the time of Constantine the Great. Of course, the equinox never shifted; the calendars did the moving!

The Faulty Julian Calendar

In 45 BC Julius Caesar introduced the "Julian" calendar which averages 365.25 days per year. Our Savior and his apostles lived in the Roman Empire where the Julian calendar had been used for decades and was known to be accurate.

But was it accurate? Both the Qumran Calendar described in the Dead Sea Scrolls and also the calendar of the Book of Jubilees had 364 days. The Book of Jubilees, dating to about the 2nd century BC, strongly emphasizes that the calendar is to have exactly 364 days. The present calendar began with the Egyptians.

The Enoch Calendar has twelve months of 30 days and 4 other days which are quarter-year markers for the four seasons. Thus, it totals exactly 364 days. The names of the months are not given, but it is clear that each season is to be reckoned as the three months following the day heralding that season.

Does The Enoch Calendar Testifies of Christ?

Undoubtedly, the Book of Enoch is a very controversial book and has been an important subject recently regarding end-time prophecy. We shall now examine this concept to see if it is a valid calendar and the key to end-time prophecy. The following is a summary written by John P. Pratt written in the Meridian Magazine in September 11, 2001. He states firstly the discovery of this controversial book, "During the Third and Fourth Centuries AD the book fell into disfavor and was removed from sacred canon, destined to become one of the 'lost books' of the Bible." It was rediscovered in 1773 in Ethiopia and is now readily available in English, but is still largely unappreciated.

Before looking at the calendar it describes, let us briefly review how it contains doctrines or phrases of our Savior.

The Bible in fact makes references to the book of Enoch in several places regarding the end-times, notice:

"And Enoch also, the seventh from Adam, prophesied of these, saying, Behold, the Lord cometh with ten thousands of his saints, To execute judgment upon all, and to convince all that are ungodly among them of all their ungodly deeds which they have ungodly committed, and of all their hard speeches, which ungodly sinners have spoken against him." (Jude 1:14-15,

While that is the only referenced quotation in the Bible, there are many indirect references which involve striking similarities. The scholar and translator R.H. Charles declared, "The influence of 1 Enoch on the New Testament has been greater than that of all the other apocryphal and pseudepigraphical books taken together." Another expert noted that "Its influence is apparent in no less than 128 places in the New Testament." The following table compares a few from the introduction to Archbishop Richard Laurence's original translation, in which the Savior apparently alludes to the Book of Enoch.

Jesus Christ	**Book of Enoch**
Blessed are the meek, for they shall inherit the earth. (Mat 5:5)	The elect shall possess light, joy and peace, and they shall inherit the earth. (Enoch 5:7 {6:9})
the Father judgeth no man, but hath committed all judgment unto the son (John 5:22).	the principal part of the judgment was assigned to him, the Son of man. (Enoch 69:27 {68:39})
shall inherit everlasting life (Mat. 19:29)	those who will inherit eternal life (Enoch 40:9 {40:9})
"Wo unto you that are rich! for ye have received your consolation. (Luke 6:24)	Woe to you who are rich, for in your riches have you trusted; but from your riches you shall be removed. (Enoch 94:8 {93:7}).
Ye also shall sit upon twelve thrones, judging the twelve tribes of Israel. (Mat. 19:28)	I will place each of them on a throne of glory (Enoch 108:12 {105:26})

PROPHETIC NUMBERS

Woe unto that man through whom the Son of man is betrayed! It had been good for that man if he had not been born. (Mat. 26:24)	Where will the habitation of sinners be . . . who have rejected the Lord of spirits. It would have been better for them, had they never been born. (Enoch 38:2 {38:2})
between us and you there is a great gulf fixed. (Luke 16:26)	by a chasm . . . [are] their souls are separated (Enoch 22:9,11{22:10,12})
In my Father's house are many mansions (John 14:2)	In that day shall the Elect One sit upon a throne of glory, and shall choose their conditions and countless habitations. (Enoch 45:3 {45:3})
that ye may be called the children of light (John 12:36)	the good from the generation of light (Enoch 108:11 {105:25})
the water that I shall give him shall be in him a well of water springing up into everlasting life. (John 4:14)	all the thirsty drank, and were filled with wisdom, having their habitation with the righteous, the elect, and the holy. (Enoch 48:1 {48:1})

The Book of Enoch was dropped from the Jewish scriptures shortly after Christ, most likely because it apparently referred to him as the Messiah. It was quoted as scripture by the early Christian Church fathers until the middle of the third century AD, accepted as a divine work having been written by Enoch himself. It then fell into disrepute and was banned from the canon of scripture in the fourth century, partly because it didn't agree with how Christianity came to be redefined after the death of the apostles.

Thus, for a variety of reasons, the Book of Enoch was systematically purged from the scriptures until it became a "lost book" of the Bible. In 1773 the famous explorer James Bruce discovered it in Ethiopia (then called Abyssinia), and brought back three copies. Fortunately, the Ethiopians had kept it in their Bible, where it was located immediately after the Book of Job.

One of the three copies was presented to the Oxford library. The first English translation was published in 1821 by Archbishop Richard Laurence, who had been a Professor of Hebrew at Oxford. Later translations included that of George

Schodde in 1881, of R.H. Charles in 1913, and by E. Isaac in 1983. The first three translations are now available on the internet. Quotations here are from the original Laurence translation, because it still appears to be the best overall translation.

The Jewish Calendar in Jubilees

Dr. Michael Segal informs us in his article, *A 364 Day Solar Year,* that:

"In contrast to the lunar-solar calendar found in Rabbinic sources, Jubilees follows a solar calendar of 364 days per year, to which it refers as a "complete year" (שנה תמימה):

"Now you command the Israelites to keep the years in this number—364 days. Then the year will be complete and it will not disturb its time from its days or from its festivals because everything will happen in harmony with their testimony. They will neither omit a day nor disturb a festival. (6:32)

"A similar calendar has been discovered in some of the Dead Sea scrolls from Qumran. A 364-day calendar is useful from the perspective that the number of days in a year is divisible by 7 (52 weeks = 364 days). Every date in the calendar is therefore anchored to a specific day of the week, and does not change from year to year. The Jubilees calendar is further divided into four quarters, each of which consists of 91 days (13 weeks of 7 days), and since this number is also divisible by 7, each date in the quarter falls out on set day of the week, without any shifts from quarter-to-quarter or year-to-year. Each quarter in the calendar begins on Wednesday, the day of the creation of the heavenly bodies relevant to time keeping (1:14-19). Every quarter throughout history is identical, consisting of two months of 30 days and third day of 31. The entire calendar is summarized in the following chart:

PROPHETIC NUMBERS

Months 1, 4, 7, 10

Sunday	Monday	Tuesday	Wednesday	Thursday	Friday	Shabbat
			1	2	3	4
5	6	7	8	9	10	11
12	13	14	15	16	17	18
19	20	21	22	23	24	25
26	27	28	29	30		

Months 2, 5, 8, 11

Sunday	Monday	Tuesday	Wednesday	Thursday	Friday	Shabbat
					1	2
3	4	5	6	7	8	9
10	11	12	13	14	15	16
17	18	19	20	21	22	23
24	25	26	27	28	29	30

Months 3, 6, 9, 12

Sunday	Monday	Tuesday	Wednesday	Thursday	Friday	Shabbat
1	2	3	4	5	6	7
8	9	10	11	12	13	14
15	16	17	18	19	20	21
22	23	24	25	26	27	28
29	30	31				

THE FOOLISHNESS OF GOD

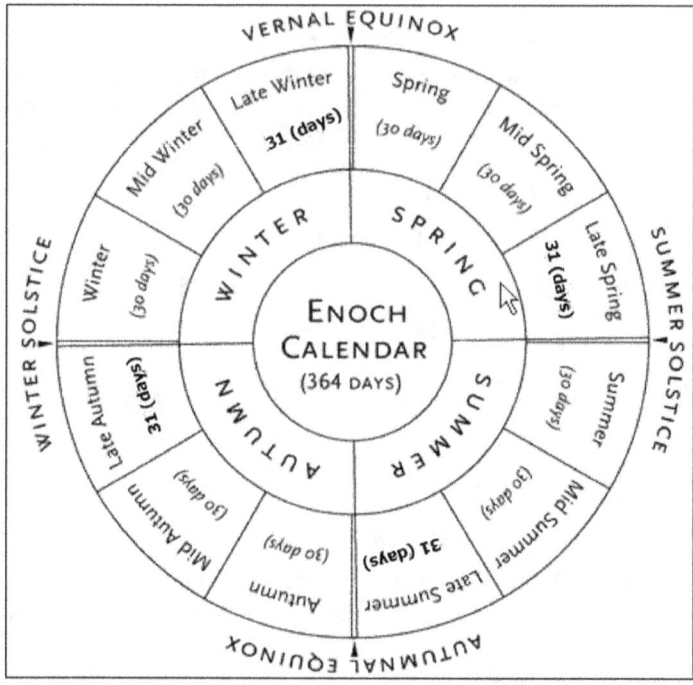

Alignment with Week. Because every quarter of the Enoch Calendar will always begin on the same day of the week, we need to know what weekday begins each quarter. One big clue is that this calendar is holy, having been revealed by an angel, and therefore most likely tied to days which God has declared holy. Both the first and last day of the week have been declared holy: the seventh day (Saturday) was the sabbath day before the resurrection of Jesus Christ. The most obvious alignment is that each quarter should begin on a Sunday just as each week begins on a Sunday. Let us try that hypothesis and see what fruit it bears.

Prophectic Dates in the Life of Christ.

There are four major events in the life of Jesus Christ that according to proponents of this belief say will line up perfectly with the Enoch Calendar, namely: his birth, baptism, beginning of public ministry, and resurrection.

The proposed dates in the life of the Savior were calculated from the Judean calendar, which was the version of the Hebrew calendar used at that time in Jerusalem. It is now clear after the fact to Christians that many of the rites of the law of Moses were symbolic of the events in the life of Christ. For example, the Passover lamb symbolized Christ who would be sacrificed (John 1:29, 1 Cor. 5:7). It is important to note that the very time at which the Savior was being crucified, the Passover lambs were also being slaughtered according to the Judean calendar.

Similarly, there is the Sheaf Offering of the firstfruits from the ground that was made shortly after the Redeemer was resurrected and became the firstfruits of them that slept (1 Cor 15:20). Thus, the timing of the various rites of the law of Moses all pointed to Christ as being the Messiah (Gal. 3:24).

Let us now consider those same events on the Enoch Calendar, remembering that the dates were derived by fitting the ritual days on the Hebrew calendar. First, let us just consider the intervals between the dates. Proponents of the Enoch Calendar believe from the beginning of our Savior's public ministry to his resurrection was exactly 3 Enoch years of 364 days. That is the very interval alignment already quoted from the Book of Enoch, namely, that after a three year period, the Hebrew and Enoch calendars align with each other.

The Temple and the Zodak Priesthood (1Chornicles 24; Ezek. 44).

1. The Zodak Priests are the only ones who are going to administer during the Millennium. The priestly order lines up perfectly using a 364 day Enoch Calendar.
2. The Israelites left Egypt on the 15th Day of the First month and also lines up using a 364 day Enoch Calendar. During the 3rd month, the same day they left Egypt (on the 15th day), they observed Pentecost.
3. The resurrection of our Savior on a Sabbath (Gr. *Sabbaton*) lines up perfectly using a 364 day Enoch Calendar.
4. Every Feast day of God's Calendar is on a fixed day of the week and will always be the same using a 364 day Calendar.

SEVENTY—PATIENCE, JUDGMENT

It is noteworthy that the interval between the dedication of Solomon's Temple (1006 B.C.) and the dedication of the second Temple (515 B.C.) was 490 years, a multiple of 7 and 10 (49 x 10). From the year succeeding the dedication of Solomon's Temple, to the year before the foundation of the second Temple was laid, was a period of 490 years of 360 days.

A like period had elapsed between the entrance into Canaan and the foundation of the kingdom under Saul. These cycles of 70, and multiples of 70 are certainly more than coincidental in Israel's history!

The Book of Enoch presents an apocalyptic account based on the seven sabbatical ages, and in (91:12-17) it adds three more—a total of ten sabbatical periods.

The Book of Jubilees records that at the creation God partitioned off time periods into sabbatical and jubilee cycles (Jub. 1:27-29). The births of Adam, Noah, Abraham, and other patriarchs were timed to coincide with sabbatical eras (4Q181, fragments 1-2). See also (Wacholder, *Interpreter's Dictionary*, Supplement, p.763).

The "Seventy Weeks" prophecy recorded by Daniel dovetails the Sabbatical Years' theme. This prophecy was the prime reference point for the advent of the Messianic age, in which the Jews were anticipating the Messiah to come in the first century. "Passover of the Sabbatical Year became the period when the redeemer's coming was expected most" (Wacholder, *Int. Dect. One Vol. supplement*, p. 763).

The nation of Israel consistently profaned God's land Sabbaths. During the period of violating 70 Sabbaticals or land rests in 430 years—the Eternal punished the nation of Israel by removing them from their land and sending them into captivity. The nation of Israel had defiled the land Sabbath for 390 years, while Judah 40 years (Ezek. 4:1-6).

Adding these totals together we obtain the sum of 430 years—the sum total of both houses' captivity. More importantly, is that Israel's punishment was for breaking God's Jubilee cycle!

The Day of Atonement *picturing* God's ultimate day of judgment was the most sacred day in Israel's history. This was the only day that the high priest of Israel was allowed to go behind the veil in the Tabernacle or Temple and into the Most

Holy Place. This event has tremendous spiritual importance in regards to Israel's final cleansing and occurred on the TENTH day of the SEVENTH month.

Here again we see the consistency of God's marvelous plan of salvation in the month and day as 7 x 10 = 70. Seven, the number of *spiritual perfection* and Ten, the number of *ordinal perfection* equaling Seventy—the number of God's Judgment!

God's entire plan is a Sabbatical plan lasting approximately 7,000 years! In fact, man's allotted life span is 70 years, after which he will be judged (Ps.90:10)!

FIFTY—RELEASE, FORGIVENESS, JUBILEE, UNITY, COHESIVENESS.

The number *fifty* denotes release from bondage of sin and to bring in everlasting righteousness. It also means "acceptance" and "unity."

The Tabernacle Moses constructed in the wilderness was covered with beautiful, high-quality curtains woven in two uneven lengths of material. They were joined with 50 hooks or clasps (Ex. 26:6, 11). The 50 attachments made the two uneven portions of linen into one curtain, one Tabernacle.

Fifty loops of blue were used as couplings for these hooks. Notice Exodus 36:12-13: **"Fifty loops he made on one curtain, and fifty loops he made on the edge of the curtain...and he made fifty clasps of gold, and coupled the curtains to one another with the clasps,** *that it might be one tabernacle.*"

It is thought Jesus began His public ministry in the year of Jubilee in the fall of A.D. 27-28. Was this by accident or was it by God's algebraic design? The year of *Jubilee* is a very important part of God's plan in dealing with the nation of Israel.

One of the Messiah's principle responsibilities will be to lead His people back to their land out of *captivity* (Isa. 49:6). Jesus proclaimed this event as He read a prophecy in Isaiah:

> **And there was delivered unto him a book of the prophet Isaiah. And when he had opened the book, he found the place where it was written, the Spirit of the Lord is upon me, because he hath anointed me to preach the gospel to the poor; he hath sent me to heal the**

brokenhearted, to preach *deliverance to the captives*, **and recovering of sight to the blind,** *to set at liberty* **them that are bruised, to preach** *the acceptable year of the Lord...* **(Lk. 4:18-19).**

Notice, the **"acceptable year of the Lord"** or His return is connected with the **"deliverance"** and setting at **"liberty"** the *captives!*
Now realize!

Jesus read this prophecy during the *sabbath* [Heb. Day of Weeks] or Pentecost (Lk. 4:16). This was during the Jubilee year of A.D. 27-28! It is worth noting that both Pentecost and Jubilee are counted by numbering seven sabbaths and adding one—rather than a set date like the other Feast days!

Calculation of the Jubilee Year

In calculating the Jubilee Year, one must count seven seven(s) of years, just as the Israelites counted seven weeks of seven days to Pentecost. Everything was based upon the weekly Sabbath day of the creation week.

Realize this very important point also! In both instances, one would end up with a total of 49. In the case of Pentecost, 7 weeks of days yields 49 days. The 50th day is Pentecost.

In calculating seven cycles of seven years, one would end up with 49 years. The 50th year or year of Jubilee also becomes the first year of the next cycle.

There were actually several reasons God instituted the year of Jubilee, namely: 1) to be the guardians of His time watch, and 2) to instill in Israel the dependency upon their Creator and to develop faith.

Prior to their coming out of Egypt, God synchronized His religious calendar with the nation of Israel through the feast days (Ex. 12:2).

Several times during Israel's dismal history—the Eternal revealed to them the true Sabbath day from which the Sabbatical cycles could be determined.

Let us contemplate. God had revealed His Sabbath day through the creation week. However, due to their slavery in Egypt, Israel was unable to worship God properly and lost track of time.

The observance of the new moons helped Israel to distinguish the months of the year (11 Chron. 2:4)—and the seventh day Sabbath was the cycle for counting the days of the month.

God told Moses that He was going to prove whether Israel was going to keep His Law by seeing if they would obey His test Commandment of the law—the Sabbath (Ex. 16:4).

During their wandering in the wilderness for forty years, God again revealed His Sabbath day by raining twice as much manna on the sixth day and withholding it completely on the seventh day (Ex. 16:26). Israel knew exactly which was the seventh day because God did not send any manna at all the day He called the seventh. God then emphasized it's importance by striking a man down for picking up sticks on the Sabbath (Num. 15:32-36).

Thus, the Eternal demonstrated to Israel that the Sabbath was "sanctified" or "set apart" for holy use—just as the entire nation was to be set aside for God's mission (Ex. 31:17).

As a boy, Jesus kept the same Sabbath day His ancestors were told to keep—and He never disputed its sequence of the weekly cycle while He walked the earth! (Mk. 2:27,28; Lk. 4:16).

To establish His religious calendar, God first revealed His weekly cycle of seven days at creation. Then, He revealed His monthly cycle through His feast days beginning with the Passover through the "new moons". Furthermore, every seven years was a bench mark in counting to the Year of Jubilee. The Jubilee Year completed a 50 year cycle [actually 49 years apart].

In other words, every 7,14,21,28,35,42 and 49th year was to be observed as a land Sabbath. Thus, through this cycle of days in a week, weeks in a month, months in a year, years in a Jubilee Year—God establishes His Jubilee cycle.

The acceptable Year of Jubilee

In Israel, every 50th year was to be hailed as a year of Jubilee. All Israelites who were debtors were released from such bondage to any of their countrymen. All debts were cancelled, notice:

And thou shalt number seven sabbaths of years

> unto thee, seven times seven years; and the space of the seven sabbaths of years shall be unto thee *forty and nine years.* Then shalt thou cause the trumpet of the jubilee to sound on the tenth day of the seventh month, in the day of atonement shall ye make the trumpet sound throughout all your land.
>
> And ye shall hallow the fiftieth year, and proclaim *liberty* throughout all the land unto all the inhabitants thereof: it shall be a jubilee unto you; and ye shall return every man unto his possession, and ye shall return every man unto his family. A jubilee shall that fiftieth year be unto you: ye shall not sow, neither reap that which groweth of itself in it, nor gather the grapes in it of thy vine undressed. For it is the jubilee; it shall be holy unto you: ye shall eat the increase thereof out of the field (Lev. 25:8-12).

The Jubilee year was the 50th year following the 7th Sabbatic year [actually 49 years apart]—(Lev. 25:8). The land was to rest even though it followed a Sabbatical rest the year before. This made for an unusual event, allowing the land to remain fallow two years in a row. The people were to live off the produce produced during the sixth year—thus testing their faith as two consecutive Sabbaths followed in a row!

Every seven years a land sabbath was to be observed, during which time the land rested: it was neither sown to a crop nor were vineyards pruned. Six years were allowed for tilling and sowing fields, pruning vineyards, and gathering the produce from them. The sixth year was to yield a triple blessing of crops which would provide food on into the ninth year; only natural produce of the land could serve as food for the Israelites during the seventh year (Lev. 25:1-7, 18-22). In addition, all loans to fellow Israelites were cancelled after the sixth year.

Rooted at the very base of God's system of economics is a unique program of land ownership. **"No land is to be sold in perpetuity, for the land is mine, and you are only guests of mine, passing wayfarers; you must allow land to be bought**

back anywhere in the country you hold" (Lev. 25:23-24). This system of land ownership which God instituted through Moses in ancient Israel provided the foundation for all economic activity of that "church in the wilderness" (Acts 7:38)

Each family had its own homestead, its own nucleus of property *never* to leave the family. Additional sons at birth received title to their own estate, compared to the present system of inheritance of land by reason of someone's death. A birth certificate was a title deed to an estate.

Every 50 years was a jubilee year during which, on the Feast of Trumpets, each man was to return to the homestead he had been given when first entering the land. Any buying or selling of land was done **"...in view of the number of years and crops till the next year of jubilee; as the years are many, you must increase the price, and as the years are few you must lower the price, for what is sold is the number of the crops" (Lev. 25:14-16).** Land was always retained by the original title holder, eliminating land speculation and fluctuating land market.

Alongside the daily, weekly, and seven-year cycles appears the God-ordained 50 year cycle. This Jubilee year is pictured as a time of joy and restoration of lands!

Jubilee and Atonement

The Jubilee year began on the Day of Atonement, and both events *foreshadow* the time of Israel's REDEMPTION and return to their land! Each Jubilee year, the land that had been divided by lot to the families of Israel, was returned to their rightful birthright owners. In the year of Jubilee, the land was to be returned to the descendants of the family God had selected to own that particular piece of real estate under Joshua.

One commentator writes: "[The Jubilee year] did not teach either the socialistic economic theory...or the free-enterprise system that allows an unlimited expansion of private property. On the contrary, it established a fixed title to the property assigned by God" (*International Standard Bible Encyclopaedia*, volume II, page 1142).

The Jubilee year was to be proclaimed, not at the beginning of the civil calendar on the Feast of Trumpets, but on the Day of Atonement, 10 days later.

God wanted the nation of Israel freed from human

oppression. But He desired much more. He wanted Israel to enjoy the same liberty Jesus Christ came to bring—freedom from sin! What is this liberating truth? Jesus explains: **"Most assuredly, I say to you, whoever commits sin is a slave of sin...If the Son makes you free, you shall be free indeed" (Jn. 8:34, 36).**

True liberty is freedom from bondage of sin. Christian liberty has its price. The apostle Paul explains:

> **Don't you know that when you offer yourselves to someone to obey him as slaves, you are slaves to the one whom you obey, whether you are slaves to sin, which leads to death, or to obedience, which leads to righteousness?...You have been set free from sin and have become slaves to righteousness (Romans 6:16-18, NIV).**

Paul continues his dissertation on Christian liberty:

> **[We] who have the firstfruits of the Spirit...[eagerly wait] for the adoption, the redemption of our body...The creation itself also will be delivered from the bondage of corruption into the glorious liberty of the children of God (Rom. 8:23, 21).**

The year of Jubilee was a *dress rehearsal* of the time that the nation of Israel will be "set free" from the bondage of their enemies as Christ returns to lead them out of captivity.

At this time, *atonement* will be made for the sins of Israel, and they will begin to inherit the blessings God has promised them!

After our Lord had finished reading this passage from Isaiah, He closed the book and declared: **"This day is this scripture fulfilled in your ears."** But why did our Lord stop in the middle of this scripture instead of completing the remainder of the verse, **"And the day of vengeance of our Lord"?**

The answer is obvious!

Our Lord Himself placed a comma in the middle of this sentence because He had only come to fulfill part of this prophecy at that time! The fulfillment of **"...the day of**

vengeance of our Lord" will only transpire upon our Lord's second and final advent in which a parenthesis of nearly 2,000 years will have elapsed!

We can now understand why the Bible says of the first century Church, that, **"...when the Day of Pentecost had fully come [Pentecost was the 50th day after the spring wave-sheaf ceremony]—see (Leviticus 23:15-16) they were all of** *one accord in one place"* **(Acts 2:1).**

What a beautiful law to reunite families!

A decade of Jubilees

Now here is something very incredible but highly significant in the understanding of prophetic events. The "seventy weeks" prophecy of (Daniel 9), which prophesies **"...the coming of the Messiah to make an end of Israel's sins, and to bring in everlasting righteousness"** is *a decade of jubilees!*

In this verse, the Hebrew word *shabua,* meaning "seven" is translated "weeks" in the *King James Version,* but is a misnomer and correct in the *Stuart's* translation! Thus, (Daniel 9:24) should read: **"Seventy** *sevens* **are determined upon thy people and upon thy holy city..."**

These "seventy sevens" technically are "seventy sabbatical cycles", and Ben Wacholder verifies this through his research of compelling evidence from Qumranic, rabbinic and epigraphic documents. He writes that the Hebrew word *shabua* clearly means "the sabbatical cycle" (Ben Zion Wacholder, pp. 202-204).

In 1956 a fragmentary text, entitled (11Q Melchizedek) was discovered in Qumran Cave 11 and cross references the Jubilee from (Lev. 25:13; Deut. 15:2; Isa. 61:1) with Daniel's Seventy Weeks Prophecy. The description of the Messianic work of Melchizedek is decribed thusly:

> **He will restore (their patrimonies?) to them and proclaim freedom to them and make them abandon all their sins. This shall take place during the sabbatical cycle (***shabua***) of the first jubilee following the ni[ne] jubilees, and on the D[ay of Atone]ment f[alling] at the en[d of the ju]bilee, the tenth; to forgive on it (the day of**

atonement) for all of (the sins) of the children of [God and] the men of the lot of Melchizedek (11 Q Melchizekek, translation by Ben Zion Wacholder, pp. 210-211).

But why prophesy seventy "sevens" instead of seventy "years"? The Hebrew word for years could have been used if only "seventy years" were God's intention concerning Israel's punishment!

Surely this is very important to God, and using His mathematical design we will now show its significance! Are there any other "sevens" of numbers mentioned in the Word of God that Daniel's people would understand? Indeed, there were!

God gave His people a week of "seven" days—the Sabbath being the *seventh* day of the week. This seventh day of the physical *rest* was a *mirror* of God's Millennial government of rest and peace upon the earth, in which the nation of Israel will be God's leading witness instrumentally!

In addition to the "seven of days" God instituted the "seven year" land rest every *seventh* year. The Israelites were to work their land the first six years, but were to let their land rest from sowing and tiling the seventh (Lev. 25:3-4). This also had similar connotation as did the seven days of the creation week!

It was upon this "seven sabbaths of years" that the foundation for counting the Jubilee year was formed! Every fiftieth year—all debts were cancelled and all real estate was returned to the rightful birthright landholders (Lev. 25:8-9).

The overwhelming evidence of the relationship of the tenth Jubilee and Daniel's Seventy Weeks is made clear from simple arithmatic. Ten Jubilee years (10 x 49 = 490), and the seventy sabbatical cycles of Daniel 9:24 (70 x 7 = 490).

Ben Wacholder adds: "...when one reads in line 18 of our fragment: 'And the herald of good tidings' (Is. 52:7a) refers to the messiah, the Spirit concerning whom it was said by Dan[iel (9:25): 'Until the coming of the messiah, the prince seven sabbatical cycles.']...It is noteworthy that, as Daniel 9:24, the last year of jubilee involves atonement for iniquity: "to forgive on it [the day of atonement] for all of [the sins]" (Ben Zion Walcholder, p. 211, Line 8, n. 87).

Another interesting point that many scholars have made in their assessment of Daniel 9, is that the Messiah or "anointed one" of (verse 25 and 26) and the "anointing" of "the most Holy" [Place or Holy of Holies] (Heb. *qodesh qodashim*) of (verse 24) may have reference to a place or a person or both.

Thus, after "seventy sabbatical cycles" the Messiah would come to cleanse the Holy of Holies [Jerusalem, the sanctuary and the holy people]. P. Grelot describes this final sabbatical cycle as "the Sabbath of Sabbaths for the tried people" (*Biblica 50*, 1969, p. 182). Andre Lacocque describes this time as "the Great Day of Forgiveness" [Heb. *Yom hakippurim*], (*The Book of Daniel*, p. 192).

This is the time that the Messiah will **"...finish the transgression, and put an end to sin, and atone for iniquity, and bring in everlasting righteousness" (Dan. 9:24).** Jesus Christ is our true High Priest, but notice what the high priest of Israel was to do in *type* on the Day of Atonement:

> **And he shall make an atonement for the holy place, because of the uncleanness of the children of Israel, and because of their transgression in all their sins...and for the altar, and he shall make an atonement for the priests, and for all the people of the congregation (Lev. 16:16; 33).**

The Jubilee and Daniel 9:24

Daniel knew that these seventy "sevens" referred to seventy *prophetic years* in the desolations of Jerusalem (Dan. 9:2). As a youth, Daniel realized the impending captivity of His people by the Babylonian Empire under Nebuchadnezzar because of the prophecies of Isaiah and Micah (Isa. 39:6; Micah 4:10). These prophets along with Jeremiah, had forecast Judah's destruction and forthcoming captivity for 70 years, almost 100 years before it happened! (Jer. 25:11,12; 29:10).

Daniel was also very familiar with God's penal code of justice for breaking His law of the Sabbatic year as stated in (11 Chron. 36:21; Lev. 26:34).

For every Sabbatic year Judah had violated—God was going to punish them one year in captivity! Because they had broken the land sabbath 70 times during the course of 490 years—God was going to punish them 70 years or seventy "sevens" of years!

How consistent this seems according to God's algebraic

design! It is as though the angel of God were saying to Daniel, **"Because the captivity of your people had been 70 years for breaking the land Sabbath, the time between the captivity and the coming of the Messiah will be *seven times* as long!"**

In the course of breaking seventy Sabbatical years [prophetic times], ten Jubilee years were also violated! Without this understanding, Daniel's seventy weeks prophecy is muddled!

Because Judah broke seventy Sabbatical cycles [land rests], they were being punished *sevenfold* or seven times each Sabbatical year of violation. Simple arithmetic of (70 times 7) equals 490 years of punishment. The first 69 weeks of punishment as recorded in (Daniel 9) have since occurred—the 70th week [consisting of seven literal years] is still future! We will study this prophecy in its entirety in the next chapter.

In God's fury, He declared to this rebellious nation:

> **Ye have not hearkened unto me, in proclaiming liberty, every one to his brother, and every man to his neighbor: behold, I proclaim a liberty for you, saith the Lord, to the sword, to the pestilence, and to the famine; and I will make you to be removed into all the kingdoms of the earth (Jer. 34:8-17).**

This historic captivity of the nation of Judah by Nebuchadnezzar's Babylonian army began **"...to fulfill the word of the Lord by the mouth of Jeremiah, until the land had enjoyed her sabbaths; for as long as she lay desolate she kept sabbath, to fulfill threescore and ten years" (11 Chron. 36:21; see also Leviticus 26:35).**

Because the nation of Judah had failed to keep God's land Sabbath for seventy years, the Eternal was going to keep it for them for these seventy missing years—by sending them into captivity!

This seventy-year period of "desolations" began with the conquering of the land and besieging of Jerusalem by Nebuchadnezzar on the tenth day of the tenth month, in 589 B.C.; and ended seventy prophetic years later [360 day years] to the exact day in 520 B.C. when the foundation of the second Temple was laid (see Haggai 2:18).

Jubilee and Pentecost

Pentecost and Jubilee are both counted by numbering seven sabbaths and adding one, rather than a set date. Both add up to "50"! Pentecost is calculated by counting seven Sabbaths of days while Jubilee is calculated by counting seven Sabbaths of years!

Surely this must be a spiritual calculus equation that only God's Holy Spirit can unlock as our school teacher! The Day of Pentecost *symbolizes* the Church's acceptance to God as "firstfruits." Because Israel also observed the Feast of Pentecost—this understanding must also apply to her!

Now Pentecost pictures the *resurrection* of FIRSTFRUITS to be *acceptable* to God as they are released from the bondage of this world!

Could it be that there will be a *resurrection* of "firstfruits" to God on some future Day of Pentecost during a Jubilee year?

Could this also be a *dual* prophecy to Israel and the Church? It appears that 144,000 *firstfruits* of the nation of Israel (Rev. 7) along with 144,000 *firstfruits* of the Church (Rev. 14:1,4) will be offered to God at some time prior to Christ's return!

Thus, we have the connecting link between Pentecost—Atonement—and Jubilee!

The Mysterious 120 Years

In (Genesis 6:3) we read the strange statement: **"And the Lord said, My spirit shall not always strive with man, for that he also is flesh: yet his days shall be 120 years."**

What is the meaning of this enigmatic verse?

Could this verse be *dual* to the actual time (120 years) to when the flood would come, and from the time of Adam to the end of the age (120 Jubilee years)?

There are exactly 120 Jubilee cycles between 4000B.C. and 2000 A.D.,or 6,000 years from creation (120 x 50= 6,000).

The Days of Noah are but a *type* of the end-time age, and Methuselah was given an additional 120 years to live in order that the gospel could be preached. We will read more of this meaning in Volume 4.

Some have thought these days represented humankind's allotted life span on the earth after the flood, but we know from the scriptures, this is not true. Humankind's allotted life span is recorded in Psalm 90:10, **"The days of our years are threescore years and ten (70); and if by reason of strength they be fourscore years (80)..."**

In other words, the average age of man would be approximately 70 years, with some attaining 80 if blessed with exceptional health. Of course, we know today that many have lived to be centenarians, including the patriarchs Abraham [175] (Gen. 25:7); Isaac [180] (Gen. 35:28); and Jacob [130] (Gen. 47:9).

Besides 120 additional years to preach the gospel, what could these 120 years possibly represent prophetically?

Could it be that God has revealed His 6,000 year plan for humankind through these 120 years?

Now take note! If the "Days of Noah" are a *type* of the end-time, and the flood a *type* of the tribulation, and Methuselah a *type* of the Church preaching the gospel—then could these 120 years possibly represent the end of God's 6,000 year plan? And could it be that God will once again grant an additional 120 years to preach the gospel as He did during Noah's day?

Is it conincidence or design that these 120 Jubilee Years add up to exactly 6,000 years? It's as though God was saying in Genesis 6:3: **"My Spirit will not contend (strive) with man forever, (only for 6,000) years, for he is mortal; his days on the earth will be a hundred and twenty (Jubilee) years."**

Assuming this concept to be correct—when do we begin counting the 6,000 years? Do we start counting 6,000 years from the creation of Adam and Eve, or from the flood? This is anyone's guess!

Through the understanding of the Jubilee Year and it's celebration on the Day of Atonement, we see a most interesting connection to Daniel's Seventy Weeks Prophecy.

The Jubilee Year *pictured* a time of Israel's *release* from *bondage* or *sin* as does the Day of Atonement. The Seventy Weeks Prophecy is based upon the Jubilee Year land violation, and Israel was to be punished for her sins! Her transgressions or iniquity was to be forgiven after a decade of Jubilee Years or "seventy sevens". Thus, we see the connecting link between Jubilee, Atonement, and Daniel's "Seventy Weeks Prophecy".

2520—THE NUMBER OF PROPHETIC SENTENCE

Nebuchadnezzar's Insanity a type of the End-Time

There are *four* time cycles of 2,520 years indicated in the scriptures. Three of these periods find their fulfillment in the last days.

We will now discuss the first of these 2,520 year time cycles.

God first pictured the succession of world-ruling governments from Nebuchadnezzar's time onward as a great imposing image of a man. This civilization was a product of *man's mind* and *heart* (intelligence and emotions). This image was described in (Daniel 2), as we have already read.

So proud was Nebuchadnezzar of the fact that he and his kingdom were its HEAD, he erected in Babylon in honor of himself an actual image of gold, and commanded all the people to worship it or face the penalty of a fiery death (Dan. 3).

God's servants Shadrach, Meshach, and Abednego would not bow down to the king's dictates and were thrown into the fiery furnace. However, these FAITHFUL servants of God were *miraculously saved,* and are a *type* of the trials that will face Christians in the last days, as the "Beast" power will impose it's *mark* on true Christians once again!

However, Nebuchadnezzar was not allowed to remain in his haughty grandeur for long. He was suddenly cut down by God, and given the mind of a *wild beast.*

Let's notice exactly what happened to King Nebuchadnezzar. The king had a second dream that troubled him greatly (Dan. 4:4-5). Nebuchadnezzar had a dream in which he saw a tree in the middle of the earth grow to a great height. The tree grew strong and tall until it reached unto heaven. The leaves of this prodigious tree produced much fruit—and all flesh was fed from it.

Then the king saw a watcher [angel] come down from heaven and said to cut the great tree down to a stump, cut off its branches, shake off his leaves, and scatter its fruit (vss. 11-15).

Then the frightened king called for his magicians and astrologers to interpret the dream, but they were unable to (vss. 6-7). Finally, the king called upon Daniel to interpret the dream.

Daniel told the vaunted Nebuchadnezzar that the tree was *symbolic* of himself—whose empire had become strong and great in the dominion of the earth (vs. 22).

The dream *pictured* the king living with the beasts of the field and eating grass like an ox, if he didn't repent. This was to be for "seven times" (vs. 25).

The dream was given at first as a warning, with a chance for Nebuchadnezzar to repent and escape the dire punishment. God is always faithful to give man a chance to repent before He punishes!

"Seven Times," in prophetic language, means seven years. Therefore, Nebuchadnezzar was to live and act like a wild beast for seven literal years before his strange madness would pass.

Nebuchadnezzar, during his insanity, *symbolized* the real nature of the prophesied Gentile empires. No longer with any real understanding, cut off from God, ignorant of the *purpose* for man's being on earth, these empires, like *wild predatory beasts*, would fight and struggle, wage war, tear and devour, down through the centuries!

The Gentile's Seven Times Punishment

Since much of Biblical prophecy is *dual*, the seven years of Nebuchadnezzar's personal punishment became a *type* of the duration of this world's human governments and their wild beast like ways. But in the *antitypical fulfillment* in the succession of human empires, each one of the "seven times" becomes not a literal year, but a *symbolic* or prophetic year of 360 days. Each such "day" itself stands for a literal year, according to the well known Biblical principle given in (Numbers 4:34 and Ezekiel 4:4-6), which show that each *symbolic* day represents an actual year in fulfillment.

And so the "times" of God's punishment on the Gentiles, allowing them to go their own way and reap the natural consequences of sin—would last for a period of 2520 years (7 x 360). During this time the world's kingdoms would act like wild beasts—until they finally learn, as Nebuchadnezzar did, that God Almighty rules in the affairs of men. The time when the great tree of Babylon fell was approximately 539 B.C.

Now here is something significant in determining *when* the "times of the Gentiles" would end. The *tree* is addressed to the *man* Nebuchadnezzar, as Daniel interpreted the tree as [you] O king—or the empire he personified (vss. 20-22). Babylon was Nebuchadnezzar, and Nebuchadnezzar was Babylon in *type*. The prophecy said 7 Times would pass over [you]—and Nebuchadnezzar was punished for 7 *literal years,* as the Gentile kingdoms in *antitype* would be punished for 7 *prophetic years*!

But what happened to Nebuchadnezzar after his 7 literal years of madness? Because he is a *type* of the Gentile world—whatever happened to him—would also happen to the Gentile world in the last days!

After 7 literal years of insanity—Nebuchadnezzar's mind was completely restored! Could this be a *duality* to what will happen to the last Gentile empire in the end-time? The 4th chapter of Daniel dealt with the person of Nebuchadnezzar, who is a *type* of the Babylonian system of this world. The very next chapter deals with the Babylonian system itself in the infamous "Handwriting on the Wall."

The Handwriting on the Wall

One of the most fascinating revelations of the entire panorama of prophecy is found in the fifth chapter of Daniel. It also concerns the duration of the Gentile world empires which had been revealed previously.

Nebuchadnezzar had suffered a punishment for "seven times" (years). Yet his kingdom was kept safe while insane (Dan. 4:26, 36), after which he *resumed* his rule until his death. Following this, several other kings reigned and died (Jer. 27:6-7).

The time finally came for the first phase [Chaldean] of world government to end, and for the kingdom to be transferred to the Medes and Persians (Dan. 5:30 31).

That night, the unsuspecting king Belshazzar [Nebuchadnezzar's son] made a great feast for his lords and ladies (Dan. 5:1-4). Then the king "saw" some strange writing on the wall, notice:

> **In the same hour came forth fingers of a man's hand, and wrote over against the candlestick upon the plaster of the wall of the kings' palace: and the king saw the part of the hand that**

> wrote. Then the kings' countenance was changed, and his thoughts troubled him, so that the joints of his loins were loosed, and his knees smote one against another" (vss. 5 6).

The queen mother summoned Daniel, now an old man to interpret the strange writing (vss. 18-22). The kings astrologers and wise men could not explain the strange writing (vs. 7), but Daniel could (vs. 17). God inspired Daniel to reveal that the strange writing, "mene, mene, tekel, upharsin" was a *sentence* that would add up to God's *judgment!*

But why was this so startling, that it made the king loose his bowels (the King James English is so colorful in describing what one goes through in fear)! But I think you get the picture!

While many are familiar with the feast he held in Babylon when the mysterious handwriting of doom appeared on the wall—they have failed to recognize, that this gathering was a *religious* gathering! The filthy and abominable practices on this occasion were part of the religious ceremonies of the Babylonian Mysteries!

Some commentaries believe Nimrod was the King and founder of Babylon, and was its first priest-king, or its religious leader as well. Belshazzar was its priest-king at that time! Says the Bible about this religious festival: **"They drank wine, and praised the gods of wood, gold, silver, brass, iron, and stone" (Dan. 5:4).**

Adding to their blasphemy of the occasion, they drank their wine from the holy vessels of the Lord which had been taken from the House of God, when Judah was taken captive by Babylon, and the Temple ransacked! Such an attempt to combine that which was holy with that which was heathenism, brought about God's swift judgment!

"Numbered", "Weighed", and "Divided"

According to *Strong's Concordance* #4484, "mene" is a number, and it means "numbered" (5: 26). "Tekel" #8625 means "to balance or weigh" (5: 27). "Upharsin" or "parsin" means "divided" as does its root word *peres* (5: 28). So, Daniel interpreted these words to mean that Belshazzar's Chaldean Empire had received a divine sentence. God had *numbered* the

PROPHETIC NUMBERS

days of the king's reign, as it had been *weighed* in God's balances, and it would soon be *divided* up among the Medes and Persians (Dan. 5:22-28).

What most Bible scholars have failed to realize about this intriguing prophecy is that it is *dual*, and not only refers to Belshazzar's kingdom and its impending doom—but it also refers to the entire Babylonish system and its final destruction upon Christ's return (Dan. 2:34,44; Rev. 17-18). This fact is also concurred by the repetition of the words "mene, mene."

The interpretation of these words "mene, mene, tekel upharsin" can only be understood by unlocking its key. Its *key* is in the common denominator of Hebrew weights designating monetary values!

Mene is the Hebrew equivalent for the *minah* weight. *Tekel* is the Babylonian spelling for the Hebrew weight *shekel*, and *parsin* is equivalent to the *peres* weight. We are told to "halve" or "divide" these weights into their lowest common denominator (like dividing dollars into pennies).

The *minah* consists of 50 shekels according to *The Interpreter's Dictionary of the Bible* ("Weights"). The *shekel* can be subdivided into *geraphs,* 20 gerahs equaling one *shekel.* *Strong's Concordance* says that *peres* #6537 is a unit of weight. Hence we have converted a number "mene", a verb "parsin" and a weight "tekel" to a common number.

Therefore, let's do as Daniel said, and divide everything into the smallest number—into gerahs:

one mene (minah)	= 50 shekels	= 1,000 gerahs
another mene (minah)	= 50 shekels	= 1,000 gerahs
a tekel (shekel)	= 1 shekel	= 20 gerahs
half a mene (peres)	= 25 shekels	= 500 gerahs
		Total 2,520

Adding up all the number of *gerahs* is 2520—the number of years of God's sentence on this Babylonian system! Ironically, this is the same number for Nebuchadnezzar's punishment of 7 x 360 days, or 2,520 days or seven years! This is also the same "seven times" punishment upon the nation of Israel!

Our Lord and Savior Jesus Christ said of the "times of the Gentiles", **"...Jerusalem shall be trodden down of the**

Gentiles, until the times of the Gentiles be fulfilled" (Lk. 21:24). The "times of the Gentiles" began with the invasion and captivity of Jerusalem in 606 B.C. by king Nebuchadnezzar's Babylonian army, and Jesus plainly states they would end only upon His return!

The succession of the four world ruling Gentile governments from Nebuchadnezzar to Christ's second Advent are outlined in the prophecies of (Daniel 2 and 7). The final Gentile power will be cut down by Jesus Christ, the supernatural "stone made without hands" that will end the "times of the Gentile powers" (Dan. 2:34, 35, 44).

2520 Years to World Peace

The number 2520 is highly significant prophetically, and has been mentioned twice already. It is used in describing the temporary worldwide insanity of Gentile governments—*symbolic* of king Nebuchadnezzar—and also the time that this Gentile insanity would end, by ushering in God's government as it is weighed in the balance!

But there is one more important prophecy regarding 2520 years—it has to do with the return of the nation of Israel, and their establishment to world PROMINENCE as a whole nation!

Ironically [by grand design] these dates coincide! At the very same time the powers of the Gentile kingdoms of this world end—the nation of Israel's power is to be RESTORED! At Mt. Sinai, God formed the nation of Israel into a theocratical model government. It was a combination of Church and State, regulated by God's 10 Commandments, statutes and judgments. This was the start of God's Church known as "The Church in the Wilderness" (Acts 7:38).

The making of the Old Covenant, as recorded in the 24th chapter of Exodus was also a MARRIAGE COMPACT! It was this marriage ceremony that established the nation of Israel as God's chosen people over all other nations of the earth! As long as Israel was faithful to her husband [Christ] in keeping God's laws—He promised to provide and protect her.

At Mt. Sinai, the people of Israel accepted the terms of this agreement and promised never to commit adulterous relations with other nations [by worshiping their false gods] (Ex. 34:12-17). If Israel remained faithful to her husband—God promised to make them "a kingdom of *priests*, and an holy nation" (Ex. 19:5-6).

However, if they became disobedient and rebellious—God also stipulated a *seven Times* punishment: **"...they that hate you shall REIGN OVER YOU...SEVEN TIMES" (Lev. 26:14-28; see also Lev. 23:24; 27:28).** A "Time" is God's "day for a year" principle (Ezek..4:4-6; Num. 14:34). In other words "one Time" would mean 360 years, each day representing a year—7 Times would be 7 x 360 or 2520 prophetic years!

Thus, God threatened to remove His government from Israel, and to allow the Gentile world to rule over them for a period of 2520 years—if Israel proved disobedient!

Israel's Seven Times Punishment.

Within a year after God made these explicit terms of the Old Covenant known to Israel, they began grossly violating the conditions of their marriage contract. At this point, the Eternal found it absolutely imperative to DIVORCE His wife and remove His government from them for 2520 long years (see Ezek. 20:13; Isa. 50:1; 59:1 2; Jer. 3:6,8).

Israel was now divorced and was taken captive by the Assyrians in 721 B.C. Soon afterward, the nation of Judah was also taken captive by the invading Gentile armies of king Nebuchadnezzar of Babylon in 606 B.C.

Both houses [Israel and Judah] were prophesied to be under Gentile domination by Daniel and Ezekiel for a duration of 2520 years.

This Gentile rule over Israel is *pictured* very graphically by the great Gentile image Nebuchadnezzar saw in his dream (which we have already elaborated upon). The authority to rule was thus handed over to Nebuchadnezzar [the head of gold] and his successors [the Persian, Greecian and Roman empires] for 2520 years!

Finally, the government of God, *pictured* by a supernatural Stone [Jesus Christ] is to SMASH the feet of this last Gentile power upon His second advent—and RESTORE *the government of God back to Israel* (Acts 3:21).

Ezekiel's Living Legend

The entire scenario of Israel's and Judah's iniquity and eventual *restoration* as a national power is graphically dramatized by an event God caused in Ezekiel's life. This event is a *type* of Israel's impending captivity. This prophecy is recorded in (Ezekiel 3:24; 4:1-8).

Essentially here's what happened. God told Ezekiel to lie on his left side for 390 days (*symbolic* of Israel's duration of iniquity) and to lie on his right side for 40 days (*symbolic* of Judah's duration of iniquity).

God spelled out His intent for Israel through this graphic illustration and declared: **"I have laid upon thee *the years of their iniquity*, according to the number of days you laid on your side" (vs. 5). "I have appointed each day for a year" (vs. 6).**

This entire *dramatization* had only one purpose—to show the length of time Israel (390 years) and Judah (40 years) were to be under Gentile domination till their *sins* would be *forgiven*! Here then is a total of 430 years of punishment that the entire house of Israel would endure until God granted them GRACE!

However, the iniquity and punishment of Israel and Judah did not end after 390 years, nor in 40 additional years! God had spoken to them previously of an additional SEVEN TIMES PUNISHMENT in Leviticus 26:18: **"If ye will not yet for all this hearken unto me, then I will punish you *seven times more* for your sins."**

It is a well established fact as recorded in (Jeremiah 29:10 and Daniel 9:2), that the duration of Judah's captivity in Babylon [representing the entire nation of Israel] would be for "seventy years." This is the captivity and partial return to their homeland in 536 B.C. recorded by Ezra and Nehemiah.

Because this was only a partial return of the Jews [described by Daniel's 70 weeks]—the remainder of the years of iniquity Ezekiel foretold still remain! This prophecy still remains for those in Israel who are still dispersed!

Realize also, that while Judah, the last remaining tribe of Israel was in captivity—the entire land of Canaan was resting, fulfilling the Jubilee rest and part of the "desolations" of Jerusalem.

By subtracting these 70 years of fulfilled captivity from the

430 years of prophesied iniquity we have a balance of sentence of 360 years. Multiplying these 360 years by 7 Times—we have 2520 years until Israel's land would be RESTORED in fulfillment of God's promise to Abraham.

But now we come to the crucial question. When do we start counting the 2520 years when Israel's punishment will end? This is a difficult question, since most historical dates are controversial. According to most Biblical and historical scholars, Israel's captivity began in 721 B.C. and Judah's in 606 B.C. Judah's captivity began in three stages and ended in 536 B.C. The first return of the Jews began seventy years later in 516 B.C.

As prophesied, at the end of the seventy years of captivity in Babylon, in the spring of 536 B.C.; in the month Nisan, under the decree of the Persian king Cyrus, a small remnant of the house of Judah returned to Jerusalem. This is the recorded historical date given by Flavius Josephus.

If we count 2520 prophetic biblical years of 360 days we get $(2{,}520 \times 360 = 907{,}000$ days). Now we must convert these days into calendar years of 365.25 days by dividing 907,000 by $365.25 = (2{,}483.8)$. Therefore, counting from 536 B.C. we arrive at the very significant date of 1948, the rebirth of the nation of Israel!

70 Sabbaticals in 430 Years

Now here is another amazing fact that few indeed realize—but once again demonstrates the *consistency* of God's master plan.

These 430 years of Israel's punishment were based upon the Jubilee cycle. During the course of 430 years, there are exactly 70 Sabbaticals or land rests. This is calculated by counting years 7,14,21,28,35,42,49,50 in one Jubilee cycle. In other words, there are 8 land rests in a 50 year period time.

I think you will agree that this is an astounding statistic and not merely coincidental that there are exactly 70 land rests during the course of 430 years!

The nation of Israel consistently profaned God's land Sabbaths. During the period of violating 70 Sabbaticals or land rests in 430 years—the Eternal punished the nation of Israel by removing them from their land and sending them into captivity. The nation of Israel had defiled the land Sabbath for 390 years, while Judah 40 years (Ezek. 4:1-6). Adding these totals together we obtain the sum of 430 years—the sum total of both houses' captivity. More importantly, is that Israel's punishment was for breaking God's Jubilee cycle!

The Day of Atonement *picturing* God's ultimate day of judgment was the most sacred day in Israel's history. This was the only day that the high priest of Israel was allowed to go behind the veil in the Tabernacle or Temple and into the Most Holy Place. This event has tremendous spiritual importance in regards to Israel's final cleansing and occurred on the TENTH

sabbatical	No. Years	Land Rests
1	49	8
2	49	8
3	49	8
4	49	8
5	49	8
6	49	8
7	49	8
8	49	8
9	38	6
Totals	430	70

day of the SEVENTH month.

2520 Prophetic Years

3 is the number of *divine perfection*.
7 is the number of *spiritual perfection*.
10 is the number of *ordinal perfection*.
12 is the number of *governmental perfection*.

The summation of 3 x 7 x 10 x 12 = 2520. Is it merely coincidence or *design* that the product of these four *perfect* numbers, results in the prophetic time period of Israel's punishment and the times the Gentiles are given to rule? I think not!

And I think you will agree that it is not merely coincidental that there are exactly 2520 biblical years from the ending of the Babylonian captivity in 536 B.C. to the rebirth of the nation of Israel in 1948!

Chapter Thirteen

DANIEL'S SEVENTY WEEKS PROPHECY

THE FIRST 69 WEEKS

Prophecy in general and Daniel's Seventy Weeks prophecy in particular has been one of the most confusing and debatable prophicies ever written. Yet it is a "key" prophecy that "unlocks" a number of other prophecies. And despite the claims made by various individuals, we shall see that this prophecy is not as clear-cut as they would have us believe.

The aim of this chapter is to expose the majority of the various viewpoints on this subject so that constructive criticism can result in a more accurate assessment and comprehension of the subject. The understanding of this prophecy is vital in understanding "eschatology", a word coined from the Greek word *eschaton* meaning (the end, last thing) and pertains to the sequence of end-time events.

There are *three* major interpretations of this most incredible prophecy currently being taught, namely, 1) the Symbolic, 2) the

Futurist, and 3) the Historical-Messianic (fulfilled in Christ).

The *Futurist* interpretation is by far the more popular interpretation and was spawned in the English-speaking world through the writings of John Nelson Darby (1800-1882), the Plymouth Brethren (1830's), and C.I. Scofield's reference Bible (1911) which incorporated Darby's views.

Darby, an Irishman, who was educated at Trinity College, Dublin, started out as a law student, and later gave up his profession to become a priest in the Church of England. He later became a leader of one of the Plymouth Brethren groups at Plymouth England, and began writing articles about the "rapture."

In around 1850, some of the Plymouth Brethen who migrated to America brought Darby's new teachings with them. Among Darby's disciples were James Inglis, James H. Brookes, Cyrus Ingerson Scofield and Lewis Sperry Chafer (see *Hermeneutics of Dispensationalism*, p. 136).

Other disciples of the *Futurist* point of view whose works have heavily swayed the minds of many in this century, are Sir Robert Anderson's, *The Coming Prince* (1909); A.J. McClain's, *Daniel's Prophecy of the Seventy Weeks* (1940); H.A. Ironside's *The Great Parenthesis* (1943); J.D. Pentecost's *Thing's to Come* (1958); and J.F. Walvoord's *Daniel the key to Prophetic Revelation* (1971).

Virtually all Bible scholars recognize that these "seventy weeks" are to be understood using the day for a year principle as recorded in (Ezek. 4:3-6, and Numbers 14:34).

For example, every day the Israelites searched the land of milk and honey, even forty days, they were punished forty years for their sins. Therefore, the 70 weeks equal (70 x 7)= 490 days or 490 years prophetically. The angel Gabriel revealed this prophecy to Daniel:

> **Seventy weeks are determined upon thy people and and upon thy holy city, to finish the transgression, and to make an end of sins, and to make reconciliation for iniquity, and to bring in everlasting righteousness, and to seal up the vision and prophecy, and to anoint the most Holy. Know therefore and understand, that from the going forth of the commandment to**

DANIEL'S SEVENTY WEEKS

> **restore and to rebuild Jerusalem unto the Messiah the Prince [Christ] shall be seven weeks, and threescore and two weeks [a total of 69 weeks or (69 x 7)= 483 prophetic years] the street shall be built again, and the wall, even in troublous times. And after threescore (60) and two weeks (a total of 62) shall Messiah be cut off, but not for himself... (Dan. 9:24-26).**

Henry Halley summarizes Daniel's Seventy Weeks Prophecy by stating in his handbook, "The 70 weeks is subdivided into 7 weeks, 62 weeks, and 1 week (25, 27). It is difficult to see the application of the "7 weeks"; but the 69 weeks (including the 7) equal 483 days, that is, on the year-day theory (Ezekiel 4:6), which is the commonly accepted interpretation, 483 years" (p. 349).

In other words, the entire time period involved is exactly specified as *Seventy Weeks* (24); and these Seventy Weeks are further divided into three lesser periods: first a period of *seven weeks;* (7 x 7 = 49) after that a period of *three-score and two weeks;* (62 x 7 = 434) and finally, a period of *one week* (1 x 7 = 7), a total of 490 years (49 + 434 + 7) (25, 27).

To put Daniel's prophecy in modern vernacular, 483 years from the time the commandment or decree given to restore and to rebuild Jerusalem—or after the "threescore (60) and two weeks", which follows the first seven weeks (69 weeks) the Messiah would make His triumphant entry into Jerusalem and present Himself as the Messiah of Israel, and shortly thereafter would be "cut off" or be crucified.

The duration from the time the commandment was given to the Messiah the Prince, is generally agreed upon to mean when Jesus would be known to Israel as their Messiah—rather than when He would be born, or baptised. Shortly thereafter, He would be crucified.

As already noted, the Hebrew word for weeks in this prophecy is *shabua* which means "seven", thus the scripture should read, "Seventy sevens are determined upon thy people and upon thy holy city..." These "sevens" have reference to God's "seven sabbaths" of years which we have just covered under the Jubilee year.

Which Commandment?

But which commandment do we begin counting from?

The starting point from which the 70 weeks were to be counted, was the decree or commandment to rebuild Jerusalem—but several decrees were issued by Persian Kings during the course of time. Henry H. Halley gives the dates of these decrees as 536, 457, and 444. According to Halley, the principle date being 457 (p. 302, *Halley's Bible Handbook*).

Jamieson Fausset and Brown *Commentary on the Whole Bible*, p. 755 on (Daniel 9:25), has this to say regarding the counting of the seventy weeks:

> **The seventy weeks date thirteen years before the rebuilding of Jerusalem; for then the reestablishment of the theocracy began, viz; at the return of Ezra to Jerusalem, 457 B.C. So, Jeremiah's seventy years of the captivity begin 606 B.C., eighteen years before the destruction of Jerusalem, for then Judah ceased to exist as an independent theocracy, having fallen under the sway of Babylon. Two periods are marked in Ezra: (1) The return from the captivity under Jeshua [Joshua] and Zerubbabel, and rebuilding of the temple, which was the first anxiety of the theocratic nation. (2) The return of Ezra (regarded by the Jews as a second Moses) from Persia to Jerusalem, the restoration of the city...Artaxerxes, in the seventh year of his reign, gave him the commission which virtually includes permission to rebuild the city, afterwards confirmed to, and carried out by, Nehemiah in the twentieth year (Ezra 9:9; 7, 11, etc); vs. 25, 'from the going forth of the commandment to build Jerusalem,' proves that the second of the two periods is referred to.**

Clearly, Halley, Jamieson Fausset and Brown and most expositors believe 457 B.C. to be the principle date to begin counting the "seventy weeks" prophecy. In order to determine the correct date, a brief history of the fall of Babylon, as well as the nation of Israel is paramount as background material.

Babylon's Fall

H.G. Wells writes of Babylon's fall:

> **The Chaldean Empire with its capital at Babylon (Second Babylonian Empire), lasted under Nebuchadnezzar the Great (Nebuchadnezzar II) and his successors until 538 B.C.; when it collapsed before the attack of Cyrus, the founder of the Persian power (*The Outline of History*, p. 169).**

Wells further states that Cyrus the Persian reigned from 550 to 529 B.C. and took Babylon in 539 B.C. (p. 195), overthrowing Nabonidus, the father of Belshazzar, the last Chaldean monarch (p. 220).

According to Well's *Outline of History*, Cyrus was succeeded by his son Cambyses who was succeeded by Darius the Persian in 521 B.C. (p. 307). See also (*Light From the Ancient Past*, p. 238, by Finegan).

Perhaps the finest summary of the period after the fall of Babylon is *Babylonian Chronology 626 B.C.-A.D. 75* by Richard A. Parker and Waldo H. Dubberstein. They confirm that Babylon fell to the Persians and Medes in the seventh month in the year of Nabondius [father of Belshazzar] in 539 B.C.

The book of Ezra gives a brief synopsis of the events that occurred after the nation of Judah had been taken captive by the Babylonian Empire under Nebuchadnezzar in 606 B.C. After they had been in captivity for 70 years for their sins, the Lord stirred up the spirit of Cyrus to make this proclamation:

> **Thus saith Cyrus king of Persia, The Lord God of heaven hath given me all the kingdoms of the earth; and he hath charged me to build him an house at Jerusalem, which is in Judah (Ezra 1:2).**

Persian Decrees

Here are some concrete historical facts concerning the Persian decrees. There were several decrees issued by Persian Kings to rebuild the Temple and the city of Jerusalem according to (Ezra 5,6; Nehemiah; Haggai) and secular history. In 536 B.C, Cyrus the Persian King made a decree to allow the captive Jews to rebuild the Temple in Jerusalem, but the building of the city was not mentioned (Ezra 1:1,2).

This was the time period in which Joshua and Zerubbabel came with the first group of exiles to build the house of the Lord. It wasn't long after they were there, when the adversaries [Samaritans] of Judah heard that they were rebuilding the Temple and offered their services. However, Zerrubabbel didn't want to have anything to do with them and replied sharply:

> **...Ye have nothing to do with us to build an house unto our God; but we ourselves together will build unto the LORD God of Israel, as king Cyrus the king of Persia hath commanded us (Ezra 4:3).**

Because of the Samaritans harassment, work on the Temple stopped until the second year of Darius (521-485) due to strong opposition, notice: **"even until the reign of Darius king of Persia" (Ezra 4:4,5,24).**

Construction of the Temple began once again by a decree of Darius, but again, this was only to rebuild the Temple, not the city of Jerusalem (Ezra 6:11,12). This decree of King Darius completed the work on the Temple in the sixth year of his reign (Ezra 6:14,15).

> **Then Darius the king made a decree, and search was made in the house of the rolls, where the treasures were laid up in Babylon. And there was found at Achmetha, in the palace that is in the province of the Medes, a roll, and therein was a record thus written: In the first year of Cyrus the king the same Cyrus the king made a decree concerning the house of God at Jerusalem, Let the house be builded, the place**

> where they offered sacrifices, and let the foundations thereof be strongly laid...(Ezra 6:1-3).

This decree allowed the captive Jews to rebuild the Temple, with the restored golden and silver vessels of the house of God, stolen by Nebuchadnezzar (vs. 5), and begin sacrificing once again (vs. 10).

The work on the Temple began once again in 520 B.C. under the direction of Haggai and Zechariah, notice:

> **And the elders of the Jews builded, and they prospered through the prophesying of Haggai the prophet and Zechariah the son of Iddo. And they builded, and finished it, according to the commandment of the God of Israel, and according to the commandment of Cyrus, and Darius, and Artaxerxes king of Persia (Ezra 6:14).**

Notice the above mentioned Persian kings from the Bible were Cyrus, Darius and Artaxerxes, who were influential in the building of the Temple, beginning with the decree from Cyrus!

The Temple was finally completed in 516 B.C., notice: **"And this house was finished on the third day of the month Adar, which was in the sixth year of the reign of Darius the king" (Ezra 6:15).**

Ezra's Commission (457 B.C.)

Thus far we have established that only the Temple had been built, but work to rebuild the city had not been mentioned. In the seventh year of Artaxerxes [457 B.C.], a decree was issued Ezra the priest (Ezra 7:7-11)—allowing him to go to the city of Jerusalem and *beautify* the Temple and to teach the statutes and judgments of God:

> **For Ezra had prepared his heart to seek the law of the LORD, and to do it, and to teach in Israel statutes and judgments (vs. 10)... Artaxerxes, king of kings, unto Ezra the priest, a scribe of**

> the law of the God of heaven...I make a decree, that all they of the people of Israel, and of his priests and Levites, in my realm, which are minded of their own freewill to go up to Jerusalem, go with thee...And to carry the silver and gold, which the king and his counsellors have freely offered unto the God of Israel, whose habitation is in Jerusalem (Ezra 7:12-15).

What was the purpose of Ezra's sojourn to Jerusalem, in which King Artaxerxes gave him all the treasures? (7:21). Was it to rebuild the city? Let's read on, **"Blessed be the LORD God of our fathers, which hath put such a thing as this in the king's heart, to** *beautify* **the house of the LORD which is in Jerusalem"** (7:27).

Observe, not one word was spoken about rebuilding the city of Jerusalem! Now notice what happened upon Ezra's arrival with the many Levite priests accompanying him (8:1-36). Judah had mixed God's holy seed with the Gentiles by intermarrying (9:1-3).

Ezra was astonished! (9:3). This was his rebuke to the abominations they had committed:

> **Since the days of our fathers have we been in a great trespass unto this day; and for our iniquities have we, our kings, and our priests, been delivered into the hand of the kings of the lands, to the sword, to captivity, and to a spoil, and to confusion of face, as it is this day. And now for a little space grace hath been shewed from the LORD our God, to leave us a remnant to escape...For we were bondmen; yet our God hath not forsaken us in our bondage, but hath extended mercy unto us in the sight of the kings of Persia, to give us a reviving,** *to set up the house of God, and to repair the desolations thereof, and to give us a wall* **in Judah and in Jerusalem (9:7-9).**

Notice Ezra's words! Not only was he sent to refurbish the Temple, but to repair the city and the wall! As we read previously, the year of this decree was in the seventh year of Artaxerxes (7:7).

Artaxerxes "Longimanus"

As we have journeyed through this most fascinating and important prophecy, we have observed several discrepancies among Bible commentaries and concordances regarding 1) which decree of the Persian kings to begin the counting of the 69 weeks, and 2) the date to begin the counting.

For those who agree that the counting should begin from the commandment given by king Artaxerxes in his twentieth year, there is some disagreement as to this date. *Dakes Annotated Bible, The Companion Bible and the New Bible Commentary Revised,* all agree that the 20th year of Artaxerxes was the correct decree to begin the counting—but each gives a different year for Artaxerxes' 20th year.

According to Dakes, Artaxerxes' 20th year was 452 B.C., [notes of Daniel], *The Companion Bible* gives the year 454 B.C., [Ap. 50, 58, 91], while the *New Bible Commentary* lists the 20th year of Artaxerxes as 445 B.C.

Who is right?

Assuming that we are counting from the right decree, obviously, if we cannot pinpoint the exact date of Artaxerxes 20th year to begin the counting—we will not end up on the correct date of the crucifixion!

The *Pictorial Bible Dictionary*, article "Artaxerxes", states that this name is actually a title given to Persian kings, like *Pharaoh, Caesar, etc.* and several Persian kings took on this title. The scholar Gesenius believes it means "strong king", and Herodotus made it mean "great warrior."

Continuing the article in the *Pictorial Bible* we read: "A Persian king (Ezra 7:1-8:1, Neh. 2:1, 5:14, 13:6) nicknamed 'Longimanus' or 'Long-handed' because of a deformity of his right hand. He granted the requests of Ezra (7:6) in 457 B.C. and of Nehemiah (Neh. 2:1-8) in 444 B.C. to go to Jerusalem and gave them power, supplies, and authority" (p. 74).

According to Rawlinson, *Herodotus*, vol. iv., p. 217: "Artaxerxes I, reigned forty years, from 465 to 425. He is mentioned by Herodotus once (vi. 98), by Thucydides frequently. Both writers were his contemporaries." H.G. Wells gives the year that Herodotus was born as 484 B.C. (*An Outline of History,* p. 320). Wells also states that Xerxes was killed in 465 B.C. and was succeeded by an Artaxerxes (p. 322). Halley's Bible Handbook also confirms the date of 465 B.C. as the beginning reign of Artaxerxes (p. 230).

Recall, it was Herodotus that narrated the birth of Cyrus, which speaks of intervention by God. If we can't believe his history of Media, who can we believe? Therefore, there is every reason to believe that Artaxerxes was the king who sent Ezra and Nehemiah to Jerusalem, and sanctioned the "restoration of the fortifications."

Archaeological discoveries during this century in Mesopotamia and Egypt have also established the beginning year of Artaxerxes to be 465-464 B.C.

An Aramaic papyrus (AP 6), written from the Jewish colony of Elephantine in Egypt states that the beginning reign of Artaxerxes began on the 18th of Kislev or the 17th of Thoth, according to the Hebrew calendar in the year 21, which corresponds to the year 464 B.C. Counting from 464 B.C. to the 20th year of Artaxerxes would bring us to the year 445-444 B.C.

Nehemiah builds the Wall (445 B.C.)

Although Ezra did in fact beautify the Temple at this time, the question still remains, "did he restore the city and the wall or was it restored upon Nehemiah's arrival 13 years later in 445 B.C.?" This was during Artaxerxes twentieth year (Neh. 2:1). Let's read this account:

> **So, I [Nehemiah] came to Jerusalem [444-445 B.C.] and was there three days. And I arose in the night, I and some few men with me; neither told I any man what my God had put in my heart to do at Jerusalem: neither was there any beast with me, save the beast that I rode upon. And I went out by night by the gate of the valley, even before the dragon well, and to the dung port, and viewed *the walls of Jerusalem,* which were broken down, and the gates thereof were consumed with fire...Then I said unto them, Ye see the distress that we are in, how Jerusalem**

> lieth waste, and the gates thereof are burned with fire: *come and let us build up the wall of Jerusalem* that we be no more a reproach (Neh. 2:11-17)

Notice it! According to most expositors, thirteen years after Ezra supposedly built the wall of the city in 457 B.C.—Nehemiah says the walls of Jerusalem were broken down, and he was going to rebuild it. This was in 445 B.C.!

Nehemiah was king Artaxerxes's cupbearer [governor] (Neh. 1:11), and was given the commission to go to Jerusalem to rebuild the wall at Jerusalem at the expense of the Persian Empire, notice:

> And they said unto me, The remnant that are left of the captivity there in the province are in great affliction and reproach: *the wall of Jerusalem also is broken down,* and the gates thereof are burned with fire (Neh. 1:3).

Despite the opposition of the Samaritans, [Judah's adversary] who wanted to stop them from building the wall (Neh. 4)—the wall was built. Let's read it!

> So the wall was finished in the twenty and fifth day of the month Elul, in fifty and two days. And it came to pass, that when all our enemies heard thereof, and all the heathen that were about us saw these things, they were much cast down in their own eyes: for they perceived that this work was wrought of our God (Neh. 6:15-16).

Not only was the wall finally built, it was dedicated with gladness and thanksgiving (Neh. 12:27). The seventh chapter of Nehemiah lists the chronology involved in the rebuilding the Temple and the restoration of national life in their homeland.

With the first decree of Cyrus in 536 B.C., 42,360 Jews and 7,337 servants under Joshua and Zerubbabel returned to Jerusalem (Ezra 2:64-65). However, the vast majority chose to remain in pagan Babylon, the land of their captivity, rather than return to their roots!

Once the foundation of the Temple had been laid, work on the Temple ceased for 15 years as a result of enemy neighbors. Interest in the Temple stopped until Haggai had a vision from God to continue building the Temple. The prophets Haggai and Zechariah aided in motivating the people to resume building at this time under the direction of governor Zerubbabel (Hagg. 1:1-2).

The Temple was completed in 516 B.C. but Ezra came to *beautify* it in 457 B.C. and reestablish the Jews national life in their homeland. His primary purpose was to *beautify* the House of God in the midst of a ruined city! Ezra came with 1,683 males and a total of approximately 8,400 people, including women and children.

The question must be raised here to those who believe the exodus under Ezra was to build the city. If he came with only 1,683 males, what were the males doing before him who arrived seventy-eight years before under Cyrus' decree and were sixfold?

Thirteen years later, Nehemiah came to rebuild the wall and restore basic religious reforms beginning the 69 weeks prophecy of (Daniel 9:25). Notice, this prophecy could only begin when the WALL was built:

> **Know therefore and understand, that from the going forth of the commandment to restore and to build Jerusalem unto the Messiah the Prince shall be seven weeks, and threescore and two weeks: the street shall be built again, and the WALL, even in troublous times.**

After the completion of the WALL had taken place, Nehemiah and Ezra began to restore basic religious beliefs including God's Feast of Tabernacles (Neh. 8:9-18).

Understanding our previous discussion of the discrepancies of the Persian kings decrees—a further point of clarification must be made in order to calculate the 69 weeks prophecy.

Failure to distinguish between Judah's national captivity for 70 years, beginning in 606 B.C., and the time period beginning the seventy weeks prophecy [69 weeks from the decree to restore Jerusalem to the Messiah being "cut off"] known as the "Desolations" has led to additional error!

Israel's dismal History

Let's recapitulate. Israel's first king was God and He instituted His laws through a system of judges for 450 years (Acts 13:20). Then Israel desired a physical king that they could see—so God obliged by giving them Saul.

After Saul was removed from office because of rebellion (1 Sam. 15:23)— God raised up David to be Israel's new king (Acts 13:22).

During this time, each tribe was independent, yet united they formed *one* nation in the same manner the United States is one nation composed of separate states.

When king David died, his son Solomon succeeded him to rule over Israel. But Solomon did not keep God's covenant or statutes, so God told him:

> **...I will surely rend the kingdom from thee, and give it to thy servant. Notwithstanding in thy days I will not do it for David thy father's sake: but I will rend it out of the hand of thy son. Howbeit I will not rend away all the kingdom; but will give *one tribe* to thy son for David my servant's sake, and *for Jerusalem's sake which I have chosen* (1 Kings 11:11-13).**

Notice the special significance God places upon Judah and Jerusalem! Except for *one tribe* [Judah] to carry out the Sceptre promise, God was going to rend the kingdom from Israel. We read in (1 Kings 11:26) where Jeroboam, the son of Nebat, an Ephraimite was made ruler over the "house of Joseph."

The northern 10 tribes became known as Israel with Jeroboam as it's king while the southern nation composed of Judah, Benjamin and some of the priestly Levites intermingling, became known as the nation of Judah. Solomon's son Reoboam was Judah's king, maintaining the kingly line as God had said *one tribe* would fulfill his promise to David.

Therefore, the name "Jew" became associated with the nation of Judah. The fact that the nation of Israel was not Jewish is clearly revealed in (11 Kings 16:6), where the nation of Israel was fighting "Jews." Israel and Judah remained separate nations with their own kings for many years.

The nation of Israel was taken captive in 721 B.C. by the Assyrians (11 Kings 17:23) while the nation of Judah was taken captive in 606 B.C. by the Babylonians (11 Kings 23:27).

The 70 Years National Captivity

"In the third year of the reign of Jehoiakim king of Judah came Nebuchadnezzar king of Babylon unto Jerusalem, and besieged it" (Dan. 1:1). This occurred in 606 B.C.

Along with the royal seed of King Jehoiakim, and the princes, came men who were skillful in wisdom, knowledge, and science [the intellectuals] chosen to teach the Babylonian ways to the Jewish captives in Jerusalem (Dan 1:3-5).

Among the bright captives, was Daniel, Hananiah (Shadrach), Mishael (Meshach) and Azariah (Abed-nego) (Dan. 1:6-7). Soon, these four men would be recognized for their exceptional understanding in all dreams and visions (Dan. 1:17-20). Recall how Daniel had interpreted Nebuchadnezzar's dream of the great image (Dan. 2). They soon found favor in the king's sight, and were appointed very lofty positions as the king entrusted them with the affairs of the Empire. Daniel was elevated to the rank of minister in the king's cabinet.

However, after being in the Babylonian Empire for 20 years, these three faithful men found themselves in the fiery furnace. These men were uncompromising in their religious convictions and would not bow down to the kings idolatrous command (Dan. 3:10-11).

The prophet Ezekiel was also a captive in Babylon. He was carried to Babylon in 597 B.C., 11 years before Jerusalem was destroyed, and 9 years after Daniel arrived. Ezekiel may have been Jeremiah's pupil, as he was preaching the same warnings in Babylon as Jeremiah was in Jerusalem!

The seventy years national captivity of Judah is calculated by subtracting 606 B.C. [Jerusalem taken captive by King Nebuchadnezzar] from 536 B.C. [Cyrus' decree] allowing the exiles of Judah to return from Babylon to rebuild the Temple in Jerusalem. Thus, 606 - 536 = 70 years!

However, the period known as the "Desolations" of Jerusalem, beginning the "seventy weeks" prophecy [not the beginning of the counting to the Messiah] were a result of further warnings of the prophets Jeremiah and Ezekiel—while Daniel was still in exile in Babylon.

The "Desolations" of Jerusalem

Meanwhile, back in Jerusalem, the prophet Jeremiah pleaded with the rebellious nation,: **"...this whole land shall be a desolation and an astonishment, and these nations shall serve the king of Babylon seventy years" (Jer. 25:11).** Realize also, these "seventy years" of "Desolations" were to begin as a result of *disobedience* and *rebellion* against the authority of the divine decree given to Nebuchadnezzar *during* their captivity—not as a result of it! Observe:

> **And now have I given all these lands into the hand of Nebuchadnezzar the king of Babylon, my servant; and the beasts of the field have I given him also to serve him...And it shall come to pass, that the nation and kingdom which will not serve the same Nebuchadnezzar the king of Babylon, and that will not put their neck under the yoke of the king of Babylon, that nation will I punish, saith the LORD, (Jer. 27:6,8).**

Now observe the time element of this prophecy. It is when Zedekiah is king of Judah (Jer. 27:12-15). It is a prophecy and warning to Zedekiah and those remaining in Jerusalem after the first siege, notice Jeremiah 27:20:

> **Which Nebuchadnezzar king of Babylon took not, when he carried away captive Jeconiah the son of Jehoiakim king of Judah from Jerusalem to Babylon, and all the nobles of Judah and Jerusalem (including Daniel).**

This same prophecy is repeated in Jeremiah 38:17-21:

> **Then said Jeremiah unto Zedekiah, Thus saith the LORD, the God of hosts, the God of Israel; If thou wilt assuredly go forth unto the king of Babylon's princes, then thy soul shall live, and**

> this city shall not be burned with fire; and thou shalt live, and thine house:

Realize also, that these "seventy weeks" of "Desolations" were to begin during the reign of Zedekiah—Judah's last ruling king! Judah's servitude of 70 years began in 606 B.C. and ended in 536 B.C. with the decree of Cyrus.

However, the period of time know as the "Desolations" in (Daniel 9:25), began in 589 B.C. when Jerusalem was besieged the third and final time by the Babylonians in fulfillment of Jeremiah's prophecy. It had been besieged a 2nd time, 9 years earlier in 598 B.C.

In 589 B.C. the city of Jerusalem was ransacked and destroyed by the invading Babylonian army. This date, beginning on the tenth of Tebeth was in the ninth year of king Zedekiah (11 Kings 25:1).

Therefore, counting seventy prophetic years of 360 days = 70 x 360 = 25,200 prophetic days from 589 B.C. brings us to 520 B.C. This date was the second year of king Darius the Persian, in which the foundation of the second Temple was laid (Hag. 2:18,19).

The "Cutting Off" of the Messiah

To disprove that the decree issued by king Cyrus in 536 B.C. as pertaining to the counting of the "Desolations" and the 69 weeks, Sir Robert Anderson comments in his renowned book, *The Coming Prince*, (xii, xvi):

> **Here is something to set both critics and Christians thinking. A decree of a Persian king was deemed to be divine, and any attempt to thwart it was usually met by prompt and drastic punishment; and yet the decree directing the rebuilding of the Temple, issued by King Cyrus in the zenith of his power, was thwarted for seventeen years by petty local governors. How was this? The explanation is that until the very last day of the seventy years of "the Desolations" had expired, God would not permit one stone to be laid upon another on Mount Moriah...And although it was a serious matter to thwart the**

> execution of an order issued by the king of Persia (Ezra vi. II), yet in this instance, as already noticed, a Divine decree overruled the decree of Cyrus, and vetoed their taking action upon it.

Anderson, as well as many Futurists believe the twentieth year of the reign of Artaxerxes was the year this decree was issued—and therefore the year we can begin counting the 483 years to the "cutting off" of Jesus Christ!

One expositor believes the counting should begin from 446 B.C., stating that Artaxerxes was in his twentieth year, and therefore only 19 years of his reign were completed. Therefore, deducting nineteen years from 465 B.C. brings us to the year 446 B.C.

Converting the 69 prophetic weeks to calendar years we would have, 69 prophetic weeks = 483 prophetic years (69 x 7) = 173,880 prophetic days (483 x 360). Dividing 173,880 prophetic days by 365.25 calendar days = 476 calendar years. In other words 483 prophetic years is equivalent to 476 ordinary calendar years.

Subtracting 445 B.C. from 476 [calendar years] brings us to the predicted year of the crucifixion of the Messiah in A.D. 32. We must add 1 year to compensate for going from B.C. to A.D. as there is no year 0. If we use the date 446 B.C. as our starting point, we would arrive at the date A.D. 31 as the year of the crucifixion.

Why 445 B.C.

Pinpointing the date of Artaxerxes decree as 445 B.C., in his well documented book, Sir Robert Anderson, one time head of Scotland Yard, wrote in 1895:

> **The Persian edict which restored the autonomy of Judah was issued in the Jewish month of Nisan. It may in fact have been dated from the 1st of Nisan...The seventy weeks are therefore to be computed from the 1st of Nisan B.C. 445. Now the great characteristic of the Jewish sacred year has remained unchanged ever since the memorable night when the equinoctial**

moon beamed down upon the huts of Israel in Egypt, bloodstained by the Paschal sacrifice; and there is neither doubt nor difficulty in fixing within narrow limits the Julian date of the 1st of Nisan in any year whatever. In B.C. 445 the new moon by which the Passover was regulated was on the 13th of March at 7h. 9m. A.M. And accordingly the 1st Nisan may be assigned to the 14th March (*The Coming Prince,* p. 121-123).

Anderson concludes:

The Julian date of that 10th Nisan was Sunday the 6th April, A.D. 32. What then was the length of the period intervening between the issuing of the decree to rebuild Jerusalem and the public advent of 'Messiah the Prince,'—between the 14th March, B.C. 445, and the 6th April, A.D. 32? THE INTERVAL CONTAINED EXACTLY AND TO THE VERY DAY 173,800 DAYS, OR SEVEN TIMES SIXTY-NINE PROPHETIC YEARS OF 360 DAYS, the first sixty-nine weeks of Gabriels's prophecy (*The Coming Prince*, pp. 127-128).

It should be pointed out that the twentieth year of King Artaxerxes (Neh. 2:1) in which he gave his famous decree to rebuild the city was also computed to be March 14, 445 B.C. by the Royal Observatory, Greenwich, United Kingdom.

However, there are certain discrepancies with Anderson's calculations, as Gerhrad F. Hasel states on page 15 of *The 70 Weeks, Leviticus, and the Nature of Prophecy:*

This reckoning can be held only on five problematical assumptions: (1) The years are not solar years but 'prophetic years' of 360 days. (2) The decree was issued on Nisan 1, 445 B.C. (3) Christ died in A.D. 32 (4) The last week of the prophecy may be moved to the future. (5) No synchronism between 'prophetic' and 'solar' years can be achieved without the

DANIEL'S SEVENTY WEEKS

Arbitrary and Subjective addition of extra days.

Although Sir Robert Anderson dates the crucifixion as A.D. 32, it is highly improbable that this was the year of the crucifixion based upon several additional historical and biblical events. And although we could debate the accuracy of these events until the day of Christ's return, including the correct date of Artaxerxes decree, the death of Herod, the completion of the Temple, and the reign of Emperor Tiberius—it only proves that *faith* is not a matter of mathematical calculation.

Based upon the sequence of events during the Passover week, the only day of the week that satisfies these conditions is Wednesday (see Appendix 156 *Companion Bible*). Now, the only years from A.D. 29 to A.D. 33 in which Passover was on a Wednesday, as verified by any work on the Hebrew calendar was A.D. 30 and A.D. 31. For an exhaustive commentary on the date of the crucifixion (see the *Seventh-day Adventist Bible Commentary,* vol. 5, pp. 251-265).

The Historical-Messianic Interpretation

The Historical-Messianic interpretation is best summarized by Gehard F. Hasel on page 28 of *Seventy Weeks, Leviticus, Nature of Prophecy:*

> **The beginning date for the 490 years is the seventh year of Artaxerxes I, now firmly established as 458-457 B.C. With Ezra returning to Palestine in 457 B.C. the prophecy finds its logical beginning with that year date. ...the interpreter of this school traces the 69 weeks or 483 years (the first two divisions: 7 + 62 weeks) on the year-day principle to A.D. 27. In A.D. 27 the baptism of Jesus occurred—noted by Luke as the fifteenth year of the Roman emperor Tiberius (Luke 3:5)—and He began His ministry as the Messiah. Three and one-half years later, 'in the midst of the week' (the spring of A.D. 31), He was crucified. The prophecy closes three and one-half years later in A.D. 34 with the death of Stephen, the**

scattering of the Christians from Jerusalem, and with the gospel going to the Gentiles. It is also possible that A.D. 34 marked the conversion of Paul.

Among earliest supporters of a Messianic fulfillment of Daniel's Seventy Weeks prophecy was Clement of Alexandria, Tertullian, Origen, Eusebius and Jerome. Recent archaeological evidence of the Qumran Dead Sea scrolls has revealed that the Essene community also held this interpretation (*Daniel 9 and the Date of the Messiah's Coming in Essene, Hellenistic, Pharisaic, Zealot and Early Christian Computation*, Roger T. Beckwith). This has also been the unamimous view of the Reformers.

Why 457 B.C.

Gerhard F. Hasel explains the reasons for the date 457 B.C. being the correct date to begin the counting of the Seventy Weeks:

> **New evidence indicates that the first decree, or edict, was made by Cyrus for the rebuilding of the temple (2 Chr 36:22-23; Ezra 1:1-4; 6:3-5) in the year 537 B.C. (Ezra 1:1). In this decree the king gives the order to build 'a temple in Jerusalem' (Ezra 1:2), namely, 'to rebuild the house of the Lord, the God of Israel' (vs. 3; cf. vss. 4-5). This decree concerned the return of the captives and the rebuilding of the temple but not a restoration of the city of Jerusalem.**
>
> **The second decree for the restoration of the temple was issued by Darius (Ezra 6:1-12) and explicitly concerns the 'rebuilding of the house of God' (vs. 8; cf. vs. 12), the temple in Jerusalem. In response to the matters related by Tattenai, king Darius had a search made of the edict issued by Cyrus. On the basis of Cyrus' decree, he issued one himself about 519/518 B.C. to reactivate it (Ezra 6:1-12). This decree is a confirming one and is limited**

explicitly to the rebuilding of the temple. It does not refer to or imply a rebuilding of Jerusalem. The third 'decree' or command (Ezra 7:11, 13, 21) was that of Artaxerxes I issued to Ezra in the king's seventh year (Ezra 7:7), the year 457 B.C. (ibid, p. 56-7).

Hasel now gives his retort to the 444 B.C. date on page 58:

The fourth and final 'decree' is that of Artaxerxes I to Nehemiah in 444 B.C., the king's twentieth year (Neh 1-2). Although this 'decree' is never called a 'decree' as such (see Neh 1-2), 'letters' were provided by Artaxerxes (Neh 2:7, 9) for safe passage and apparantly in support of the rebuilding of 'the city of my father's tomb' (Neh 2:5). When Nehemiah arrived in Jerusalem he inspected 'the walls of Jerusalem which were broken down and its gates which were consumed by fire' (Neh 2:13) and involved himself in the process of rebuilding. However, the bulk of the work must have been accomplished already under Ezra. The evidence is that Nehemiah finished the walls and gates in only 52 days (Neh 6:15).

Arthur J. Ferch also a firm believer in the 457 B.C. date adds additional support to this starting point:

According to Ezra 4:7-23 several lower state officials in the Persian province known as 'Beyond the River' of which Judah was a part wrote a letter against the Jews to Artaxerxes. In the letter these officials complain that 'the Jews who came up from you to us have gone to Jerusalem. They are rebuilding that rebellious and wicked city; they are finishing the walls and repairing the foundations' (vs. 12).

This communication seems to imply (1) a migration of Jews from Babylon to Jerusalem, and (2) a royal consent to rebuild the foundations, city, and walls of Jerusalem. The phrase, 'from you to us,' suggests a migration of Jews authorized by Artaxerxes himself. This written scenario finds its best historical counterpart in the migration of Ezra and his fellow Jews as recorded in Ezra 7 in the year 457 B.C. Nehemiah's journey to Jerusalem 13 years later was a solitary trip and in no way parallels the migrations of the Jews under Zerubbabel and Ezra...

Ferch concludes:

In comparison with the migration of Jews after the decrees of Cyrus (538/537 B.C.) and Artaxerxes (457 B.C.) Nehemiah's journey was quite different. It was not part of a migration. The decision of the king was not a publicized proclamation. The purpose of Nehemiah's visit was kept secret, and its work consisted primarily in repairing the walls and gates damaged only a few years earlier. Given these facts, it is evident that Nehemiah's journey in 445/444 B.C. does not match the specifications of Daniel 9:25... (ibid p. 73). Nehemiah's work in 445/444 B.C. was limited primarily to repair work on the walls and gates damaged earlier through the Samaritan outrages. His task was accomplished in 52 days... (ibid, pp. 74, 76).

Unanimously, the chronological evidence of both history and archaeology confirm the date of Artaxerxes' seventh year as 458/457 B.C., as verified by the Olypmiad dates, Ptolemy's Canon, Elephantine Papyri, and the Babylonian Cuneiform tablets. However, the question still remains, "is this the correct date to begin the counting from?"

457 B.C. Rebuttal

Professor Dewey M. Beegle responds to the traditional

Historical-Messianic interpretation that the proper starting point is the order given Ezra by king Artaxerxes I in 457 B.C. Professor Beegle takes a sharp view of Hazel's conclusions:

> Where does Hasel find a basis for his claim? He refers to Ezra 4:7-23 where it is reported to Artaxerxes that the Jews are 'finishing the walls and repairing the foundations of Jerusalem' (4:12)...But one cannot 'safely' come to Hasel's conclusion because after Artaxerxes heard the report of rebuilding he said, 'Therefore make a decree that these men be made to cease, and that this city be not rebuilt, until a decree is made by me' (Ezra 4:21). Artaxerxes had authorized Ezra to start a religious reform, not rebuild the city, and so he ordered the fortification of the city stopped. If Hasel is right, then Artaxerxes was schizophrenic. There is no evidence that Artaxerxes ever followed through and authorized Ezra to rebuild Jerusalem... The Jews needed walls to protect themselves from raids and harassment by their neighbors...The battered walls and burned gates reported to Nehemiah were the rubble left from Nebuchadnezzar's destruction. The returning exiles built the temple and constructed homes in area cleared of debris, but they did little with the wall system (*Prophecy and Prediction*, p. 117-18).

Dr. Beegle's conclusions:

> There is not one bit of evidence to show that in 457 B.C. there was a royal decree, or even one from God, ordering the rebuilding of Jerusalem. Gerhard Hasel has done as thorough a job as possible under the difficult circumstances. This critique of his views should not be taken as an attempt to 'hassle' him personally. The examination is really a refutation of all conservatives who try to start

> the 490 years in 458 or 457 B.C....Hasel admits that his theory cannot account for the destruction of Jerusalem in A.D. 70 even though he thinks the 'prince' mentioned in Dan. 9:27 was Titus (ibid. p. 119).

Payne, in his *Theology*, p. 277 also confirms Beegle's findings:

> **In the very year of Daniel's prophecy (538), Cyrus of Persia did issue an earlier decree which encouraged the return of the Jewish exiles to Palestine and authorized the rebuilding of the temple (Ezra 1:1-4; cf. Isa 44:28). But this decree of Cyrus did not mention the rebuilding of the city or its walls. Such restoration came to pass only in the following century, in the reign of Artaxerxes I (465-424), under Nehemiah in 444. There had been, however, under the same monarch, a previous attempt at restoring the walls, which had been thwarted by the Samaritans (Ezra 4:11, 12, 23). This original effort must have occurred under Ezra in 458, whose decree from Artaxerxes granted him such extended powers (7:18, 25; 9:9).**

Summary

As we have viewed this very intricate prophecy, we have seen the confusion of the various Persian decrees as a starting point. Even if we could agree on a starting point, we would then have to agree on whether to count prophetic years of 360 days, or calendar years of 365.25 years. If we use the traditional date of 457 B.C. as the Persian decree and count 483 calendar years, we would arrive at the date of Christ's beginning ministry in A.D. 27. This would make the crucifixion (3 1/2 years later) in A.D. 31.

However, if we use the date of the Persian decree in 446 B.C. and count 483 prophetic years (476 calendar years) we would arrive at the date of Christ's crucifixion in A.D. 31. Both dates would satisfy a Wednesday crucifixion.

ChapterFourteen

DANIEL'S 70TH WEEK

Much understanding about the sanctuary, Temple and Tribulation can be understood from the 70 weeks prophecy [a multiple of 7] in (Daniel 9:24-27)—yet this is one of the most controversial prophecies of the Bible.

As already noted, most Bible scholars agree the first part of this prophecy [69 weeks] refers to Jesus the Messiah [when He would be crucified], but there are vast differences of opinion concerning the interpretation of the last part of this prophecy.

One school of thought believes that this prophecy is speaking exclusively about Jesus Christ, while the other school of thought believes the last part of the prophecy beginning in (verse 26) refers to the "False Prophet." They reason, in (verse 25), it speaks of Jesus, the "Messiah" (capital letters...where small letters are used in (verse 26) to describe "the people of the prince"), who will come and destroy the city and the sanctuary and the end thereof shall be with a flood, and unto the end of the war desolations are determined. Here's how Daniel 9:26-27 reads:

And after threescore and two weeks (62) shall Messiah be cut off, but not for himself: and the people of the prince that shall come shall destroy the city and the sanctuary; and the end thereof shall be with a flood, and unto the end of the war desolations are determined.

And he shall confirm the covenant with many for one week (7 years): And in the middle of the week (3 1/2 years) he shall cause the sacrifice and the oblation to cease, and for over-spreading of abominations he shall make it desolate, even until the consummation, and that determined shall be poured upon the desolate.

The crux of this disagreement revolves around WHO confirms this covenant for *seven* years—Christ or Anti-christ?

As noted earlier, virtually all Christian expositors believe the first 69 weeks of this prophecy applies to the *anointing* and crucifixion of Jesus Christ. It is this final 70th week or last seven years that brings about a vast difference of opinion.

Many have reasoned that the 70th week of Daniel refers to Jesus being "cut off" after 3 1/2 years of His public ministry and that He still has 3 1/2 years remaining. That Christ will use these 3 1/2 years through the "Two Witnesses" who will be preaching the gospel at Jerusalem prior to Christ's return.

Believers of this persuasion feel Jesus used the first 3 1/2 years to *confirm* the covenant [New Covenant] and by His death caused the sacrifice to cease.

Others believe this covenant is confirmed for only 7 years, while the New Covenant is *everlasting*, and therefore could not be referring to Jesus Christ.

Those who believe in this exegesis believe this cannot be the Messiah, nor is it the Messiah who causes "the sacrifices and oblation to cease" in the midst of the last week [which is still future], as is clear from (Daniel 8:11-13; 11:31; and 12:11), which it is also connected with the setting up of the "abomination of desolation."

Adherents of this belief, contend the 26th verse describes the present dispensation from the crucifixion of Christ to the rise of the Antichrist, while the 27th verse describes the last week [or seven years of Antichrist's actings], divided as it is into two parts of 1260 days, (3 1/2 years or 42 months). Advocates of the *seven years* of the "False Prophet" ask: "why would Jesus and His people destroy the city of Jerusalem and the sanctuary?"

To support their argument, "seven year False Prophet proponents" point out that practically every Bible [including the Companion, Cambridge, Scoefield, International] and Bible commentaries have marginal references or appendixes that explain the last week or seven years of Daniel's Seventy Weeks relating to the Anti-christ.

Two major events are said to transpire after the sixty-ninth week and before the seventieth week, namely, 1) the "cutting off" or crucifixion of the Messiah, and 2) the destruction of the city and the Temple in Jerusalem. As we have observed, the crucifixion of our Lord took place within a few days after He entered Jerusalem and presented Himself as Israel's Messiah, or when the sixty-ninth week ended.

However, the destruction of the Temple did not occur until 70 A.D.—or until 40 years after the termination of the sixty-ninth week when the Roman general Titus entered Jerusalem and destroyed the Temple and the city.

From our understanding of the *types*—it seems apparent that there is another *duality* between Jesus Christ and Satan presented in this prophecy. Satan is a master *counterfeiter* and duplicates everything in God's plan. It seems evident that he would also duplicate God's end-time seven year plan for Jesus Christ.

Assuming that the 70th week applied to Jesus Christ only, undoubtedly the Devil would also desire seven years to counterfeit God's plan!

The Seventieth Week and Christ

As noted earlier, virtually all Christian expositors believe the first 69 weeks of this prophecy have found its fulfillment to the letter in Jesus Christ's first Coming. It is this final 70th week or *last seven years* that brings about a vast difference of opinion. The following reasons are given by advocates who believe Jesus fulfilled the remaining seventieth week:

- Jesus confirmed a covenant for one week (7 years) and in the midst of it (after 3 1/2 years) was "cut off" by being killed. A prophecy concerning Christ's death is found in (Isaiah 53:8) which states: "**...He was *cut off* out of the land of the living...**" The covenant Jesus confirmed of course was the New Covenant.

- There is no mention of "Anti-christ" in this scripture, but only "Most holy", "Messiah", and "Prince."

- Nothing is said of a covenant restoring sacrifices or breaking a covenant.

- Christ confirmed the New Covenant as mentioned in (Matthew 26:28; Malachi 3:1, and Hebrews 8:6; 12:24).

- Jesus did cause the sacrifice of animals to cease by becoming the only true sacrifice for sin (Hebrews chapters 9 and 10:18,26).

- This prophecy is continual and does not allow for a 2,000 year gap of time.

The Anti-Christ Version

This is the more popular view and is held by many television evangelists including Jack Van Impe, Hal Lindsey, Howard Estep and prophetic writers Salem Kirban, John F. Walvoord, and Allen Beechick to name a few. Actually, this belief is nothing new, and was written about in the first part of this century by H.A. Ironside and Sir Robert Anderson. But this concept dates even further than this century, and is as old as the writings of the Ante-Nicene Fathers which included Irenaeus.

Proponents of this view contend, trying to fit 7 years of prophecy into 3 1/2 years is like trying to put a size 10 foot into a size 5 shoe!

Here's what the *Companion Bible* says of this 70th week in (Appendix 89 & 90):

> **There are five specific periods of 'time' and 'days' mentioned in the Book of Daniel (7:25; 8:14; 12:7,11,12). In addition to these five, we have the great period of the 'seventy sevens' (or**

weeks) of years in chapter 9. *Sixty-nine* of these were completed at the 'cutting off' of the Messiah; the last or 'seventieth seven' is yet to come. All the other five periods of time in the book are to be referred to, and are *standardized*, so to speak, by this last 'seven'. The 'seventy weeks' (sevens) are confessedly to be reckoned as *years*. Therefore, on the basis of a Jewish year of 360 days, one 'seven' is 360 x 7=2,520 days.

The *terminus a quo* is manifestly determined by the term 'in the midst of the week' (the last 'seven' of years), of the *standard*, that is 1,260 days, or 3 1/2 years from either end of the column. 'The prince that shall come' (Antichrist) 'will make a covenant with many for one week' (i.e. *seven years*) (9:27). After 3 1/2 years, on grounds not stated, he breaks this covenant (or 'league', 11:23), the daily sacrifice is 'taken away', the 'abomination' set up, and 'Jacob's trouble' (Jer. 30:7) commences and continues for the remainder of the 'seven', vis: for the 1,260 days or 3 1/2 years. It is this 'midst of the week' that determines both the *a quo* and the *adquem* of these Numbered Days. In 8:14 it is stated, 'then shall the Sanctuary be cleansed'. With regard to this 'cleansing', all the periods synchronize at the end, while the last two columns are *extended* and prolonged beyond the close of the 1,260 days by two significant periods of days, viz. 30 days and 75 days, respectively.

The first of these, 1,290 days is 1,260 + 30. And the 90 days here may be taken as a 'Ve-Adar' or intercalary month of 30 days of 'cleansing' following directly after the destruction of the false Messiah; and the break up of his confederacy. These *thirty* days may possibly be the period allotted for the construction of the new and glorious 'Sanctuary' of Ezekiel 40-43, which is to be erected *after* the destruction and removal of the Jewish temple which will have been built by the sons of Israel some time previously to its profanation by the Antichrist— as the antitype of Antiochus Epiphanes. With regard to the 1,335 days of 12:12:

This 1,260 days with an excess of 75 days. This again being an excess of 45 days beyond the 1,290 of 12:11. 1,335 is, therefore 1,260 + 30 + 45. If the 30 days are occupied with the 'cleansing', i.e. with the 'justifying' or 'making righteous' a new and glorious 'Sanctuary', then it may be that the further 45 days, over and above the 1,290, will cover the preparation time for the fulfillment of the forty-fifth psalm (such preparation including the resurrection to life of those concerned in 12:2), in order that the nuptials of the king may be celebrated as described in such wonderful and minute detail in that psalm (Ap. 89 & 90).

The Gap Theory

The beginning of the first 69 weeks began with the commandment to rebuild Jerusalem, which was issued by the Persian king Artaxerxes in 445 B.C.

From this well established date, to the coming of the Messiah as Israel's "Prince" would be exactly 69 prophetic weeks or 483 years. This event has already occurred as both schools firmly believe!

But now we come to what one school of thinking calls the *continuous* interpretation of this prophecy, while the other school labels the separation of the 69th and 70th weeks as the *gap* interpretation.

Those who believe in the continuous interpretation, contend there is no division of time lapse between the 69th and 70th week of Daniel's "Seventy weeks" prophecy—and therefore the prophetic events mentioned here have already been fulfilled!

Contrary to this view of thinking are the advocates of the *gap* interpretation of the 70th week, who maintain that there is a division of thousands of years between the 69th and 70th week, and the 70th week therefore is yet future!

Advocates of this exegesis contend that a great parenthesis of time between the 69th and 70th week is made evident from several related passages, which our Lord Himself inspired.

This is the viewpoint held by H.A. Ironside and A.J. McClain as summarized by Pentecost on pp. 247-48 of his book, *Things to Come*.

To disprove the *continuous* interpretation of this prophecy, *gap* enthusiasts point out that the events which led to Jerusalem's destruction in A.D. 70 along with the Temple and Sanctuary were nearly *forty years after* the fulfillment of the first 69 weeks!

History informs us that the invading Roman legions of General Titus destroyed Jerusalem around A.D. 70. For this to be the interpretation of the *continuous* theory would prove in actuality a *gap* between the 69th and 70th week. Surely, if even one year would be acknowledged longer than the last two weeks of this prophecy, it would be an admission to the gap interpretation!

Since Christ came in A.D. 27 and died 3 1/2 years later—this leaves an obvious gap of nearly forty years to the supposed fulfilment of this prophecy by Titus in A.D. 70. This is a definite problem to reckon with for advocates of the continuous philosophy!

P. Mauro rebukes this concept for the following reasons, as he states his interpretation of God's prophecies:

> **...there is an absolute rule, admitting of no exceptions, [namely] that when a definite measure of time or space is specified by the number of units composing it, within which a certain event is to happen or a certain thing is to be found, the units of time or space which make up that measure are to be understood as running continuously and successively (*The Seventy Weeks, Leviticus, and the Nature of Prophecy* p. 23).**

Furthermore, proponents of the gap interpretation ask: When did God ever 'finish the transgression'—'make and end of sins'—'make reconciliation for iniquity'—'bring in everlasting righteousness'—'seal up the vision and prophecy' and 'anoint a most holy place' (A.R.V. margin) for Israel?

This most certainly was not done within a prophetic week (7 years) after Christ's death! There is no mention of such things occurring in the book of Acts! Contrariwise, we find the apostle Paul grafting in Gentiles to the Church because of Israel's sins! There is no mention of forgiveness to Israel here—rather mercy extended to the Gentile!

Now one final point is given by *gap* proponents to prove their interpretation is the correct one. They refer to the prophecy in (Isaiah 61:1-2), in which our Lord quoted from in (Luke 4:18,19). This refers to His public ministry of preaching the gospel and healing the sick—to a 2,000 year gap in which he would fulfill the last part of the prophecy by delivering the captives of Israel out of slavery!

The Seventy Weeks and Israel

John F. Walvoord, gives his interpretation of the Seventy Weeks prophecy as it relates to the nation of Israel:

The seventy weeks of Daniel, properly interpreted, demonstrate the distinct place of the Christian church and Israel in the purposes of God. The seventy weeks of Daniel are totally in reference to Israel and her relation to Gentile powers and the rejection of Israel's Messiah. The peculiar purpose of God in calling out a people from every nation to form the church and the program of the present age are nowhere in view in this prophecy (*Is Daniel's Seventieth Week Future?*, Bibliotheca Sacra, 101:30, January, 1944).

Summary of the Anti-Christ Version

The following are points of difference between the advocates who believe Daniel's 70th week refers to the coming of Antichrist and is yet future:

- This covenant is confirmed for only *7 years*, while the New Covenant is *everlasting!*

- The entire prophecy deals with the nation of Judah and

Jerusalem as (verse 24) refers to *Daniel's people* and *Daniel's city*! (see also verses 2,7,12,16,18,19,25).

- There indeed is a *gap* from the 69th to the 70th week. The death of the Messiah, and the destruction of Jerusalem nearly 40 years later in A.D. 70 by the invading armies of Titus—were not a continuous prophetic year! There is a further 2,000 year gap between our Lord's first and second Coming!

- Two different "princes" are alluded to as the "Messiah the *Prince"* refers to Jesus Christ (vs. 25)—but "the *prince* that shall come" describes a different prince—the "False Prophet" or "little horn".

- The fulfilment of the events in (verse 24), "to finish the transgression", "to make an end of sins", "to make reconciliation for iniquity", "to seal up the vision and prophecy", "to anoint a most holy place" (A.R.V. margin), have not happened to the Jewish people or their city as yet!

- The death of Christ did not cause the sacrifices to stop—for they continued until the city and the Temple were destroyed by Titus' Roman legions nearly forty years later! Since the death of Christ in the middle of the week did not stop the sacrifices, this prophecy could not be referring to the Messiah the Prince!

- Only when Christ returns in power and glory can specific great blessings be poured out upon Judah! This can only happen *after* the "seventy weeks" have been fulfilled! There is also indication, although highly controversial that upon Christ's return, He will institute a place of Temple worship with sacrificial system for all nations to worship Him properly! This is when He will "anoint a most holy place" for the Millennial Temple!

- Daniel 7,8,9,11,12 all refer to the Anti-christ ("little horn") taking away the daily sacrifice, setting up the Abomination of desolation, and making war with God's people. Why assume that in the middle of these chapters any change of thought occurs?

- The close of the seventieth week was to bring full blessings to Judah resulting from the Messiah's death. But Judah's transgression is yet to be restrained, and his sins to be sealed up. The Hebrew verb *caphar* [to make atonement or reconciliation] means literally "to cover over" sin. It implies the removal of the punishment between the sinner and God, or the obtaining of forgiveness for the sin. This verb *caphar* is used in (Exodus 32:30) in reference to doing away with a charge against a person by means of bloodshedding. This same word was used in (Genesis 6:14) for "pitch" in reference to "covering" Noah's Ark. This was a *type* of "covering" or "atonement" for sin that protected the individual inside the Ark. In all references where the Hebrew word *caphar* is used, it means "atonement" or "forgiveness" (Girdlestone's *Synonyms* O.T., p. 214). But the time of "atonement" for Israel and complete "forgiveness" of her sins will only occur upon the return of the Messiah when He fulfills the Day of Atonement!

- The seven year end-time plan is revealed by God through the *types*. The 7 years of famine in Egypt during the time of Joseph is merely a *type* of the 7 years of famine coming prior to Christ's return. King Nebuchadnezzar's "seven times" punishment and "seven years" of actual insanity is a *type* of the Gentile madness that will exist in the Babylonian system at the end of this age (Dan. 4:25). Ironically, a "seven times" punishment was stipulated to the nation of Israel if they became disobedient and rebellious (Lev. 26:14-28). Bible students are aware that a "time" is God's day for a year principle in prophecy (Ezek. 4:4-6; Num. 14:34). Both of these prophecies [the Gentile domination, and the removal of Israel's power] dovetail each other and add up to a duration of 2520 years. After this time, God will restore His kingdom to the nation of Israel.

- The prophecy has to do with the anointing of "the most holy" (margin: *Most Holy Place*). The "Most Holy Place" can only refer to the Holy of Holies in the Temple. Since the Temple was destroyed in A.D. 70 by the Roman General Titus—there has not been a "Most Holy Place" in Jerusalem because there has not been a Temple!

- In (Daniel 11:31), speaking of the evil Antiochus Epiphanes, who is a *type* of the Beast to come, we read that his forces will "pollute the *sanctuary of strength,* and shall take away the daily sacrifice, and they shall place the abomination that maketh desolate." Antiochus polluted the Temple of God, and placed a statue of himself in the "Holy of Holies." Since this was a *type* of the coming Beast, then he must do the same type of things. For this to occur, a Temple or sanctuary must exist with a "Holy of Holies"!

- If the 69th week has a literal interpretation, then it follows that the 70th week would also be taken literally.

Joseph in Egypt and 7 Years of Famine

We have already shown how Joseph is a *type* of Christ—now we shall show how the famine conditions that existed in the days of Joseph were a *prototype* and a *prelude* to the famine to occur in these last days!

After being sold into slavery by his jealous brothers into Egypt, Joseph became renowned as an interpreter of dreams. One night, Pharaoh had a remarkable dream that disturbed him tremendously. When Pharaoh's chief counsellor's magicians, soothsayers, and priests failed in their attempt to interpret his dream—he called upon the services of Joseph.

Pharaoh had dreamed that seven fat cows fed in a meadow, but after them seven lean cows ate up and consumed the seven fat cows! After this he dreamed again, and this time seven fat ears of wheat came up on one stalk, full and goodly to behold; but then seven thin ears came up, blighted with the east wind, and devoured the seven fat and full ears. The lean cows, Pharaoh told Joseph, were so skinny that they were **"such as I never saw in all the land of Egypt for badness."** This was a most incredible dream, and this was Joseph's interpretation for the Pharaoh:

> **The dream of Pharaoh is one: God hath shown Pharaoh what He is about to do. The seven good cows are *seven years*; and the seven good ears are *seven years*: the dream is one. And the seven thin and ill favored cows that came up after them are *seven years*; and the seven empty ears blighted with the east wind shall be *seven years* of famine.**

Joseph explained to the Pharaoh of Egypt that there was coming a time in which there would be seven years of great plenty throughout all the land of Egypt, followed by seven years of famine.

What few realize is that this *seven years of famine* in the days of Joseph, as well as the last seven years of the *"times of the Gentiles"* pictured by Nebuchadnezzar's temporary insanity, represent the *seventieth week* of (Daniel 9:27). This was merely a *type* of what is going to happen on this planet, before the glorious return of Jesus Christ!

The "Times of Jerusalem"

We have just examined several interrelated prophecies concerning the nation of Judah which correlate to the holy city of Jerusalem. Coincidentally, all of these prophecies dovetail into one theme—the termination of the Gentile powers rule on earth known as "the times of the Gentiles" and the reestablishment of the nation of Israel as God's supreme nation upon the earth.

These prophecies can best be summarized as follows:

- **The "times of the Gentiles"**—the nation of Israel was God's chosen nation over the hierarchy of the nations upon the earth. Israel was to be a "model nation" for all the world to see and emulate. They were a kingdom literally "set on a hill" [Jerusalem] to be a shining example for the Gentile world around them.

- However, due to spiritual infidelity, the Lord divorced His wife and sent her into captivity. Judah and Jerusalem would be *synonymous* as they possessed the holy land and were

DANIEL'S SEVENTIETH WEEK

the last tribe to go into captivity (1 Kings 11:11-13). They would also be the tribe to give birth to the Messiah!

- At this point, the Eternal had now decided to transfer the kingdom to the Gentile powers pictured by the two visions of king Nebuchadnezzar of Babylon as recorded in (Daniel 2 and 7).

- The vision of Nebuchadnezzar's great image (Dan. 2) and the lion, bear, leopard and beast with iron teeth and ten horns (Dan.7) both *portray* the succession of Gentile powers on the earth until Christ would return and *restore* again the kingdom to Israel.

- During Jesus' day, His disciples understood that the kingdom, with all authority to govern, whether civil or Church government had been taken away from their people, and turned over to the Gentiles. Recall how they asked Him, **"Lord will thou at this time restore again the kingdom to Israel" (Acts 1:6).**

- As already inferred, the "times of the Gentiles" began in 606 B.C. when God decided to send Judah into captivity by the first Gentile power (Babylon) represented by Nebuchadnezzar's dreams. "The "times of the Gentiles"will end upon Christ's second Advent when He returns as the supernatural "stone made without hands" to smite the final Gentile power represented by Nebuchadnezzar's dreams (Roman).

- Jesus Christ will at this time *restore* the kingdom of God to Israel once again as they will be His model nation to begin the Millennium. **Israel's "seven Times Punishment"**—because the nation of Israel had become disobedient to her husband [Jesus Christ] they were going to be punished for 7 TIMES or 2520 prophetic years (Lev. 23:24; 26:14-28; 27:28). In other words, they would be under Gentile domination for a period of 2520 biblical years of 360 days.

- After seventy years of servitude, a partial return of the nation of Judah was allowed to return to their homeland by king Cyrus the Persian in 536 B.C. Therefore, if we count 2520 prophetic years from 536 B.C. we would arrive at the very significant year of 1948—the year in which Israel was "reborn" as a nation and established in their homeland!

- **The Gentiles "seven Times Punishment"**—after the captivity of God's chosen people, king Nebuchadnezzar of Babylon became very proud and haughty. God was going to cut him down to size. This should be a lesson to all of us as, "Pride goeth before destruction" (Prov. 16:18).

- The 4th chapter of Daniel describes the fate of Nebuchadnezzar in a dream of the great tree. The dream was a warning to the king that his empire was about to crumble and he would become as a wild beast for seven years.

- This seven years of literal insanity was characteristic of "seven Times" or 2520 years of Gentile insanity, after which a brief restoration to sanity would occur prior to our Lord's return.

- **Daniel's Seventieth Week**—as already mentioned, Daniel's seventy weeks prophecy was a decade of Jubilees! It was upon the breaking of God's Jubilee cycles that the "desolations of Jerusalem" were calculated. In the course of breaking seventy sabbatical years, ten Jubilee cycles were also violated!

- Therefore, God was going to punish Judah *sevenfold* or "seven Times" or 490 prophetic years (70 x 7 = 490) till their land would be returned to them. Then the Messiah would "make an end of Israel's sins" and "bring in everlasting righteousness" and "anoint the most holy place"—Jerusalem!

God had promised Abraham that his descendants through the lineage of Judah would inherit the birthright promise which includes the land of present-day Palestine.

Prior to entering the promised land, God sent this rebellious nation into 70 years captivity for breaking His land Sabbaths during the span of 490 years. Then, God gave them an additional 490 year sentence before the kingdom would be restored again to Israel. The land was restored to them in 1948—when the Messiah returns—the Kingdom will be restored again to Israel in fulfillment of God's promise to Abraham. This is the capstone of all the prophecies of the Bible!

After sixty-nine prophetic weeks of Daniel's prophecy, the kingdom was offered once again to Israel by Jesus Christ—but they rejected Him! At that time they could have inherited their land and the kingdom would have been restored to them!

However, because of their rejection of the Messiah—their is a gap between the 69th and 70th week of Daniel's Seventy Weeks prophecy until they will fulfill this prophecy. Then, Jesus will say to them—"Come ye, inherit the kingdom that has been prepared for you."

SIGNIFICANT PROPHETIC DATES

1451 B.C.	Israel [consisting of all 12 tribes] crosses the Jordan to settle in Canaan.
721 B.C.	The nation of Israel consisting of 10 tribes taken captive by the Assyrians (11 Kings 17:23).
606 B.C.	The nation of Judah, consisting of Judah, Benjamin and a sprinkling of Levites, taken captive by Nebuchadnezzar's Babylon Empire (11 Kings 23:27). Daniel and the royal house taken to Babylon.
597 B.C.	Ezekiel taken as a captive to Babylon.
589 B.C.	Jerusalem besieged by

THE FOOLISHNESS OF GOD

	Nebuchadnezzar, the desolations of Jerusalem begin. (11 Kings 25:1).
539 B.C.	Nebuchadnezzar's Babylonian Empire falls to the Persians (Dan. 5:30-31).
536 B.C.	Cyrus the Persian allows a partial return of the Jews to their homeland to rebuild the Temple (Ezra 1:1-2).
520 B.C.	Work on the Temple continued under Haggai and Zechariah (Ezra 6:14) in Darius' 2nd year (Hagg. 2:18-19). The 70 years desolation of Jerusalem ended when the foundation of the second Temple laid.
515 B.C.	The Temple completed in the 6th year of Darius (Ezra 6:15). The dedication of the second Temple completed (Ezra 6:15).
465 B.C.	The beginning of king Artaxerxes reign.
457 B.C.	The seventh year of Artaxerxes of Persia who gave a decree to Ezra allowing him to beautify the Temple and teach God's laws (Ezra 7:7-11).
445 B.C.	The twentieth year of Artaxerxes. Nehemiah builds the wall. Beginning of the 70 weeks prophecy.
A.D. 31	The Messiah "cut off" fulfilling the first 69 weeks (Dan. 9:25).
A.D. 1948	The rebirth of the nation of Israel.

www.ingramcontent.com/pod-product-compliance
Lightning Source LLC
Chambersburg PA
CBHW070529010526
44118CB00012B/1086